Geoffrey D. Klinger
Jennifer Adams • Kevin Howley

Money Talks

Alan Greenspan's Free Market Rhetoric and the Tragic Legacy of Reaganomics

palgrave
macmillan

Geoffrey D. Klinger
DePauw University
Greencastle, IN, USA

Jennifer Adams
DePauw University
Greencastle, IN, USA

Kevin Howley
DePauw University
Greencastle, IN, USA

ISBN 978-3-031-00818-4 ISBN 978-3-031-00816-0 (eBook)
https://doi.org/10.1007/978-3-031-00816-0

This Palgrave Macmillan imprint is published by the registered company Springer Nature Switzerland AG.
The registered company address is: Gewerbestrasse 11, 6330 Cham, Switzerland

This book is dedicated posthumously to Dr. Klinger's two beautiful daughters Celeste and Sage. They were the light of his life and carried all his hopes for the future. He was so very proud of them both.

Acknowledgments

Our dear friend and colleague, Geoff Klinger, died of a sudden heart attack in May 2021. He was 54 years old. In addition to his teaching and scholarship, Geoff worked tirelessly to affirm, defend, and promote shared governance at DePauw University, his beloved alma mater. He planned to ready this manuscript for publication over the summer months. With the blessing of Geoff's parents, J. Philip and Nancy Klinger, his brother Kevin, and his daughters Celeste and Sage, we took up the bittersweet task of completing our friend's work. Despite heavy hearts—made lighter by our comrade's incisive analysis and well-crafted prose—we assumed responsibility for securing an altogether fitting outlet for this timely and deeply relevant book. We offer our sincere gratitude to Wyndham Hacket Pain at Palgrave Macmillan, and Karthika Devi Ravikumar and Nirmal Kumar Gnana Prakasam at Springer Nature for their editorial support.

Professor of Rhetoric & Interpersonal Communication Jennifer Adams
DePauw University

Professor of Media Studies Kevin Howley
DePauw University

Contents

About the Author

Geoff Klinger (1966–2021) was Professor of Rhetoric and Director of Forensics at DePauw University, USA. His research and teaching interests included the connection between rhetoric and social theory; political communication; presidential, civil rights, and business rhetoric; and Supreme Court decisions.

List of Figures

CHAPTER 1

Introduction: Painting by Numbers—Decoding the Discourse of Economics

In the 2005 film, *Batman Begins*, Ra's al Ghul, leader of the League of Shadows, conspires with a local crime leader and corrupt hospital administrator to poison the citizens of Gotham City with a powerful hallucinogen. Ra's al Ghul, played by Liam Neeson, reveals to Batman that this is not the League of Shadow's first attempt to destroy Gotham City. The first "weapon" that they used was "economics." The idea behind this plot was that the free market and the love of money would eventually ignite greed, corruption, and class warfare, and the citizens of Gotham would literally rip each other apart causing their society to implode. That plan failed, however, because of altruistic philanthropists such as Bruce Wayne's parents and this undermined the natural deleterious consequences of the free market.

The idea of using economics as a weapon is a powerful metaphor for understanding how economics functions within our society. Importantly, it is not simply a metaphor. As Warren Buffet, one of the richest people in the world, recognized in a 2006 column in the *New York Times*: "There's class warfare, all right, but it's my class, the rich class, that's making the war, and we're winning" (Stein, 2006). And while we continue to hold out hope that rich philanthropists, Buffet among them, will save us from the unsettling natural tendencies of the free market, history seems to teach us that voluntary philanthropy comes up short as an answer to the problems of an economy based on the principles of the free market. Robert

G. D. Klinger et al., *Money Talks*,
https://doi.org/10.1007/978-3-031-00816-0_1

Reich, the former Secretary of Labor under President Clinton, and currently the Chancellor's Professor of Public Policy at the Goldman School of Public Policy at the University of California at Berkeley, writes, "The generosity of the super-rich is sometimes proffered as evidence they're contributing as much to the nation's well-being as they did decades ago when they paid a much larger share of their earnings in taxes. Think again." He continues, "[A] large portion of the charitable deductions now claimed by America's wealthy are for donations to culture palaces—operas, art museums, symphonies, and theaters—where they spend their leisure time hobnobbing with other wealthy benefactors" (Reich, 2013). Citing work from Dylan Matthews of the *Washington Post* and Indiana University's Center for Philanthropy, Reich notes, "[E]ven under the most generous assumptions only about a third of 'charitable' donations were targeted to helping the poor." Further, and ironically, the rich donate less of their income in percentage terms than do the poor. Writing in *The Atlantic*, Ken Stern, observes, "One of the most surprising, and perhaps confounding, facts of charity in America is that the people who can least afford to give are the ones who donate the most." In 2011, for example, "the wealthiest Americans … contributed on average 1.3 percent of their income to charity. By comparison, Americans at the base of the income pyramid … donated 3.2 percent of their income" (Stern, 2013). This phenomenon is "accentuated by the fact that, unlike middle-class and wealthy donors, most [lower class donors] cannot take advantage of the charitable tax deduction, because they do not itemize deductions on their tax returns" (Stern). It seems that it is only in films where Batman is waiting in stately Wayne Manor to save us from ourselves.

Since 1980, those in power have done a Herculean job of what Jim Aune (2001) aptly called, *Selling the Free Market*. While surely many of the changes that took place were structural, those in power still had to justify dismantling key aspects of an economic system that had dominated our thinking and policy making for over a half-century. To do so required a powerful rhetoric. McNamee and Miller (2014) concur: "For a system of inequality to be fair over the long run, those who have more must convince those who have less that the distribution of who gets what is fair, just, proper, or the natural order of things. The greater the level of inequality, the more compelling and persuasive these explanations must appear to be" (p. 3). Importantly, this is a place where two modes of inquiry dovetail together: rhetoric and economics. My own education, studying both communication and economics, prepared me well to understand the nature and implications of this powerful confluence.

The idea that economics is fundamentally rhetorical is an important frame for this entire argument. While this point may seem obvious to many, it runs counter to the prevailing view of economics, a view that maintains that economics is a non-normative science. Indeed, nineteenth-century writer Thomas Carlyle once called it "the dismal science." William Greider (1987) writes, "[Economists] cloaked their observations in dense, neutral-sounding terminology that was opaque to nonscientists. The neutral language masked the political content of economics and the social rituals of capitalism" (p. 55). The contention that economics is more rhetorical than scientific is one that challenges core assumptions about the nature of money and economics. Among other things, a rhetorical view of economics invites an analysis of the ideology and discourse that both undergirds and cloaks particular economic systems. In other words, understanding economic discourse is the key to unraveling the complexities of any economic system. In short, words matter more than numbers, a realization that was a key component to the popularization of economics that has steadily unfolded over the last 40 years. Although proponents of the "free market" often characterize it as a "natural" state of affairs, it is a purposeful choice among many other competing alternatives, and its supporters have mobilized a persuasive discourse in order to justify its place in our society. Indeed, the very claim that the free market is natural is a significant rhetorical maneuver.

Before continuing to examine the specific rhetorical tropes involved with selling the free market, it seems prudent to briefly discuss the theoretical and practical connections that exist between rhetoric and economics since it is so important to this project. Despite the claims of some, particular systems of economics, such as the free market, are not natural, and they do not justify themselves. Instead, certain people, typically those with a vested interest in advancing a particular economic agenda, must persuade others that the economic system that they endorse is one that is the best for all members of the community. In other words, economics has a symbiotic relationship with rhetoric or persuasion. This revelation, of course, is nothing new. Indeed, it goes back as far as the beginnings of modern capitalism, if not before. Adam Smith, who many consider to be the intellectual inspiration for the modern capitalist state, had this to say regarding persuasion:

> Men always endeavor to persuade others to be of their opinion even when the matter is of no consequence to them. If one advances any thing

> concerning China or the more distant moon which contradicts what you imagine to be true, you immediately try to persuade him to alter his opinion. And in this manner every one is practicing oratory on others thro the whole of his life. (1978, p. 352)

The connection between Smith's view on the nature of rhetoric and his better-known principles of economics is not coincidental. For Adam Smith, a model of rhetoric based on the free exchange of opinions was fundamental to his economic model based on a free marketplace that facilitated the exchange of goods and services. They both found legitimacy in his view of human nature: humans have a natural tendency to truck, barter, and exchange. Importantly, Smith did not intend for this natural tendency to manifest itself unchecked in the marketplace. Rather, Smith's understanding of both rhetoric and economics had important connections with his moral philosophy that outlined the ethical implications for action under either an economic or a rhetorical paradigm. Thus, from the very beginning, Smith's principles of economics were inextricably bound to his conception of rhetoric and his theory of moral sentiments. This third connection is an especially interesting one. Since, as I will contend in the pages that follow, economists often speak of their discipline as an inherently non-normative enterprise, Smith's connections between rhetoric, economics, *and* moral action suggest that critics should re-examine this claim of non-normativity. Deirdre McCloskey (1990) raises similar concerns: "Concealing the ethical burden [of economics] under a cloak of science is the master move of expertise, the secret ingredient of snake oil. Adam Smith was a professor of moral philosophy. John Stuart Mill was a moral and political philosopher. … [T]he subject of economics is ethical, which makes a claim to sidestep ethics worrisome" (p. 135).

Importantly, I believe that Adam Smith is far from an unapologetic advocate for complete laissez-faire capitalism. I find it somewhat ironic that many contemporary economists, Alan Greenspan included, appropriate his work in defense of the free market. After a close reading of Smith's main economic texts under the tutelage of Professor Siep Stuurman at the University of Amsterdam, coupled with an independent and concurrent close reading of Smith's lesser-known *Lectures on Rhetoric and Belles Lettres*, *Lectures on Jurisprudence*, and his *Theory of Moral Sentiments* at the same time, I am convinced that Adam Smith was a proponent of capitalism, but not an advocate for an unregulated free market. In his *Theory of Moral Sentiments*, Smith (1976) wrote:

> [T]his disposition to admire, and almost to worship, the rich and powerful, and to despise, or, at least, to neglect persons of poor and mean condition, though necessary both to establish and to maintain the distinctions of ranks and the order of society, is, at the same time, the great and most universal cause of the corruption of our moral sentiments. (I, iii, p. 28)

Smith also recognized the connections between politics and economics, and the important role that persuasion and public posturing played in both. Many people know of, or appropriate Adam Smith, but precious few have actually read his work, a fact that Noam Chomsky recognized when he quipped during a lecture at University of Massachusetts, Amherst, in 2012: "[Adam Smith is] someone we are supposed to worship but not read. He was—a little subversive when you read him sometimes" (Chomsky, 2012).

This is a realization that not all economists recognize, let alone embrace. Indeed, as I note above, many economists often present themselves as engaging in a non-normative enterprise. A close examination of the discourse surrounding economics reveals that this is simply not the case. Indeed, several noted economists have arrived at this very conclusion as they develop the relationship between rhetoric, economics, and ethics first theorized by Adam Smith.

There has been increasing attention in recent years to the ways in which academic disciplines and professional practices conduct themselves rhetorically. Specifically, there has been a particular interest in the ways that these disciplines and practices gather, study, and disseminate their claims to increased knowledge and understanding. One of the early conclusions of such work is that there are marked similarities in the ways that seemingly disparate disciplines conduct inquiry.

Perhaps the central text emblematic of this movement is *The Rhetoric of the Human Sciences: Language and Argument in Scholarship and Public Affairs*. The aim of the project was outlined early in the preface:

> [The] essays explore an emerging field of interdisciplinary research on rhetoric of inquiry, a new field that stems from increased attention to language and argument in scholarship and public affairs. It examines how scholars communicate among themselves and with people outside the academy, and it investigates the interaction of communication with inquiry. (Nelson et al., 1987, p. ix)

This book was the culmination of a 1984 Humanities Symposium held at the University of Iowa, the central task of which was to bring together scholars from a spectrum of academic disciplines that roughly represented what the symposium called the "human sciences." One of the consequences of that symposium was the creation of the Project on the Rhetoric of Inquiry, or POROI, a group that I had the pleasure of working with while I was in graduate school at the University of Iowa.

The ultimate hope of the project was to find the intersections between disciplines in the ways that they seek and disseminate knowledge. The central intersections taken seriously by these scholars were rhetoric, argumentation, and persuasion: "[A]rgument is more unified than is commonly understood, and far more unified than the fragmentation of academic fields might imply. Every scientist or scholar, regardless of field, relies on common devices of rhetoric: on metaphors, invocations of authority, and appeals to audiences—themselves creatures of rhetoric" (Nelson, et al. p. 4). Thus, rhetoric became the touchstone from which scholars associated with this project began to establish intellectual linkages between their fields of study. Indeed, such linkages provided opportunities for biologists to converse with economists, for example, and for legal scholars to talk with anthropologists.[1]

A second unifying thread in this movement is the critique of modernist presuppositions in academic practice: "Rhetoric of inquiry turns away from modernism and foundationalism in the philosophy of science. It rejects the notion that there can be a single and autonomous set of rules for inquiry" (*Rhetoric* ix). The rhetoric of inquiry movement presents itself as an alternative construct through which one can examine and come to understand claims of knowledge. Given the centrality and pervasiveness of the positivist impulse in most academic disciplines, the rhetoric of inquiry project was both an ambitious and important move.

The rhetoric of inquiry movement transformed disciplinary debate within economics, in particular. Arjo Klamer notes that economists, much like their colleagues in other disciplines, often believe that they are engaging in a value-neutral enterprise. Klamer critiques such a view of economics through an incisive analysis of one of the grounding presuppositions of microeconomics, the rationality assumption: "[T]he fundamental

[1] For more developed work in the rhetoric of inquiry, see *The Rhetorical Turn: Invention and Persuasion in the Conduct of Inquiry* (1990). See also, J. Lyne, "Rhetorics of Inquiry" (1985).

assumption is that any economic choice is rational to the extent that it is consistent with the outcome of the optimization procedure: a rational choice is the optimal choice" (1987, p. 168). This assumption underlies most theoretical models in microeconomics. The idea, of course, is that we can build models to understand microeconomic actions, such as an individual's choice of a particular product, only if we assume that market participants act rationally. However, empirical and anecdotal evidence indicates that market participants often do not act in a rational way. Yet, despite evidence to the contrary, the rationality assumption remains. Importantly, the rationality assumption is more than just the basis for building economic models for individual preference and choice; it pervades economists' ways of thinking about that which they do; further, Klamer warns, "The denotation of the rationality assumption as a technique also seems to preclude any discussion of its meaning" (p. 170).

Klamer observes that contemporary economists often overlook, or ignore important normative aspects involved in the process of economic choice. They work from a model of economics that favors modernist reason, capitalist self-interest, and utilitarian optimization, while suppressing other normative considerations such as "the emotional facets of a relationship, or the influence of traditions, power, or cultural perceptions on relationships" (pp. 176–177). The end result, Klamer laments, may be the continued intellectual hegemony of the neo-classical tradition: "The [rationality] filter works, from the radical perspective, in favor of those who seek control through technology and bureaucratic institutions" (p. 180).

Klamer offers an alternative conception of the neo-classical formulation: "At this point we can recognize that speaking in terms of individual rationality constitutes a way of being. The rationality assumption, then, is a cultural artifact. Its role becomes transparent when we interpret it as a filter that brings some aspects of the world alive and suppresses others" (p. 174). Thus, Klamer wants his readers to think of economics less scientifically and more culturally. He argues that the discourse surrounding economics has important material consequences in society and culture. For example, although professional economists often claim that the enterprise in which they engage is non-normative, or apolitical, the impact of their economic rhetoric has immediate normative and political consequences. Indeed, there are cases where Alan Greenspan, former chair of the Federal Reserve, publicly argued that the Fed should be insulated from political concerns. In 1988, for example, after he received a letter from

Assistant Treasury Secretary, Michael Darby, Greenspan "objected quite strongly" to the Reagan Administration for attempting to politically pressure the Fed (Pine, 1988). In his biography, though, Greenspan seems to have softened his stance on the connections between politics and economics, something that I will discuss in later chapters.

The ways in which economic discourse is both constituted by and constitutive of a larger political and ethical community support the view that economics is an inherently normative enterprise. As Samuels (1990) similarly recognizes, "[I]t is possible, and arguably even necessary if not also desirable to contemplate economics (and the other disciplines) as comprising modes of discourse embracing and giving effect to a system(s) of belief, to a particular paradigm(s) with its distinctive set(s) of preconditions" (pp. 3–4).

McCloskey, who was an important early voice in the POROI movement I mention above, recasts economics in similar terms in what is considered the foundational book conjoining rhetoric and economics, *The Rhetoric of Economics.* "Economics," McCloskey argues, "uses mathematical models and statistical tests and market arguments, all of which look alien to the literary eye. But looked at closely they are not so alien. They may be seen as figures of speech—metaphors, analogies, and appeals to authority" (1998, p. xvii). Like scholars in other disciplines urging a rhetorical view of that which they study and practice, McCloskey opposes the neo-classical tradition specifically and the modernist project more generally. While "philosophers agree that strict logical positivism is dead," economists have not "caught up" in the wake of this intellectual transformation (p. 12). McCloskey notes that many economists, from Samuelson to Friedman, are still using modernist methodology and scientific assumptions, and this fact clouds a fuller understanding of economics.

Other economists reinforce and extend this thesis. Samuels, for example, emphasizes the interplay between economists and their relevant audiences, and the ways in which economic rhetoric shapes the political community in which it functions by engaging in the process of interpretation and meaning building: "Economics as a language is part of the total communication system of society, part, therefore, of the total symbolic, myth, and code system of society that governs meaning and signification" (p. 7). Thus, like the artist who seeks to create representations or interpretations of that which they paint, economists use numbers and statistics to "paint" interpretations of particular economic artifacts, or systems. Indeed, different economists may, and very often do, paint very different pictures using the same set of statistics. Samuels notes that one should expect multiple interpretations of particular statistics from economists. In his words:

> It seems that the economy is characterized by enormous complexity, heterogeneity and kaleidoscopy of subject matter. These aspects of diversity permit, perhaps indeed require, plural or multiple interpretations and analysis. In any event, students of the economy approach its subject-matter from a multiplicity of interpretive standpoints or perspectives. The result is multiple interpretations or specifications of economic reality, in whatever sense "real" is taken. (p. 9)

Scholars of rhetoric have described this process of linkage between rhetor/artist and audience in terms of dramas (Burke), fantasy themes (Bormann), narratives (Fisher), and myths (Rushing). Each of these perspectives equips us to better understand the rhetorical campaign underway over the last 40 years to sell us the free market.

Other economists have developed similar insights, as well. As James Kenneth Galbraith (1988) recognizes: "Rhetoric is a matter of language, and language is dual, a matter of transmission and reception. Between economics and politics, transmission and reception must occur across a cultural divide. ... To understand [political economy] properly you have to have a sense of the nuance in both cultures" (p. 221). Thus, Galbraith contends that understanding the "rhetoric of translation" is fundamental for understanding the ways in which the various discourses of economists reshape political communities. In other words, the best way to understand economics is to view it as an act of communication, one that is inextricably tied to politics and ideology.

Translation and interpretation are two of the key tools for decoding and assessing the rhetoric of economics generally, and the selling of the free market, specifically. One of the key figures is this rhetorical program over the last 40 years was Alan Greenspan. While there are others along the way that helped with the sales job, Greenspan was the central pitch person, given his unabashed intellectual commitment to the principles of the free market. During his tenure as chair of the Fed, Greenspan spoke with tremendous ambiguity, and entire markets seemed to turn on his every word. Oftentimes, markets had to wait for political and economic pundits to decipher the enigmatic rhetoric of Greenspan, who seemed to delight in keeping everyone guessing. But I am ahead of the story here.

Before getting to Greenspan, we need to set the stage and work through a so-called political and economic revolution.

In the 2008 film, *The Dark Knight*, Batman again has to confront a super-villain intent on sowing the seeds of political and economic chaos. This time, the Joker, played brilliantly by the late Heath Ledger, represents the angst felt by so many of the disenfranchised in society. His goal seems to be to upset an inherently unequal status quo. At one point, he remarks, "Introduce a little anarchy. Upset the established order, and everything becomes chaos. I am an agent of chaos." Not surprisingly, one of his targets is Batman, a billionaire with seemingly unlimited financial, political, legal, and quasi-military resources. Surely, Bruce Wayne, despite his philanthropic initiatives, personifies an economic and political system built upon fundamental inequality. Most people, however, have been duped into believing that this system is palatable, even desirable. The Joker realizes the deep and lamentable irony of this fact when he poignantly quips, "Nobody panics when things go 'according to plan.' Even if the plan is horrifying." Many have come to accept an economic and political system that works against their own self-interest. It is quite remarkable to hear disingenuous politicians, many of whom are millionaires or better, fumble all over each other to champion the cause of the so-called middle class precisely at a time when the middle class is largely disappearing as a discrete political and economic group. Rarely do you hear these politicians talk about how much they want to help those who need it the most, namely, the lower class, the untouchables of capitalist economics, simply because it is not politically expedient to do so. How did we get to a place where a precious few control the vast majority of all economic resources, and this situation is deemed normal? This is a question that has vexed me my entire life. It surely has roots that go back hundreds, even thousands of years, but the significant and growing economic inequality that marks our time finds its unique origin in 1980. It is now time to tell the story of how we got from there to here.

References

Aune, J. A. (2001). *Selling the free market: The rhetoric of economic correctness*. Guilford.

Chomsky, N. (2012). Who owns the world? Lecture delivered at University of Massachusetts at Amherst. Retrieved July 21, 2021, from https://chomsky.info/20121026/

Galbraith, J. K. (1988). The grammar of political economy. In A. Klamer, D. N. McCloskey, & R. M. Solow (Eds.), *The consequences of economic rhetoric* (pp. 221–239). Cambridge University Press.

Greider, W. (1987). *Secrets of the temple: How the federal reserve runs the country.* Simon and Schuster.

Klamer, A. (1987). As if economists and their subjects were rational. In J. S. Nelson, A. Megill, & D. N. McCloskey (Eds.), *The rhetoric of the human sciences: Language and argument in scholarship and public affairs* (pp. 163–183). University of Wisconsin Press.

McCloskey, D. N. (1990). *If you're so smart: The narrative of economic expertise* (2nd ed.). University of Chicago Press.

McCloskey, D. N. (1998). *The rhetoric of economics* (2nd ed.). University of Wisconsin Press.

McNamee, S. J., & Miller, R. K., Jr. (2014). *The meritocracy myth* (3rd ed.). Rowman & Littlefield.

Nelson, J. S., Megill, A., & McCloskey, D. N. (1987). *The rhetoric of the human sciences: Language and argument in scholarship and public affairs.* University of Wisconsin Press.

Pine, A. (1988, February 25). Greenspan discloses attempt to prod fed to ease policy. *Los Angeles Times.* Retrieved July 21, 2021, from https://www.latimes.com/archives/la-xpm-1988-02-25-mn-45243-story.html

Reich, R. (2013, December 14). Rich people's idea of charity: Giving to elite schools and operas. *Salon.* Retrieved July 21, 2021, from https://www.salon.com/2013/12/14/the_wealthy_give_to_charity_elite_schools_and_operas_partner

Samuels, W. J. (Ed.). (1990). *Economics as discourse: An analysis of the language of economists.* Springer.

Smith, A. (1976). *Theory of moral sentiments.* Clarendon Press.

Smith, A. (1978). *Lectures on jurisprudence* (R. L. Meek, D.D. Raphael, & P.G. Stein, Eds.). Oxford University Press.

Stein, B. (2006, November 26). In class warfare, guess which class is winning. *New York Times.* Retrieved March 3, 2011, from https://www.nytimes.com/2006/11/26/business/yourmoney/26every.html/

Stern, K. (2013, April 23). Why the rich don't give to charity. *The Atlantic.* Retrieved July 21, 2021, from https://www.theatlantic.com/magazine/archive/2013/04/why-the-rich-dont-give/309254/

CHAPTER 2

American Dream: Manufacturing Monetary Miasma

In the summer of 2014, my partner, Genina, and I visited London. I was there primarily to do some work at the Benjamin Franklin House. Franklin, of course, besides being the United States' first ambassador to France for the new fledgling nation, also served as the official agent to the Crown for several colonies during his almost 20 years in London from 1757 to 1775. Since this was Gena's first trip to England, we decided to do some typical touristy things in our down time. One morning, we stared in dismay at the huge line already assembling outside Westminster Abbey. We thought we had arrived early enough to avoid the crowd, but since that was not the case, we changed our plans. We quickly consulted our map and found, much to our delight, that the Florence Nightingale Museum was just across the River Thames from where we were. Tellingly, there was no line at the Nightingale Museum despite her unmatched contributions to healthcare, generally, and nursing, specifically. Among other things, Gena is a nurse, so this was an especially meaningful and serendipitous experience. For me, it was more illuminating than I had anticipated.

In particular, I was drawn to a story of Nightingale's experiences during the horrific Crimean War. In 1854, she was dispatched to the Ottoman Empire along with 38 volunteer nurses, and 15 nuns, to attend to the wounded from the war. She served at the Selimiye Barracks in modern-day Istanbul. During her first winter there, over 4000 soldiers died in the Barracks from diseases such as typhus, typhoid, cholera, and dysentery.

G. D. Klinger et al., *Money Talks*,
https://doi.org/10.1007/978-3-031-00816-0_2

Nightingale believed that the spread of these diseases was because of unhygienic conditions due to overcrowding, poor ventilation, and defective sewers. In short, she blamed much of the spread of the contagions on the fact that the hospital operated on what was essentially a cesspool. This experience inspired Nightingale to develop what is now dubbed "Miasma Theory." The idea is that the sanitary conditions of the care facility, including good ventilation, pure water, proper sanitation, personal hygiene, and natural light, were just as important as the actual medical care itself, and that "miasmas" contributed to the spread of contagion and disease. In *Notes on Nursing*, Nightingale wrote, "There are five essential points in securing the health of house:—1. Pure air, 2. Pure water, 3. Efficient drainage, 4. Cleanliness, 5. Light. Without these, no house can be healthy. And it will be unhealthy just in proportion as they are deficient" (1969, p. 24).

Previously unfamiliar to me, discovering this theory prompted me to do more research on miasmas. Merriam-Webster defines miasma as "a vaporous exhalation formerly believed to cause disease." It further defines miasma as "an influence or atmosphere that tends to deplete or corrupt." In Greek mythology, miasma means "a contagious power that has an independent life of its own." The latter definitions made me come to an important realization: to view miasmas solely in a medical context was to see them too narrowly. When we view miasmas as toxic environments, or contagious power, the theory has much broader applications.

In my estimation, the United States has become a political and economic miasma in recent years, and many have suffered tremendous negative consequences because of this state of affairs. Not only have we literally poisoned and polluted our environment, but we have embraced an immoral and unsustainable economic system, as well. The signs of this are everywhere, from ever-widening income inequality to obesity, drug use, violence, and mass incarceration. The so-called American Dream is proving to be unobtainable by a growing percentage of the population.

The American Dream is a slippery concept that has an interesting history. In his 1931 book, *Epic of America*, James Truslow Adams, whom many consider to be the first person to coin the phrase "American Dream," wrote: "But there has been also the *American dream*, that dream of a land in which life should be better and richer and fuller for every man, with opportunity for each according to his ability or achievement" (1931, p. 415). It is significant that Adams was writing on the cusp of the Great Depression. In many ways, his book is a response to the excesses of the 1920s. Indeed, in the very next line of *Epic of America*, Adams continued: "It is a difficult dream for the European upper classes to interpret adequately" (p. 415). The American Dream, it seems, at least as initially articulated, was decidedly anti-elite. It sought equality of opportunity for all, not merely the enrichment of the upper class with the hope that the economic prosperity enjoyed by the rich would "trickle down" to those less fortunate. Adams specifically resisted this class-based aspect of the American Dream: for the dream to grow to its "fullest development," it must be "unrepressed by social orders which had developed for the benefit of classes" (416).

Despite its initial articulation, the concept of the American Dream has changed over time, and it has been redefined at various junctures by those with a vested interest in articulating a specific meaning for the same. The American Dream is what Communication scholar Michael McGee (1980) has termed an "ideograph." These words are unique in that the words themselves do not have an underlying ontic from which one could fix and measure its meaning, instead they are complex amalgams of discourse and ideology. In a disagreement about the meaning of the word "car," "dog," or "tree," one can point to the actual object to resolve the dispute, but that is not the case with words such as "freedom," "justice," and "equality." Such terms become funded with meaning not through ascertaining the nature of that ontological existence (if, indeed, there is one at all), but by concrete, historical practice as manifested in culturally contingent discourse. "Freedom is as freedom does," as McGee was fond of saying; or, rather, that "[t]he important fact about ideographs is that they exist in real discourse, functioning clearly and evidently as agents of political consciousness" (p. 7). McGee calls such usages "ideographs" because these symbols are "the basic structural elements, the building blocks, of ideology" (p. 7). Ideographs do not have fixed or universal meanings, and they can mean remarkably different things for different people and communities. They can, therefore, both serve to unite and divide us. An investigation into the discourse of the American Dream then at once penetrates beyond discursive parameters; it provides us with clues into the ideology, the social and political theory, and the countervailing norms and warrants of different historical moments and political cultures. In short, the meaning of the American Dream has been contested from the time of its original articulation.

Communication scholar Walter Fisher observes, "[T]he American Dream is two dreams, or, more accurately, it is two myths that we all share in some degree or other, and which, when taken together, characterize America as a culture" (1973, p. 160). Fisher calls the two primary myths that have historically infused the American Dream with meaning in the United States are the "materialistic" myth, and the "moralistic myth." He outlines the key aspects of materialistic myth in particular:

> [It] is grounded in the puritan work ethic and relates to the values of effort, persistence, "playing the game," initiative, self-reliance, achievement, and success. It undergirds competition as the way of determining personal worth, the free enterprise system, and the notion of freedom, defined as the freedom from controls, regulations, or constraints that hinder the individual's striving for ascendency in social-economic hierarchy. (p. 161)

Importantly, he continues, "In naked form, the materialistic myth is compassionless and self-centered: it encourages manipulation and leads to exploitation" (p. 161). Fisher wrote this article in 1973, and it seems that the materialistic myth has gained even more traction since that time. A significant turning point occurred after the presidential election in 1980. Writing in 1982, John Horton commented: "Today, in the 1980's, we are seeing the reassembling of the American Dream into its right wing mold" (1982, p. 123). Specifically, the Reagan Administration changed the meaning of the "American Dream" by rearticulating a particular ideological agenda, one that linked traditional notions of the American Dream to tropes centered upon economic deregulation, economic self-interest, and the free market. Ronald Reagan spun a tale about increased opportunity for all, but the policies that he enacted during his time as president told a very different story. While demonizing those less fortunate, he constructed and implemented an economic system that favored big businesses and the rich under the banner of "Reaganomics," an interesting ideograph itself, and one that we will revisit in later chapters. Reagan packaged and sold Reaganomics by blending free market rhetoric with the ever-evolving myth of the American Dream. This rhetorical package seduced people across political groups and economic classes despite the historical evidence that the vast majority of people during the Reagan presidency and in the years that followed it did not see a noticeable improvement in their income or quality of life.

Over the years, the media have been complicit in reinforcing this particular retelling of the American Dream. In their study of the 120 top-grossing Hollywood business films from 1927 to 1995, media scholars Pileggi, Grabe, Holderman, and Montigny identified two seemingly contradictory narratives regarding the American Dream, the cautionary and the hopeful. Based on their close reading of relevant texts, they contend that although "few American lives exemplify the dream, media content perpetuates the myth that achieving the American dream is within everyone's reach. Structural barriers to social mobility such as demographic heritage and limits on potential financial gain are underplayed. Ultimately, this narrative structure provides a social space that benefits the economic system" (reference omitted) (2000, p. 208). In his study of the films *Wall Street* (1987) and *The Firm* (1993), J. Emmett Winn reaches a similar conclusion regarding Hollywood's explicit reinforcement of the American Dream myth. Specifically, he contends, "[T]he films communicate an understanding of social order that rationalizes the social limits placed on the working class while simultaneously the myth of abounding success opportunities for all Americans. In the end, the protagonists' upward mobility stalls because of their own personal failure—not because the myth [of the] American Dream is unsound" (2003, p. 308). These films, exemplars of Reagan's remaking of the American Dream myth in the 1980s, seem to function as critiques of greed, but that greed is cast as a personal failure, not a shortcoming of the American Dream itself. Consequently, the underlying message of the films is "working class characters who pursue material success risk giving into greed and forsaking their own morally superior working class values. Ultimately, the protagonists fail to achieve upward mobility because of their greed (personal failure) rather than an inegalitarian social system" (p. 311). Despite their surface critique of greed, the films end up subtly, but unmistakably reinforcing inherently unequal class structures in society hidden beneath the promising, but unreachable myth of the American Dream.

Hollywood is not alone in its complicity. In her article, "The Great Middle American Dream Machine," Lynn Berk contends that corporate media tend to obscure class divisions while advancing the cause of the American Dream: "No bias is so thoroughly supported by networks and so ignored by critics and viewers as the bias of class. The nature of this bias is, of course, obscured by the myth of a classless America, or more accurately, the myth of a middle-class America" (1977, p. 27). Significantly, she contends, "Andrew Levinson insists that 60 percent of Americans are working class. … Yet, until recently, network television virtually ignored the American working class" (p. 27). Instead, Berk argues, the media tend to spin tales of upward mobility and the merits of middle- to upper-class living. Consequently, while a majority of Americans are firmly entrenched in the working class, the media lead them to believe that they are middle to upper class, or that achieving this class status is both desirable, and obtainable through hard work and determination. Most soon discover, however, that their hard work only means longer hours, more stress, and little to no additional compensation. For a vast majority of Americans, the American Dream is quite literally an unobtainable myth with no grounding in reality.

The tendency of the American Dream myth, as used by those in power, to reinforce existing the social class structure, and to get people to accept their station in an inherently unequal economic system, plays out in virtually every aspect of our lives with great consequence. Take, for example, the National Basketball Association's promise of basketball stardom as the ticket out of poverty for so many aspiring young basketball players. While we know the success stories all too well through sports celebrities like Michael Jordan, Charles Barkley, Shaquille O'Neal, Kobe Bryant, and LeBron James, the reality is that only a small fraction of players actually make the pros. In 2014, Andrew Flint reported in *Hoopsvibe* that of 545,844 high school basketball players over the past several years, and 17,500 college players, only 48 players were actually drafted. Thus, only 2.9% of players move from high school to college basketball, 1.3% make the jump from college to the pros, and only .03% move from high school to the pros. Based on these numbers, Flint (2014) observed, "This means out of every 10,000 kids playing basketball in high school only 3 will make it to the pros." These numbers jibe with the 2012 *NCAA Sports Sponsorship and Participation Rates Report* prepared by Erin Irick (2012) that studies participation rates in sports from 1981–1982 to 2011–2012. Importantly, this does not mean that basketball players who break through will be NBA superstars with lucrative salaries and endorsement contracts; it simply means that they will be drafted. Flint concludes, "The reality is it doesn't matter how much you are dominating the local, state, or even national scene the odds are stacked against you." Sadly, though, tens, even hundreds of thousands of young people devote their whole lives to basketball, seduced by the myth that they can be one of the next NBA superstars if they only work hard enough. They will often forgo gainful employment, even adequate devotion to their education to pursue this nearly unobtainable dream. The end result is that the vast majority of players who pinned all of their hopes for future success on making it to the NBA are left without the educational preparation, work experience, or life skills to substantially improve their lot in life.

In the 2014 edition of their book, *The Meritocracy Myth*, Stephen J. McNamee and Robert K. Miller Jr. contend, "The notion of raw artistic talent as a means to upward social mobility is even more suspect" (2014, p. 27). They continue, "The presumed link between raw talent and celebrity athletes and artists reinforces the meritocracy myth. The presumption that if *some* celebrities with these talents came from these origins, then *anyone* who had those potential talents could do the same" (p. 27). However, the reality is, as I noted above, only .03% of basketball players from high school forward will actually be drafted by an NBA team. Importantly, these seemingly insurmountable odds are not unique to the sport of basketball: "The NCAA has calculated similar long-shot odds for reaching the professional level in football, baseball, ice hockey, and soccer" (p. 27). The end result, as I note above, is what McNamee and Miller call a mobility trap: "The illusion of potential success in glamorous areas such as sports or entertainment ends up being a mobility trap for many youthful aspirants who end up investing time and effort in the long-shot pursuit of fame and fortune at the expense of more realistic avenues of social mobility" (reference omitted) (pp. 27–28).

Sports are just an illustration of a much deeper problem in the United States. Indeed, the lessons we glean from this example apply to nearly all aspects of our economic lives:

> Recently, however, the prospects for attaining the American Dream have diminished. The American Dream implies not just a general hopefulness about the future and a formula for success but also a sense of what the fulfillment of the dream would look like. Although specifics vary, several outcomes are generally associated with the fulfillment of the American Dream, home ownership, improved life chances for children (especially defined as now sending children to college), opportunities to get rich, and a secure and comfortable retirement. The prospects for fulfillment of the American Dream have dimmed in recent years, and Americans appear to be responding by being more pessimistic about the future (references omitted). (McNamee & Miller, pp. 11–12)

Despite this reality, a significant majority of people still believe in the promise of the American Dream: "Survey data from a 2005 *New York Times* national poll show that 80 percent of Americans believe that it is possible to 'start out poor in this country, work hard, and become rich'" (McNamee & Miller, p. 14). Recent empirical evidence suggests, however, that this belief is misguided and based largely on an illusion. According to Hargreaves (2013), "The American Dream is supposed to mean that through hard work and perseverance, even the poorest people can make it to the middle class or above. But it's actually harder to move up in America than it is in most other advanced nations." Citing evidence from University of Ottawa economist and Russell Sage Foundation Fellow Miles Corak, Hargreaves notes, "Among the major developed countries, only in Italy and the United Kingdom is there less economic mobility." One of the main factors that contribute to this self-reinforcing class structure is the level on income inequality: "The more unequal a society is currently, the greater chance that the children will be stuck in the same sphere. This is because wealthy families are able to provide things like tutors and extracurricular activities—and the time to pursue them—that poorer families cannot" (Hargreaves).

If you do not have the good fortune to be a CEO of a behemoth corporation, you are an employee who is dependent on your employer for your livelihood, and if you are especially lucky, some measure of additional benefits. Current wage and salary levels in this country for the vast majority of people prevent individuals from reaching the full promise of the American Dream: "With the decline of family farms and businesses and the ascendency of corporations in the twentieth century, however, rates of self-employment plummeted. New business starts are notoriously risky. For most Americans, these factors have decreased rather than increased the likelihood of 'rags-to-riches' scenarios" (McNamee & Miller, p. 14). While there are demographic factors at work that continue to increasingly limit economic mobility, we also live in an economic and discursive system that promises great things, and delivers on them to only a very few: "If why Americans have a harder time making it into the middle class is a bit of a mystery to economists, why Americans cling to the belief that it's still easy to do is even more baffling" (Hargreaves).

America is assuredly one of the richest countries in the world. According to Credit Suisse, in 2013, America was home to 42% of millionaires in the world; Japan is second at merely 8% (Luhby, 2014). One of the things that always mystified me is the fact that while the United States has the world's largest economy and is one of the richest countries on the planet, it never seems to crack the top-ten list of the happiest places to live on earth. Perhaps this is just further proof of the old adage: "money cannot buy happiness," but I suspect there is more to it than that. In their book, *The Spirit Level: Why Greater Equality Makes Societies Stronger*, Richard

Wilkinson and Kate Pickett argue persuasively that "[n]ot only have measures of wellbeing and happiness ceased to rise with economic growth but, as affluent societies have grown richer, there have been long-term rises in rates of anxiety, depression, and numerous other social problems" (2010, pp. 5–6).

The myth of the American Dream has cloaked staggering inequality that has only increased in recent years. In 2011, *The Economist* reported, "There was not a single year between 1952 and 1986 in which the richest 1% of American households earned more than a tenth of the national income" ("Beautiful & Damned," 2011). However, "after rising steadily since the mid-1980s, reckon Thomas Piketty and Emmanuel Saez, two economists, in 2007 the income share of the richest percentile reached a staggering 18.3%. The last time America was such an unequal place was in 1929, when the equivalent figure was 18.4%" (Economist). That figure was only 8% in 1981, so the top 1% of income earners in the United States more than doubled their share of income in about 25 years (Luhby). Growing income inequality is only one aspect of the problem. Wealth inequality is arguably even more pronounced, with the top 1% controlling 42% of the nation's wealth in 2014 (Sullivan et al., 2015, p. 5)

It is important to note here that there is an unmistakable element of race involved in the growing income inequality in the United States that is too often masked by a singular focus on class. In a study conducted by Demos and Brandeis University, researchers noted that in 2011, "the median white household had $111,146 in wealth holdings, compared to just $7113 for the median Black household and $8348 for the median Latino household" (Sullivan et al., p. 1). Wealth inequality is perhaps a more important marker for the future than income inequality because of the potential for wealth to transfer between generations. As such, the study concludes, "The result is that the racial wealth gap perpetuates from generation to generation, with profound implications for the economic security and mobility of future generations" (p. 6). Significantly, as was the case with wealth inequality in general, the disparity seems to be growing along racial lines, as well: "The gap between Black and white household wealth quadrupled from 1984 to 2007, totally discrediting the conventional wisdom that the U.S. is slowly and fitfully moving toward racial equality, or some rough economic parity between the races" (Ford, 2010).

Growing wealth inequality is not just an American phenomenon. Ahead of the World Economic Forum in 2014, Oxfam reported that .7% of the world's population owns $99 trillion, while the lowest 68.7% own only $7 trillion (Luhby). In 2015, Oxfam's report was even more startling: "[T]he richest 1% will have as much wealth as the other 99% combined" (Karimi, 2015). Still, the growing income and wealth inequality in the United States receives the most attention because as the world's largest economy, and the paragon of capitalism, it is model for other capitalist countries. The example that the United States sets for them is tremendously unsettling, and the consequences are unmistakable. In 2009, citing a study by Mark Rank of Washington University in St. Louis published in *Archives of Pediatrics and Adolescent Medicine*, CBS reported, "Half of American kids will live in households receiving food stamps before the age of 20" (Szabo, 2009). The problem only seems to be getting worse. In 2014, CNN reported that "48 million Americans were receiving food stamps—the highest number since the program began in 1969" (Kurtz, 2014a). In 2012, economists predicted that poverty rates will "climb to levels unseen in nearly half a century, erasing gains from the war on poverty in the 1960s amid a weak economy and fraying government safety net" (Yen, 2012). An estimated 47 million people in the United States, over 15% of the U.S. population, was poor in 2011 (Yen).

Peter Edelman, director of the Georgetown Center on Poverty, Inequality, and Public Policy, identified a key component contributing to the rise in poverty: "The problem is that the tidal wave of low wage jobs is dragging us down" (Yen, p. A3). Employers continue to exploit workers by demanding higher productivity while cutting salaries and benefits. They are often told that they should consider themselves lucky to even have a job after the "Great Recession" of 2008. That claim, of course, is used to justify low wages and salaries, reduced hours, and diminished benefits. Employers also take advantage of legal loopholes. My youngest took her first job at Dairy Queen her junior year in high school. They made her work as many hours as they possibly could, and more than any of us liked, without crossing the line to the point where she would qualify for benefits. While her story is anecdotal, it seems to be happening with increasing frequency across the United States. According to a study by University of Massachusetts economists Randy Albelda and Michael Carr, "Over the last 30 years, the number of all U.S. workers has grown 40%, roughly in line with the adult population. But over that same period, the number of low-wage workers who also live in low-income households has climbed 94%" (Kurtz, 2014b). Importantly, they note, it's not just teenagers, or spouses earning a second income, an increasing number of primary breadwinners are forced to take these low-wage jobs. They now make up about 14% of all workers in the United States, the highest level since the 1980s (Kurtz, 2014b). These are people who make enough to not be classified as poor, but hardly make enough to support themselves and their families. Economists often refer to this class as the "working poor." So, the poverty rates I cite above underestimate the magnitude of the issue.

Another way that statistics are used to cloak underlying economic inequities is in government reporting about employment numbers. In June 2014, for example, the government reported that the U.S. economy added a "surprising" 288,000 jobs which, of course, gave the stock market a boost. Hidden in this report, though, was the fact that the number of people who said they felt compelled to take part-time jobs even though they would prefer full-time jobs, jumped from 275,000 to 3.5 million in the same period (Davidson, 2014). In addition, although former President Obama wore improving numbers in unemployment like a badge of honor for his presidency, those figures distort the troubling reality of the situation. Annalyn Kurtz (2014c) noted that the U.S. job market was weaker than most economists had projected months earlier. And despite the unemployment rate falling to 6.7% in December 2013, "the drop came mainly from workers leaving the labor force. ... Only 62.8% of the adult population is participating in the labor market now—meaning they either have a job or are looking for one. That matches the lowest level since 1978."

This might be an easier pill to swallow if everyone was sharing in the suffering, but evidence suggests otherwise. In 2011, Matt Krantz and Barbara Hansen noted, "At a time most employees can barely remember their last substantial raise, median CEO pay jumped 27% in 2010 as the executives' compensation started working its way back to prerecession levels" (2011, p. 1B). Workers in private industry, on the other hand, saw their compensation rise only 2.1%, according to the Bureau of Labor Statistics (p. 1B). Besides CEO's, the other group that is benefitting from the economic recovery is big corporations in general, and their wealthy shareholders: "At around $15.8 trillion a year, the United States produces more in annual economic output than ever before, but it's not the worker that's benefitting. Instead corporate profits now account for the largest slice of that pie on record, whereas the slice for workers has been steadily declining" (Kurtz, 2014a). So, while the economy is arguably more productive than ever, it seems to be enriching only those who are already at the top. In short, workers are not reaping the benefits of their increased productivity; they are working harder, and for longer hours, but with less overall compensation. Instead, employers continue to exploit their workers, and enjoy even more of the fruits of their labor. According to Thomas Piketty and Emmanuel Saez, whom I cite above, the "richest 1% of American families have captured 95% of the income gains in the recovery period spanning 2009–2012" (Kurtz, 2014a). The end result, of course, is that fewer and fewer people are able to achieve the increasingly elusive American Dream. The actual numbers are quite revealing: "An analysis by *USA Today* shows that living the American Dream would cost the average family of four about $130,000 a year. Only 16 million U.S. Households—about 1 in 8—earned that much in 2013, according to the U.S. Census Bureau" (Gold, 2014, p. 6B). In other words, only about 12% of U.S. households are living the American Dream. Still, people seem to cling to the idea despite ever-worsening odds, and overwhelming evidence to the contrary.

The impact of the growing economic inequality has taken a significant toll on our collective well-being in several different ways. Christine Dugas (2009) reported that business bankruptcies were up 240% since 2006; the vast majority of these failures are small businesses. Stephanie Armour warns that a second wave of home foreclosures loom (2009, p. 1B). Julie Hirschfeld Davis calculated that the recession of 2008 caused Americans' retirement accounts to lose $2 trillion in value (2008, p. A6). U.S. Representative George Miller commented, "It's clear that [American's] retirement security may be one of the greatest casualties of this financial crisis" (Davis). The end result, of course, is that a growing number of American workers, already overworked and under compensated, now feel that they will have to work beyond retirement just to make ends meet. It is not just our pocketbooks and houses that are taking a hit. According to *Time* magazine, "Among people earning less than $50,000 a year—roughly half of U.S. households—34% have not gone to the doctor because of the cost, 31% have been out of work at some point, and 13% have been hungry" (Gibbs, 2009). Additionally, "Forty percent of people at all income levels say they feel anxious, 32% have trouble sleeping, and 20% are depressed." Our growing economic inequality is reflected in our worsening mental and physical health. Perhaps part of the reason why clinical obesity, heart disease, and premature death is such a significant problem in the United States is because employees are constantly stressed because of their jobs, workers have to eat fast food for lunch because they are only afforded 15 minutes to eat, and people are not afforded enough time to exercise because they are too busy trying to hold down two jobs. Sharon Jayson (2008) observes, "Economic stress is taking its toll on the

United States' emotional and physical health, new survey data show: More than half of Americans report irritability or anger, fatigue or sleeplessness, and almost half say they self-medicate by overeating or indulging in unhealthy foods" (p. A3). Indeed, the high rates of alcoholism, tobacco consumption, drug abuse, divorce, crime, and mental illness in the United States are additional signs of a body politic in distress.

Our collective suffering because of economic inequality often comes out in more insidious ways as well. Far too many people are angry about their life situations, and they regretfully turn to violence to express their angst. Elliott Rodger, the young man who brutally murdered others his age during a shooting rampage near the campus of the University of California, Santa Barbara in 2014 left behind a 107,000-word manifesto in which he tries to explain his actions. Entitled "My Twisted World: The Story of Elliott Rodger," three passages in particular stand out. First, he claimed, "I couldn't help but feel a bitter form of envy at all of the rich kids at the concert. They grew up in lavish mansions, indulged in excessive opulence, and will never have to worry about anything in their pleasurable, hedonistic lives. I would take great pleasure in watching all of those rich families burn alive" (Duke, 2014). Second, he noted, "Wealth is one of the most important defining factors of self-worth and superiority. I hated and envied all of those kids for being born into wealth, while I had to struggle to find a way to claim wealth for myself. I had to be ruthless, and do whatever it takes to attain such wealth" (Duke). Finally, he sadly believed:

> I knew I was always destined for great things. This must be it! I was destined to be the winner of the highest lottery jackpot in existence. I knew right then and there that this jackpot was meant for me. Who else deserved such a victory? I had been through so much rejection, suffering, and injustice in my life, and this was to be my salvation. With my whole body filled with feverish hope, I spent $700 dollars on lottery tickets for this drawing. As I spent this money, I imagined all the amazing sex I would have with a beautiful model girlfriend I would have once I become a man of wealth. (Duke)

At the start of this chapter, I talked about disease, and how quickly a contagion can spread when one lives in a miasma. We are born into a system where we are told that if we apply ourselves, and work hard enough, we can achieve the American Dream. As we have seen, though, we are also born into a system where achieving that dream is structurally and practically impossible for the vast majority of people. That assuredly creates a sense of false hope, and often a deeply felt resentment, when the promise doesn't meet our reality. We can blame others, or the system, for this undeniable fact, but we also must share some of the blame ourselves. We believed the hype, we jumped on the bandwagon, we ignored the suffering of others as we tried to get to the top, and we enabled an inherently exploitative economic environment. Although we may not like to hear it, Nancy Gibbs raises an important point: "Our institutions watch for economic vital signs. But maybe, for individuals, the sickness is what came before—the hallucination that debt would never need to be repaid, that values only rise, that bubbles never burst. When the markets collapsed, that fever broke" (Gibbs). One additional heartbreaking story illustrates that point. On December 2, 2008, *The Indianapolis Star* reported that a worker was trampled to death when 2000 customers stormed into a Walmart in Minneola, New York, the day after Thanksgiving, in the annual ritual of what has been appropriately termed, "Black Friday," the busiest shopping day of the year ("Trampled Worker," 2008). Stores offer massive discounts, and cash-strapped consumers only too willingly take the bait, often camping out days before in store parking lots to get the best deals, and employees often have to be in stores hours before the sun rises to deal with the anticipated mob scene. These companies take advantage of people's economic vulnerabilities and foment near economic anarchy because, after all, profits are more important than encouraging people to spend quality time with family during the holidays. The worker who was trampled to death by crazed customers in this case was a double tragedy. Not only did he lose his life, but he also had only been working at that Walmart for about a week with no formal crowd control training. He was a member of the "working poor" who had been hired through a temp agency. If he had made it through the weekend alive, he probably would not have had a job waiting for him on the other side.

Before "affluenza" was a clever, but specious legal argument for excusing culpability in an otherwise indisputable case of intoxication manslaughter, it was an outstanding public television program (De Graaf & Boe, 1997) and later adapted as a book in 2001. The beginning of the film defines affluenza as follows: "**Af-flu-en-za** n. 1. The bloated, sluggish and unfulfilled feeling that results from efforts to keep up with the Joneses. 2. An epidemic of stress, overwork, waste and indebtedness caused by dogged pursuit of the American Dream. 3. An unsustainable addiction to economic growth." The film offers some fairly stark statistics. For example, by 1990, the average house has more than doubled since 1950 (3000 sq. ft.

v. 1100 sq. ft.); the average garage space is now an average of 900 sq. ft., almost as large as an entire home in 1950. By 1987, the United States had more shopping malls than high schools, and we shop an average of 6 hours a week, but only play with our children 40 minutes a week. The trend has only worsened: the number of malls has almost doubled since that time, from 69,596 in 1987 to 107,773 in 2010 (Statista, 2016). According to the U.S. Department of Education (2016), there were a total of 37,100 public and private secondary schools in the United States in 2001. The push to get people to consume more and more is a reflection of our misaligned priorities. Significantly, "credit card debt tripled in the 1980's," as we were seduced into believing that our economic lives were improving while the reality was that most people's income was stagnating, at best (De Graaf & Boe). The end result should hardly be surprising: "In 1996, more than a million Americans declared personal bankruptcy, more than graduated from college" (De Graaf & Boe). The comparative statistics offered by Michael Moore (2009) in *Capitalism: A Love Story* are even more startling: between 1980 and 2000, average working wages increased only 1%, household debt increased 111% to make up for the fact that wages were stagnant, bankruptcies increased by 610%, incarcerations increased 355%, anti-depressant sales increased 305%, and the ratio of CEO to worker pay increased by 649%. During the same time, of course, the Dow Jones Industrial Average increased by 1371%, enriching the lives of a fortunate few before even that was taken away from the average American in the Great Recession of 2008. In all, the evidence is overwhelming that consumerism and materialism have created an economic, political, even spiritual miasma. All of our efforts to treat the symptoms—giving pharmaceuticals to those who are depressed, giving alcohol and drugs to those who are stressed, giving extra hours to those who are already overworked, giving happy meals to those who are already poorly nourished—will do little to cure the disease unless we address the underlying causes that result from an inherently unequal and unfair economic system. American songwriter Bruce Springsteen once said, "I have spent my life judging the distance between American reality and the American dream." This project is written toward the same end.

References

Adams, J. T. (1931). *The epic of America*. Little, Brown, & Company.

Armour, S. (2009, November 19). Next wave of foreclosures loom. *USA Today*, 1B.

Berk, L. M. (1977). The great middle American dream machine. *Journal of Communication, 27*(3), 27–31.

Davidson, P. (2014, July 6). Rise in part-time workers worries some experts. *USA Today*. Retrieved July 19, 2015, from https://www.usatoday.com/story/money/business/2014/07/06/part-time-workers/12185871/

Davis, J. H. (2008, October 7). Pension plans lose trillions. *ABC News*. Retrieved July 19, 2015, from https://abcnews.go.com/Business/Economy/story?id=5976063&page=1

De Graaf, J., & Boe, V. (Producers). (1997). *Affluenza*. KCTS Television.

Dugas, C. (2009, June 30). Small business vital to economic recovery go bankrupt. *ABC News*. Retrieved July 19, 2015, from https://abcnews.go.com/Business/story?id=7973776&page=1

Duke, A. (2014, May 27). Five revelations from the "twisted world" of a "kissless virgin." *CNN*. Retrieved July 19, 2015, from https://www.cnn.com/2014/05/25/justice/california-shooting-revelations/index.html

Fisher, W. R. (1973). Reaffirmation and subversion of the American dream. *The Quarterly Journal of Speech, 59*(2), 160–167.

Flint, A. (2014, January 2). The odds of playing in the NBA. *Hoopsvibe*. Retrieved July 19, 2015, from https://www.hoopsvibe.com/features/285631-the-odds-of-playin-in-the-nba

Ford, G. (2010, May 19). Study finds blacks will never gain wealth parity with whites under the current system. *Black Agenda Report*. https://www.blackagendareport.com/content/study-shows-blacks-will-never-gain-wealth-parity-whites-under-current-system. Accessed 24 May 2010.

Gibbs, N. (2009, April 15). The great recession: America becomes thrift nation. *Time*. Retrieved July 19, 2015, from http://content.time.com/time/nation/article/0,8599,1891527,00.html

Gold, H. R. (2014, July 4). Price tag for the American dream: $130K a year. *USA Today*, 6B.

Hargreaves, S. (2013, December 18). The myth of the American dream. *CNNMoney*. Retrieved December 19, 2013, from https://money.cnn.com/2013/12/09/news/economy/america-economic-mobility

Horton, J. (1982). Class struggle and the American dream. In T. McCormack (Ed.), *Studies in communication: Culture, code and content analysis, 2* (pp. 114–141). Jai Press.

Irick, E. (2012). *Student athlete participation: 1981–82–2011–12.* NCAA sports sponsorship and participation rates report, NCAA.

Jayson, S. (2008, October 8). Poll: Financial fears are affecting health. *Indianapolis Star*, A3.

Karimi, F. (2015, January 19). Wealthiest 1% will soon own more than the rest of us combined, Oxfam says. *CNN.* Retrieved January 20, 2015, from https://www.cnn.com/2015/01/19/world/wealth-inequality/index.html

Krantz, M., & Hansen, B. (2011, April 1). CEO pay soars while workers' pay stalls. *USA Today*, 1B–2B.

Kurtz, A. (2014a, January 24). 7 setbacks for the middle class. *CNNMoney.* Retrieved February 12, 2014, from https://money.cnn.com/2014/01/24/news/economy/middle-class-economy/index.html

Kurtz, A. (2014b, February 6). Rise of the low-wage breadwinner. *CNNMoney.* Retrieved February 7, 2014, from https://money.cnn.com/2014/02/06/news/economy/low-wage-breadwinner/index.html

Kurtz, A. (2014c, January 10). 2013 ends with weakest job growth in years. *CNNMoney.* Retrieved February 7, 2014, from https://money.cnn.com/2014/01/10/news/economy/december-jobs-report

Luhby, T. (2014, August 5). America's middle class: Poorer than you think. *CNNMoney.* Retrieved July 19, 2016, from https://money.cnn.com/2014/06/11/news/economy/middle-class-wealth/index.html

McGee, M. C. (1980). The "ideograph": A link between rhetoric and ideology. *The Quarterly Journal of Speech, 66*(1), 1–16.

McNamee, S. J., & Miller, R. K., Jr. (2014). *The meritocracy myth* (3rd ed.).

Moore, M. (Director). (2009). *Capitalism: A love story.* Overture Films.

Nightingale, F. (1969). *Notes on nursing: What it is, and what it is not.* Dover. (Original work published 1860).

Pileggi, M. S., Grabe, M. E., Holderman, L. B., & de Montigny, M. (2000). Business as usual: The American dream in Hollywood business films. *Mass Communication and Society, 3*(2–3), 207–228.

Statista.com. Retrieved July 19, 2016, from https://www.statista.com/statistics/208059/total-shopping-centers-in-the-us/

Sullivan, L., Meschede, T., Dietrich, L., & Shapiro, T. (2015). The racial wealth gap: Why policy matters. *Demos.* Retrieved July 6, 2016, from https://heller.brandeis.edu/iere/pdfs/racial-wealth-equity/racial-wealth-gap/racial-wealth-gap-why-policy-matters.pdf

Szabo, L. (2009, November 2). Study: Half of U.S. kids on food stamps. *CBS News.* Retrieved November 3, 2009, from https://www.cbsnews.com/news/study-half-of-us-kids-on-food-stamps

The beautiful and the damned. (2011, January 22). *The Economist*. Retrieved July 19, 2015, from https://www.economist.com/finance-and-economics/2011/01/20/the-beautiful-and-the-damned

Trampled worker has no crowd training. (2008, December 2). *Indianapolis Star*, A7.

US Department of Education. High school facts at a glance. Retrieved July 19, 2016., from https://www2.ed.gov/about/offices/list/ovae/pi/hs/hsfacts.html

Wilkinson, R., & Pickett, K. (2010). *The spirit level: Why greater equality makes societies stronger*. Bloomsbury.

Winn, J. E. (2003). Every dream has its price: Personal failure and the American dream in Wall Street and The Firm. *Southern Communication Journal, 68*(4), 307–318.

Yen, H. (2012, July 23). U.S. poverty nearing 1965 levels. *Indianapolis Star*, A3.

CHAPTER 3

Bread and Circuses, or Poppies to Make You Sleep

In the *Wizard of Oz*, the Wicked Witch of the West used poppies to drug the people of Oz into submission. The witch and the poppies, of course, are very compelling metaphors that represent key aspects of Western capitalist economics. The Yellow Brick Road, the Emerald Palace, and the infamous Wizard of Oz are similarly important symbols of capitalism. From 1980 onward, money, greed, and the illusion of economic gain were the poppies that drugged people into quiet complacency and complicity. Of course, this love of money was nothing new. Greed, profiteering, and exploitation are as old as humankind itself. But, as I noted in the last chapter, this was a trope of modern capitalism that had lain dormant for much of the twentieth century.

The promise of easy money seduced perhaps three generations of young people. In my estimation, there was no more compelling image for the times than Nirvana's "Nevermind" album cover, released in 1991. That image featured a baby floating in water being lured in by a dollar on a hook. It represented precisely the dominant theme of the times. Those in power were trying to lure a new generation into accepting greed, self-interest, and the love of money as the guiding principles of their lives. I was able to watch this unfold during my formative years. Reagan took office my first year in high school, he was reelected my first year in college, and George H. W. Bush was president during my early graduate school years. My economics class in high school, taught by one of the more

G. D. Klinger et al., *Money Talks*,
https://doi.org/10.1007/978-3-031-00816-0_3

animated teachers in our school, helped draw me to this subject when I was in college. I decided to major in economics, as well as communication. Little did I know then what connections I would eventually find in the interplay between these two disciplines.

Many of my peers in college were studying economics to enter the business world, and to discover ways to become richer faster. President Reagan had set the tone for my generation: the quest for the almighty dollar had begun. I was interested in economics, though, for different reasons. I was interested in how economics created divides between people and classes. I dropped my "Investment Analysis" class at my Alma Mater in favor of an "Economics of Inequality" class my junior year while I was studying in England. In the former class, students had to create a mock portfolio of investments, and the person who made the most money at the end of the semester was deemed the "winner." It was like a slightly more advanced game of monopoly where the goal was to ignore the boundaries of ethical behavior to make the most money possible. Embracing ethics, it seemed, such as long-term investing in socially responsible companies, was the surest way to lose this competition. Also, since the course was only a semester long, it simultaneously encouraged students to rethink investment time frames. The goal: quick, short-term profit with little to no effort. The winners always seemed to be the ones who took big risks that paid off. This, I believe, created a new investor: somebody willing to accept significant risks, somebody investing with a short-term horizon, somebody hoping for huge gains with minimal work, or outlay. The children of the (Reagan) revolution were being trained to be tomorrow's day traders. By and large, they seemed to embrace this role with little hesitation. Like the baby on Nirvana's album cover, they had been hooked by the allure of a quick buck.

This generation helped shape an entire community built on these principles. In the years subsequent to 1980, everything was transformed into a commodity, and business sensibilities penetrated every aspect of our culture. Indeed, even the Academy, one of the last independent loci for social critique, had been co-opted by this new economic-centered transformation. During the nineteenth century, colleges and universities had been places where students learned to be moral participants in an increasingly complex world. The primary mission of many of these schools, especially private liberal arts colleges, was to train young clergy who often preached against the moral excesses of the industrial revolution and the capitalist state. Slowly, however, their mission seemed to change. Now these schools seem to be training grounds for new members of the capitalist hierarchy.

College and university presidents, once philosophers and ministers, were now being replaced by corporate-style CEOs. The mission of these presidents was no longer to teach responsible social critics, or enrich intellectual lives, but to raise the size of the endowment. Our students became "clients," and business speak permeated nearly every aspect of academic life. I remember in graduate school attending a seminar at the University of Iowa where University administrators advanced the merits of running the University like a business, and encouraged all of us to implement common corporate strategies like "Total Quality Management," or TQM, which was geared mostly toward maximizing customer satisfaction. Challenging our students to think critically often clashed with their satisfaction, it seemed, so the University's mission had to change, they argued. As Yuxia Qian (2013) observes, "The higher education environment has been undergoing tremendous changes the past two decades. … As a consequence, higher education institutions have to engage in planned changes to adapt to the shifting educational environment" (p. 67). Qian continues, "One particular trend in planned changes is that leaders increasingly resort to profit-driven business practices to improve efficiency and effectiveness. However, higher education institutions are guided by values such as 'intellectual creativity,' 'academic freedom,' and 'shared governance,' more than just by the 'bottom-line performance' in corporate organizations" (reference omitted) (p. 67). Under this new business paradigm, our job is now to give students what they wanted: technical training, and a stamp of approval in the form of a diploma to allow them to participate in an ever-expanding corporate machine. Schools of liberal arts, while still clinging to the principles that made them intellectually unique, were being transformed into training grounds for the business world. The main reason this is so unsettling for an educator with an eye to the future is, as Abraham Lincoln once warned, "The philosophy of the school room in one generation will be the philosophy of government in the next."

This began a vicious and self-reinforcing cycle. Those who had succeeded in the business world were precisely the ones who helped grow these cherished endowments. Now government and corporate influence in the previously isolated "Ivory Tower" was commonplace. Business leaders now increasingly populate college and university Boards of Trustees that have had a subtle, but unmistakable impact on their institutions' missions and, significantly, even their curriculum. Importantly, this phenomenon has not been limited to higher education. Channel One News, loaded with corporate and government advertising propaganda, made significant inroads in elementary and secondary schools, Coke and Pepsi were buying up the rights to control school beverage choices, corporate sponsorship of buildings and athletic teams seemed to be the new norm. A report in *Advertising Age* in 1995 noted, "Schools in El Paso County District 11 [Colorado] are counting the cash they've earned in the past 13 months for ads carried everywhere from calendars, maps, parent newsletters and staff magazines to school hallways and buses" (Parker, 1995). It was believed at the time that they were the first public school corporation to allow advertising upon and within school property. The school corporation raised just over $100,000 with just over half of that, $57,000, going to the school district and the remainder going to the advertising agency. Bus advertisements included offerings from Burger King and a 7-Up, among others. Burger King, for example, paid $12,500 to advertise on five buses. Inside the school, Pepsi paid $5000 to place two ads by student lockers and in the cafeteria. Interestingly, the American Association of School Administrators named District 11 Superintendent Kenneth Burley national superintendent of the year in 1993. In 2005, CBS News reported that the school district now reaps $650,000 from commercial advertising and, perhaps not surprisingly, enjoys newly placed Coca-Cola vending machines on school property (Kopp, 2005). The unsettling precedent had been set, and other schools have quickly jumped on the bandwagon. As Trevor Hughes reported, "Financially struggling schools nationwide are increasing the volume of advertising that children see in the halls, at football games and even on their report cards" (2012, p. 3A). Although public relations experts for this public school system try to spin the economic advantages of these programs while downplaying the costs, one only needs to look at the national statistics for childhood obesity and Type-2 diabetes to recognize what a shameful legacy these so-called educators have created. Indeed, "[c]onsumer advocates say marketers want to get in front of kids to build customers for life. Kids are especially vulnerable to persuasive advertising while they are still learning how to think critically, says Elizabeth Ben-Ishai, a spokeswoman for the Washington D.C.-based consumer-advocacy organization Public Citizen's Commercial Alert" (p. 3A) (Fig. 3.1).

Despite the well-placed concerns here, these amounts pale in comparison to what we are seeing in higher education. For example, the University of Maryland "reaped $20 million over 10 years for naming rights to the

Fig. 3.1 The iconic image from Nirvana's *Nevermind* album captures the lure of the almighty dollar for a new generation. (Records/Alamy Stock Photo)

Terrapins' basketball arena and another $5 million for naming rights to the arena's floor" (Wieberg & Berkowitz, 2009, p. 2A). The University of Kansas recently signed an 8-year contract with Adidas for $26.67 million; now their uniforms display the Adidas three-stripe logo (p. 2A). This, of course, is dwarfed by the 11-year, $169 million apparel deal the University of Michigan signed with Nike in 2015, the highest collegiate apparel contract in history (Rovell, 2015). The NCAA tournament in 2009 generated $591 million in TV and marketing revenues (p. 1A). And, since the beginning of 2007, "35 schools have guaranteed themselves almost a combined

$1.7 billion by bundling and selling their multimedia rights" (p. 2A). In what I consider to be the most poignant move of all, "[s]everal schools and conferences allow advertising and promotions by casinos in their arenas or game programs" (p. 2A). We all know, however, that money often comes with strings attached, even if those strings are only subtly interwoven at their inception. When the regulatory and ethical walls came down, government and corporate influence over education steadily increased.

The rise of athletics is one particularly telling place where both educational institutions lost sight of their mission and society at large lost touch with a moral life. The average salary earned by a major league baseball player in the 2007 season was just over $2.8 million dollars. The minimum salary earned by a bench player on a major league baseball active roster in 2008 was $390,000. While I was writing this chapter, Manny Ramirez signed a 2-year, $45 million contract with the Los Angeles Dodgers. In contrast, the average salary for a teacher in my home state of Indiana in 2007–2008 was $48,508. I do not mind saying that there is something fundamentally wrong with this discrepancy. I daresay that in terms of meaningful contributions to our world, teachers handily outperform professional baseball players. In addition, I do not know of one teacher who "retired" in disgrace for using Performance Enhancing Drugs as Ramirez did in 2010. The New York Yankees major league payroll, comprised of 25 roster players, was just over $209 million in 2008. By comparison, the GDP of the entire Republic of Palau in 2007 was $162 million. In short, a baseball team makes more than an entire sovereign nation. Yet, we live in an economic system where it is the professional athlete who receives the most significant rewards. This is the free market in action, and it leads, in my estimation, to some very unsettling consequences. Still, people seem entertained by these circuses of contemporary capitalist life. The ancient Roman ruling class used bread and circuses to maintain control of the people. The idea, of course, was to keep people entertained and, more importantly, distracted so that they were unaware that their rights were being steadily eroded, and their livelihood steadily undermined. Such is the case with modern professional sports.

But the problem is not isolated to the professional sports arena. Colleges and universities have allowed athletic departments to dominate the budgets and overall spirit of the Academy. Among other things, this squeezes the funds available for academics, and it undermines the mission of higher education. A little-known fact is that only "half a dozen of the 330 Division I programs operate in the black—absent school subsidization—each of the last five years [2004–2008], according to the NCAA" (Wieberg & Berkowitz, p. 2A). Urban Meyer, who was the football coach when I taught at the University of Utah, agreed to "one of the riches contracts in college sports history" to coach at Ohio State in 2011: "$24 million plus a country club membership and private plane for personal use" (Gregory & Webley, 2011, p. 51). In 2014, Nick Saban, football coach at the University of Alabama, earned over $7 million in total compensation. In contrast, Judy Bonner, who served as the President of the University of Alabama from 2012 to 2015, earned a $535,000 base salary. There is an urban legend that federal employees cannot make more than the President of the United States, but in 2014, both the Army and Navy football coaches earned over $1.5 million, making them the best paid Department of Defense employees while President Obama earned a $400,000 base salary the same year. If we ever find ourselves in a future war, maybe we should just challenge the other side to a game of football since that seems to be where we are placing a significant portion of our defense resources! The astronomical rise in coach's salaries is not limited to a few nationally recognized programs: "According to Duke University economist Charles Clotfelter, salaries for football coaches at 44 major public universities have grown 750%, on an inflation adjusted basis, since 1985" (Gregory & Webley, p. 51). As a point of comparison, "[s]alaries for professors at these schools have risen 32%" (p. 51). Our priorities, both nationally and in the Academy, are completely out of sync, and our students seem to be following our lead. As a college professor, I continue to be dismayed by the fact that 30,000 fans will crowd into an arena to watch a Division I athletic competition, but typically no more than 100 students will attend a highly acclaimed public debate featuring some of the brightest minds in our world. Of course, the media contribute significantly to this bread and circuses mentality. Writing on the place of sports in general, and football hooliganism in particular, cultural theorist Stuart Hall (1978) contends:

> [W]e know that we are encountering a phenomenon of very great public resonance when we discover stories which break out of the segregated enclave of the sports pages, and gain a wider, more general coverage on the front page of the paper. This signals that something has happened which connects sport, dramatically, with other news. It often means—again to put it metaphorically—that sport has gone political. (p. 18)

Further, and perhaps more insidious, athletics often reinforces an "us versus them" mentality. It legitimizes a mindset where there are always "winners" and "losers," and that this outcome is both normal and acceptable. The ancient Greeks used to theorize athletic competitions the same way that they theorized war: there is no true victory until the enemy/opponent is defeated and vanquished. Indeed, media coverage of sports today is peppered with language and images that evoke a warlike mentality. We teach our children at a very young age to hate their rivals, and I believe this creates artificial barriers to communication, interaction, and understanding. Importantly, it also normalizes violence. What we need in this world is to learn how to get along, rather than inventing new ways to hate "others." Given the pervasiveness of this mentality, it is perhaps not surprising that the whole of human history has been dominated by wars. Sadly, despite well-intentioned programs in conflict and peace studies, the modern Academy has done much to reinforce this war mentality as is evidenced by the unchallenged rise of intercollegiate athletics within and between our institutions of higher learning, among other things. Given that we teach our children at a young age to play board games like Monopoly, Rich Uncle, Risk, Acquire, Easy Money, and King Oil, games that reinforce a sense of economic and political domination, they are a receptive audience for this type of thinking. It is deeply ironic that the games we play often turn on normalized violence and conquest while we are simultaneously shocked and outraged at violence that occurs between fans at sporting events, and in society at large. Further, by normalizing conquest and domination in our games, it makes exploitation, destruction, and humiliation of others in the "real world" acceptable. Forcing people into bankruptcy, overcharging for rent, price-gouging consumers, and foreclosing on homes are allowed, even encouraged, because we are taught that this is the way that you "win the game" in Monopoly, and so it should be in life. To this end, Stuart Hall writes, "We see the violence of the street brawl or the pub fight, but not the violence implicit in poverty, unemployment or racism" (p. 29).

This relates to another important point, something I have termed the "casinoization" of everyday life. Once we accept this winner/loser paradigm as the normal and preferred state of affairs, it permeates every aspect of our lives. Casinos are interesting places to visit for a student of economics. I have spent a fair amount of time in various casinos not so much to gamble but to learn how they operate and how they gained traction in states that have historically resisted gambling. One of the first things that strikes me about casinos is that one never seems to find the faces and names of the losers, only the winners, who are emblazoned on posters, and promotional literature throughout. When somebody wins the "jackpot" on a slot machine, everyone knows because of the light and noise parade that emanates from a winning machine. Some believe that the "loosest" slot machines are positioned close to entrances so as to maximize the popular impression that everyone is winning big. The same is true of state-sanctioned lotteries and the media, our so-called watchdog of the government, has been complicit in advancing the cause of the unbridled capitalist agenda. The corporate media continues to be only too happy to publish the ever-growing size of the Powerball lottery, and the fact that there were no "winners" the previous week, feeding the buying frenzy. They also do not hesitate to publish reports about how much the lottery "benefited" the state, the job market, the education budget, and local communities. Ping-pong ball programs showed the live result of the lottery, rebroadcast several times a day. Indeed, there were even quasi-game shows like "Hoosier Millionaire," that allowed preliminary winners to compete for the "ultimate" prize. As I note above, the media during this time has been co-opted by corporate and government institutions; it had become more a mouthpiece for, rather than a watchdog of the government. And it seemed all too willing to sell itself to the insidious influences of the gambling industry. After all, money talks, and ethical responsibility did not pay the bills, and it assuredly did not turn a profit. Media organizations are for profit enterprises, so they share at least that motivating influence with the capitalist state. But they assuredly did not want to stand in the way of the state-based rhetoric of unlimited progress and profit. In their seminal book, *Manufacturing Consent*, Edward S. Herman and Noam Chomsky astutely observe, "[T]he media serve, and propagandize on behalf of, the powerful social interests that control and finance them" (2002/1988, p. xi).

I should spend a moment to discuss the casino-like transformation of the financial markets, and the U.S. economy, generally. My father was a Hoosier Methodist minister, the end of the line of four generations of Hoosier Methodist ministers. He was a strong and constant voice of opposition to the encroachment of gambling in our society. Gambling is, as he put it, a "tax on the poor." In other words, those who can least afford it tend to be the ones, collectively, who lose the most by gambling. This is nothing new to his profession, of course; Methodist ministers have a long history of speaking out against vices such as gambling, prostitution, and drinking, stretching as far back as their infamous circuit rides to various camps along the Western frontier in the nineteenth century. I remember visiting my grandmother's house when I was young. My brother and I were not even allowed to play cards during our visits, even seemingly innocuous games like hearts, or gin rummy (which was especially bad because it also referenced alcohol). Her position was that harmless card games, even when no money was involved, desensitized players to games of chance, and inevitably led to gambling later in life. Needless to say, it was no fun to visit grandma's house, but she was more prescient than I then realized at the time. In the same vein, parents should think twice before taking their children to places like Chuck-E-Cheese; they are training grounds for future gamblers, and simply one step removed from casinos.

Driven by a sense of financial need, and the promise that anybody can be the next "Hoosier Millionaire," gambling had become more than a mere metaphor for our society. We were being bombarded by the "get rich quick" mentality. Now, if you have "fast fingers" you could qualify to be a part of "Who Wants To Be a Millionaire?" You could even call in from home to be a part of this game show that advanced the ultimate rhetorical question, further enticing an all too willing public to embrace gambling as a centerpiece of their lives. You could also be a millionaire by doing nothing more than eating a Big Mac at McDonalds, or if you "supersized" your French Fries and drink, you could "earn" even more chances to win. Fast fingers and Big Macs only fed the no risk, no effort mentality that many people accepted as the surest path to easy money. In one particular revealing case, families in need were played off each other to exploit their economic vulnerabilities. On the Reality Television show, *The Briefcase Game*, which first aired in May 2015, two families were given briefcases with $101,000 and were instructed to decide if they should keep the money, or give some, or all of the money to the other family. This show was, in my estimation, economic exploitation at its worst, and it was emblematic of the greed and self-interest that mark our current political-economic culture. It also illustrated how others can and do profit by taking advantage of an inherently unequal economic system. Since others quickly reached the same conclusion, the show was canceled later the same year.

I watched the step-by-step encroachment of the gambling industry in my home state of Indiana. Indiana, a historically conservative agrarian state, had always resisted gambling within its borders. But constant pressure from the deep pockets of the gambling industry and lobby finally convinced some state leaders that they stood to benefit from allowing limited gambling within the state. First came limited horse racing, not full thoroughbred racing, but trotters, featured at places like the Indiana State Fair. One could not bet on the trotters, but it was the first step in normalizing competitive gaming in the state. The money was not far behind. In the 1988 election, Hoosier voters approved a lottery referendum by an overwhelming 62%. Shortly thereafter, the Indiana legislature passed the Indiana Lottery Act, and Governor Evan Bayh signed it into law. Gambling was now legal in Indiana. It started timidly as one might expect given Indiana's long-standing resistance to gambling, originally as a scratch-off game, until it eventually thrust its way onto the television, the radio, the newspaper, and nearly every convenience store in the state. Once the floodgates opened, the permutations of the Hoosier Lottery since that time have risen in number and scope. The names of the games are telling: Hoosier Millionaire, Lotto Cash, Daily 3 and Daily 4, Powerball, Lucky 5, Tax Free Million, Quick Draw, Double Play, Colts Cash, Mega Millions with Megaplier, $1 Million Cash Extravaganza, Indiana's Lucky Dog, Indiana's $5 Million Club, Tag 6, Money Bag Multiplier, Cash 5, Cash for Life, and EZ Match, to name a few. In 2003, Indiana passed a law that prohibited cigarette vending machines from places where minors had direct access to these products. Imagine my surprise when I recently saw Hoosier Lottery Ticket vending machines in the Indianapolis Airport, allowing anyone unfettered access to the same despite the fact that lottery tickets are just as illegal as cigarettes for minors to purchase. Double standards, it seems, are to be expected when the gaming industry is involved, a group that is apparently even more powerful than the once-mighty tobacco industry. Billboards along major interstates and highways in the state, as well as stories and advertisements in local newspapers and on local television, now proudly proclaim how much money the gaming industry has brought to the state, and how many jobs it has created. The initial trope that seemed to work on the people of the traditionally conservative Hoosier state, advanced simultaneously by the gaming industry and the state government, is that a percentage of the gaming industries' profits would be specifically earmarked for education, something that can and should create an ethical dilemma for school corporations. Still, how could one resist the rhetorical lure of allegedly more money for education, even though it was being raised by a tax on the poor? Of course, we now know that the schools were not actually receiving more money overall; it was just part of an elaborate shell game as the money previously allocated to education was diverted to other places in anticipation of this new gambling revenue.

As I note, though, the encroachment of the gambling industry on the state was slow and deliberate. Like other Midwestern states, Indiana reluctantly accepted casinos, but only with strict rules and regulations. The Indiana Riverboat Gaming Act passed in 1993. One of the more amusing requirements was that casinos could only be on boats on a body of water. The idea that if the casinos were not actually attached to the physical territory of the state that this was somehow a morally acceptable situation was laughable. In Iowa, the boat actually had to leave the dock before gambling could commence. Iowa was the first state to legalize riverboat gambling in 1991. Ironically, the boats began operating on April Fools' Day. Players were limited by how much money they could bring on board, $200 initially, and were issued vouchers in exchange for cash before the boat departed. You could not simply take out more money on the boat. The public justification for this policy was to limit losses, but it also limited how much people could gamble, a maximum $5 bet initially, and other rules, like preventing players from doubling down in blackjack, actually worked against players by limiting their winning potential, and led to more money flowing to the casinos.

One of the more amusing consequences of the law in Indiana was the recently opened French Lick casino. This casino is actually a building, attached to the ground with cement, but it has a small moat built around three of its sides, a couple of faux paddle wheels stuck on its outside walls, and houses an engine that cannot and will not ever be used unless a massive flood strikes the area and somehow breaks the "boat" away from its cement mooring. It was also required to staff a "crew" for the "boat." Eventually, state legislators realized how ridiculous things were, and allowed for a broadened range of gambling activities in the recently opened casino in Anderson that made no claims to be any kind of a boat. The distinction for these land-based casinos was that they were not allowed to house "live" table games. To circumvent these restrictions, though, the casinos offered three different types of alternative table games. The first was a table where players would sit in front of a video dealer who dealt virtual cards, the second was a table where real cards were used, but they were enclosed in a glass bubble and dealt by a mechanical arm, and my personal favorite, a table that actually had a live person behind the table, but whose only job was to push a button and "deal" virtual cards to video screens in front of players.

Ironically, the regulations put in place to "protect" consumers, and the moral integrity of the state, oftentimes worked against both. Further, because the state limited the number of casinos that were allowed to operate to less than ten initially (there are now only seven casinos in the Casino Association of Indiana), these casinos had de facto monopoly power over the gambling community. On a given weekend, one would often have to wait to get on a table, and the minimum bet was usually many times higher than one would see in places like Las Vegas, where one could bet as little as $1. Also, unlike Indiana, which typically has a six-deck shoe for blackjack, Las Vegas offered single-deck blackjack which some gamblers believe improves players' ability to make calculations about probable card draws.

Despite these limitations, the casinos soon began taking massive amounts of money from residents and visitors alike while at the same time telling the people of the state how much gambling is actually helping the state. On their website, the Casino Association of Indiana has a rolling banner that proclaims that Indiana casinos pay $7 billion in taxes, save Hoosiers billions in property taxes, have created 17,500 jobs, and have given $1.8 billion for community projects. With all of that outlay, one wonders how they even stay in business! The answer, of course, is that the gambling industry remains quite profitable, but it is not something they will say much about on their website. In 2007 alone, Indiana casinos netted over $2.64 billion in revenue, according to the Indiana Gaming Commission. That is money that is being taken from the pockets of people who can afford it the least, and it has a net negative impact on the state economy given that only a small portion of these proceeds are diverted back to the state. The casinos pocket the lion's share of this stolen money as it enriches only the gaming industry, not the people of the state.

Despite best efforts otherwise, once the step-by-step encroachment started, once the money started flowing, there was little to hold back the steady expansion of gambling in Indiana and other states. In fact, based on a huge lobbying effort in 2015 by the casino industry, Indiana has finally relented, and is now allowing the Tropicana Casino, a riverboat formerly known as Casino Aztar, in Evansville, to spend $50 million to develop a fully land-based casino with all previous restrictions regarding table games now completely removed. When it comes to the gaming industry, resistance proves to be futile. Grandma, it seems, was right after all.

This is an experience, of course, that is not unique to Indiana. Another telling chapter in how the gaming industry skirts regulations is the development and expansion of Native American casinos. In other states that prohibited gambling, Native American reservations were often allowed to circumvent state law and run fully functioning casinos. Award-winning filmmaker Alex Gibney's (2010), *Casino Jack and the United States of Money*, tells the story of Jack Abramoff, who took Native American casino money and lobbied various political decision-makers to deregulate the industry. In many ways, Abramoff was one of the first people to formally peddle political influence for money, and created the first *de facto* exemplar of what we today term "Political Action Committees." According to the film, Abramoff charged the Choctaw tribe $3.5 million in lobbying fees in exchange for $120 million in Federal assistance in the form of grants, and deregulation. In some cases, he played local tribes off each other, rewarding the tribe that paid him the most while launching campaigns to undermine the efforts of other tribes who would not "pay to play."

Abramoff's reach was not limited to casinos, a fact that illustrates the confluence of gambling and politics. The chair of the College Republican National Committee from 1981 to 1985, Abramoff was a self-described "free market knight." Another example of how he attempted to enable clients to avoid economic regulations was by lobbying against regulatory efforts aimed at addressing the exploitation of immigrant workers in Saipan, capital of the Commonwealth of the Northern Marianas Islands (CNMI). While CNMI is an American territory, it was not subject to the same legal, environmental, and economic regulations as the United States. At the time, there were no effective immigration, labor, or minimum wage laws in place. As a result, Abramoff and his law firm helped facilitate the importation of 40,000 foreign workers to run garment factories under inhumane conditions in exchange for $6.7 million in lobbying fees paid by the CNMI government. Workers, for example, had to pay huge up-front fees for the right to work essentially making them indentured servants. Among other charges, workers were allegedly forced to live behind barbed wire enclosed factory housing that did not have indoor plumbing, many were forced into sex slavery, and pregnant workers were encouraged to have abortions to keep them in the factories. When regulators finally moved to reveal the political and economic scandal, and close the legal loopholes that allowed for this exploitation, the garment factories pulled out, leaving an eco-catastrophe and thriving sex worker trade in their wake. Indicted by several grand juries in various jurisdictions, Abramoff was sentenced to a total of six years in federal prison for mail fraud, conspiracy to bribe public officials, and tax evasion. He only served 43 months of his sentence. As an aside, since I mentioned it earlier, one of Abramoff's clients from 1993 to 2001 was Channel One News, a company that made significant inroads in our educational system despite its pre-packaged advertising that schools were obliged to accept.

Casinos specifically, and gambling generally, became a powerful metaphor for economic life in the United States. Today, financial markets have the feel of a casino. Instead of betting on the red or black of a roulette wheel, investors bet on the red, or green of the Nasdaq stock market. Historically, the market would enjoy only modest gains or losses on any particular trading day, but now market moves of well over 5% seem commonplace almost every day. From 1985 onward, record movements in one direction or the other seemed to happen with increasing frequency, as well. Further, options markets, margin accounts, and complex derivatives only multiplied the amount any individual investor could gain or lose at any given time. Given the growing linkage between policies of the Federal Reserve and the financial markets, something I will discuss in later chapters, one could even bet on the size of interest rate adjustments in the markets. While I admit it felt good at the time, the $1.3 billion tax cut bill that President George W. Bush signed into law in 2001 that led to unprecedented "rebate checks" of between $300 and $600 mailed from the Internal Revenue Service to each individual taxpayer felt a little bit like a slot machine giving you a few dollars back to keep you gambling before it finally took all of your money.

Over the last several years, the government and financial markets made it easier for individual investors to risk more in the market. Investments were traditionally the domain of large investment companies insofar as individual investors had limited access to timely information, and transaction fees were often prohibitively expensive. Indeed, access to real-time market quotes for free is a fairly new evolution in the financial markets. Further, the rise of the internet also decreased reliance on brokers, and fees dropped significantly. This led to an increase in day traders, those who would buy a stock, option, or commodity online early in the day, and then sell the position before the end of the day, often garnering enormous profits, or losses. This, I believe is one of the fundamental problems with an unregulated free market. It allows people to make outrageous sums of money with little to no commitment to an actual company. At its height, fortunes were made and lost on single days during the dot-com and technology frenzies of the last 30 years.

This phenomenon, of course, was not limited to the financial markets. This is the problem when fundamentally immoral financial ideologies and mechanisms are uncritically accepted. I remember watching with great disbelief as natural gas providers, such as the El Paso Corporation, and electricity providers, such as Duke Energy, squeezed the residents of California because they had de facto monopoly power over a state that had tremendously inelastic demand for energy in 2000–2001. On May 25, 2001, California's Independent Systems Operator (Cal-ISO) filed charges of price gouging against several energy providers with the Federal Energy Regulatory Commission, or FERC. In its filing, Cal-ISO alleged:

> The energy suppliers have reaped vast profits from the deregulation of the energy market. In 2000, Reliant Energy's adjusted earnings rose 164 percent to $838 million. The company more than doubled its 2001 first-quarter profits over last year, earning $274 million. Close behind was AES Corporation, which saw net income in 2000 jump 189 percent to $658 million. Dynegy, which earned $452 million in 2000, increased profits by 210 percent over the previous year. The Williams Corp. reported $873 million in income for 2000, and more than a 200 percent rise in first-quarter earnings. (Cappannari, 2001)

Significantly, these outrageous profits were directly tied to the deregulation of the energy market in California in 1998, another reminder about the dire consequences of an unregulated free market. Governor Gray Davis and the State of California filed suit against FERC, a government organization designed to ensure "just and reasonable" energy prices, given its inaction, but a Federal judge dismissed the lawsuit. The *New York Times* subsequently unmasked an apparent conflict of interest between Kenneth Lay, CEO of Enron, and Curtis Hebert, Chair of the FERC, a revelation that was one of many pieces in the infamous Enron Scandal, a controversy that implicated the highest levels of the George W. Bush Administration. While Hebert denied being unduly influenced by Mr. Lay to support Enron's push to deregulate the energy markets, he felt like his job was being threatened if he did not comply:

> Though the accounts of the discussion differ, that it took place at all illustrates Enron's considerable influence in Washington, especially at the commission, the agency authorized to ensure fair prices in the nation's wholesale

> electricity and natural gas markets, Enron's main business. Mr. Lay has been one of Mr. Bush's largest campaign contributors, and no other energy company gave more money to Republican causes last year than Enron. And it appears that Mr. Herbert may soon be replaced as the commission's chairman, according to Vice President Dick Cheney, the Bush administration's point man on energy policy. (Bergman & Gerth, 2001, p. 1A)

The next day, Senator Dianne Feinstein called for a Congressional investigation into possible improprieties between members of the FERC and private energy interests. Also that day, the Senate confirmed two of President Bush's appointees to this five-person agency. In a follow-up article, the *New York Times* reported that the appointees were: "Patrick Wood, a former head of the Texas Public Utilities Commission, which deregulated electricity in the president's home state, and Nora Brownell, a Pennsylvania utility regulator. [Vice-President] Cheney has indicated that Mr. Wood will take over as chairman" (Marquis, 2001, p. 11A).

Despite the enormous amount of money involved, the California energy crisis was merely a small test case of what was to come. Once energy markets proved themselves easy to manipulate, with little to no government intervention, it was only a matter of time before the profit-based experiment was tried at the national level. In a period of just a few years, the price of gasoline tripled across the United States. While the price gouging was spread out over millions of customers, it had a tremendous microeconomic impact on personal disposable income. Other energy markets also tested the boundaries of acceptable price manipulation, but the price-fixing in the gasoline and diesel markets received the most attention. Oil companies made record profits during this time and, again, the government did next to nothing to check this egregious abuse of unregulated monopolistic power. More than one critic decried the efficacy of having two former oil executives in the White House as they pursued policies to enhance the profit margins of the oil industry. The manipulation of the energy markets was only one aspect of this profiteering, and other commodities, such as food, precious metals, and real estate were soon to follow. And these, of course, were intertwined with broader aspects of the economic collapse of 2008, something that I will discuss in more detail toward the end of the book.

It was becoming clear from these and other events that a new economic paradigm, largely motivated by greed, had taken root, nourished by deregulated markets and industries, and reinforced with a discourse about the merits of a free market. This new paradigm seemed to encourage speculation geared toward quick profit with little to no substantive commitment. It also seemed to encourage a belief shared by many Americans, especially those in the lower and middle classes, that they can and should be riding this new wave of economic expansion, even though evidence over the intervening years has proved otherwise. It enticed the public into risky economic choices and living beyond one's means. Deficit spending, it seemed to many, worked for the Reagan Administration, so it should work for average citizens, as well. It is worth noting that a good part of the so-called economic expansion during the Reagan years was fueled by a credit-induced spending spree from those who could perhaps least afford it. It put many Americans in an incredibly vulnerable economic position, as illustrated by the ever-increasing rise in home foreclosures and bankruptcies. These were the losers in the great gamble of the free market. It is a game that, like a casino, requires many players, and many losers, in order to enrich the few who took advantage of the inherently unequal complexities of this economic system.

In the critically acclaimed short story, "The Lottery," Shirley Jackson (1949) describes a community that is committed to the life and death determinism of a lottery. The lottery losers were presumably stoned to death, a powerful metaphor for modern capitalism. The lottery had become a ritual, a defining principle of this community, even though its original intent had long since slipped into obscurity. Toward the end of the story, Jackson laments, "Although the villagers had forgotten the ritual and lost the original [lottery] black box, they still remembered to use stones" (p. 301). So many of us remembered how to use the stones, the bricks and mortar of the free market, and too many of us carelessly allowed it to happen despite the fact that we knew, based on historical precedent, what the consequences would be.

Before closing this chapter, it would be prudent to return to Oz for another brief moment. It is difficult to blame the average person for being gullible and allowing this spectacle to unfold. Those in power are both subtle and relentless in their step-by-step encroachment on our moral foundations. It is also difficult to hang blame for the current state of affairs on one, or even a few people. Still, as there is a Wizard who lured Dorothy and her companions to the Emerald Palace with the promise of a heart, a brain, courage, and a journey home, there are those whom we have been elevated to Wizard-like status in our society. As we will learn, however, the belief in an all-powerful Wizard is nothing but a collective delusion of grandeur, as we realize when we look behind the curtain, enabling us to boldly pronounce: "The Emperor has no clothes!" In the museum at Ellis Island, there is an excerpt from a letter written by a nineteenth-century Italian immigrant who had recently arrived in America with high hopes. He wrote, "I came to America because I heard the streets were paved with gold. When I got here, I found out three things. First, the streets weren't paved with gold; second, they weren't paved at all; and third, I was expected to pave them." The myth of and belief in unlimited riches continue to dominate the contemporary American psyche as people continue their Oz-like quest to "follow the yellow brick road." Although the Roman and American Empire are separated by over 1500 years, it seems that the use of "bread and circuses" by the ruling elite to amuse and distract the masses has stood the test of time.

References

Bergman, L., & Gerth, J. (2001, May 25). Power trader tied to Bush finds Washington all ears. *New York Times*, 1A.

Cappannari, A. (2001, June 9). More evidence of price-gouging in California energy market. *World Socialist Web Site*. Retrieved July 20, 2021, from https://www.wsws.org/en/articles/2001/06/cal-j09.html

Gibney, A. (Director). (2010). *Casino Jack and the United States of money*. Participant Media.

Gregory, S., & Webley, K. (2011, December 12). Penn State of mind. *Time*, 46–51.

Hall, S. (1978). The treatment of "football hooliganism" in the press. In R. Ingham (Ed.), *"Football hooliganism": The wider context* (pp. 15–36). Inter-Alia.

Herman, E., & Chomsky, N. (2002/1988). *Manufacturing consent: The political economy of the mass media*. Pantheon.

Hughes, T. (2012, June 4). Advertising offers cash-strapped schools a lifeline. *USA Today*, 3A.

Jackson, S. (2005). *The Lottery and other stories*. Farrar, Straus, and Giroux. (Original work published 1949).

Kopp, C. (2005, December 28). School buses now roll with ads. *CBS News*. Retrieved March 3, 2011, from https://www.cbsnews.com/news/school-buses-now-roll-with-ads

Marquis, C. (2001, May 26). Senator calls for hearings into energy regulators' moves. *New York Times*, 11A.

Parker, T. (1995). Schools learning new ad lessons. *Advertising Age, 66*(7), 27.

Qian, Y. (2013). Beyond the BOHICA syndrome: Social construction of employee cynicism toward organizational change. *Florida Journal of Communication, 41*(2), 67–79.
Rovell, D. (2015, July 15). Michigan officially unveils Nike apparel deal worth $169M. Retrieved July 20, 2021, from https://www.espn.com/college-football/story/_/id/13260992/michigan-11-year-deal-nike-worth-169m
Wieberg, S., & Berkowitz, S. (2009, April 2). Has college sports marketing gone too far? Casino ads, video deals reflect urgent push for revenue. *USA Today*, A1–A2.

CHAPTER 4

Children of the Revolution: Reaganomics as Free Market Redux

It was the summer of 1976. I was a child of ten and seemingly did not have a care in the world. It was a magical summer. It was America's bicentennial, the skies were filled with fireworks, the streets were filled with parades, the nation was filled with a renewed sense of perhaps naive patriotism, and our pockets jingled with newly minted bicentennial coins. My brother and I were already avid collectors of coins, and stamps, and sports cards, and rocks, and beer cans, and just about anything that young boys could collect. These new coins, though, were all the rage. It had been years since American money had received any sort of facelift, and everyone seemed ready to celebrate anything new, including a compelling blend of economy and ideology.

We lived in South Bend, Indiana, during those years. Our neighbors to the south, Indiana University, won the national championship in 1976 under the leadership of their infamous coach, Bob Knight, the last NCAA Division I program to complete a perfect season. Still, in South Bend, everything seemed to revolve around Notre Dame football. I remember Notre Dame's quarterback, a promising young gun named Joe Montana, visiting our Cub Scout Troop one weekend. I still have and treasure his autograph, signed on a piece of our pack's notepad paper. I remember attending Notre Dame football games during those years, in awe of the gleaming golden dome, and the infamous "touchdown Jesus," the relief of Jesus with his arms outstretched on the Hesburgh Library, the largest

G. D. Klinger et al., *Money Talks*,
https://doi.org/10.1007/978-3-031-00816-0_4

collegiate library in the world when it opened in 1963, within eyesight of the football stadium, seemingly signaling another Notre Dame touchdown.

Imagine my dismay when I learned years later that Notre Dame, a symbol for all that was true and right with the world for a young child, accepted $1.8 million, more than any other institution of higher learning in the United States, from Chase Bank in 2009 to market high-interest credit cards to its young stewards, the under-protected students of Notre Dame (Haimerl, 2010). That fact alone demonstrated to me that both the Academy and religion, two of strongest bulwarks against the excesses of the capitalism, had finally been compromised. Needless to say, I read Robert Benne's (2001) book, *Quality with Soul*, that identified Notre Dame as one of six colleges and universities that had avoided the "darkening trends" of secularization in higher education with a healthy dose of skepticism.

I also vividly remember people in our Midwestern city painting all of the city's fire hydrants. Fire hydrants, of course, already look like little people, so somebody thought it would be a clever idea to paint them to look like patriots from the American Revolution in honor of the United States bicentennial. We all thought it was pretty cool, and was yet another symbol of the growing sense of renewal, hope, and patriotism that had infected the United States. Perhaps our naive patriotism lulled us into a false sense of security, and left us unprepared for the changes that were to come.

In 1977, George Lucas and company released *Star Wars*, a film that transformed the industry and the country. Appropriately sub-titled, "A New Hope," *Star Wars* set the tone for a new generation. I remember seeing the film nine times while it was still in the theater, something that seemed to be the norm among younger audiences for this groundbreaking film. My friends and I would wear how many times we saw *Star Wars* as a badge of honor of sorts, constantly comparing notes, and trading stories. It was with great regret that we watched the Reagan Administration co-opt the name "Star Wars" to describe its proposed, and ill-fated, laser-based missile defense system.[1] The "Star Wars" program, also sometimes termed the "Strategic Defense Initiative," or the "High Frontier" system,

[1] There is some disagreement about who first coined the term "Star Wars" to characterize Reagan's space-based weapons and defense program. It may have been the late Senator Ted Kennedy in his comments to the *Washington Post* the day after Reagan's infamous "Star Wars Speech," in which Reagan outlined the rough details of his ambitious proposal (Lang).

was widely criticized as being unrealistic, unscientific, and costly. Nevertheless, the United States spent nearly $40 billion on the project deemed an important weapon in the Cold War. More than a viable military project, it was one piece of what Communication professor Gordon Mitchell (2000) called a "Strategic Deception," in his outstanding book entitled the same.

Also in 1977, Apple Computer released the Apple II computer. Founded in 1976, and incorporated in 1977, Apple Computer represented a "new hope" of sorts in another domain: technology and consumer electronics. My brother and I were fascinated with computers when they first came out, and I still remember our early days of navigating our difficult and cumbersome TRS-80, the dominant machine on the market at that time, along with the Commodore PET. Apple represented a revolutionary break with these other computers because of, among other things, its commitment to open architecture. Apple continued to milk this revolutionary trope in the years to come, developing one of the most loyal customer bases in the computer and personal electronics industries. The infamous Orwellian-themed "1984" commercial, which aired nationally only one time, during Super Bowl XVIII that same year, coincided with the launch of the first "Macintosh" computer, and Apple's place as market and corporate contrarian was cemented in history. Like *Star Wars*, Apple built off the tropes of the "evil" Empire pitted against the "noble" rebels, another set of *Star Wars* themes that Ronald Reagan co-opted when he characterized the Soviet Union as an "Evil Empire," while calling the U.S. backed, and illegally funded, Contra rebels in Nicaragua "Freedom Fighters."

There was one other significant event that illustrated the changes that were forthcoming in the years to come. I remember my mother taking us to a local bank to try out one of the new Automated Teller Machines, or ATMs, that had been recently installed at one of our local banks. I remember it was celebrated as a "grand opening" of sorts with a line stretching around the bank as people waited their turn to try out this new machine. On the day of its opening, people were simply being trained how to use the machine. You would enter certain account information, enter an amount, and the machine would magically dispense fake paper money. To entice people to try the machine, the bank randomly inserted real $20 bills, so every once in a while, somebody would scream with joy that they had received a real money reward in addition to the fake bills. People were immediately enchanted. While Chemical Bank introduced the first networked ATM, originally called the "Docuteller," in New York City in 1969, their widespread use did not take hold until the intervening years of the 1970s. Today, it is estimated that there are almost 2 million ATMs in use. The ATM was a powerful symbol of the forthcoming popularization of economics. Chemical Bank's advertisement announcing the opening of the first networked ATM proudly pronounced: "On Sept. 2 our bank will open at 9:00 and never close again" (Zetter, 2010). Writing in *Wired* magazine, Kim Zetter notes, "[T]he machines were good for banks … eventually letting them cut costs, reduce teller lines and, of course, charge outrageous user fees." This was an early lesson further reinforced in subsequent years: money never sleeps, and it was about to become the centerpiece of everyone's lives. Further, this greased the wheels of the capitalist machine increasing access to, and consequently, the velocity of money.

On the surface, it seemed, America had recovered from the debacle of Vietnam, the oil price shocks and stagflation of the early 1970s, and the humiliating resignation of President Nixon. Jimmy Carter represented a "new hope" for a country groping for political and economic direction. He helped broker a historic peace agreement between Egypt and Israel at Camp David, one of the most significant (and underestimated) political and presidential accomplishments of our time. He was and is a humble, thoughtful, and soft-spoken man. He led the nation with kindness and temperance. He was recognized for all of the good things that he has done in his life with the Nobel Prize in 2002. He was perhaps too nice to be president given the harsh political realities that continue to confront that office. Since he felt that he still had work to do after being voted out of office in 1980, Douglas Brinkley (1998) aptly called Carter's time in office and the years that followed it an "unfinished presidency" in his book entitled the same. Almost eerily anticipating the greed and self-interest that were to become the hallmarks of the coming years, President Carter lamented toward the end of his Presidency in a speech delivered on July 15, 1979, that "too many of us now tend to worship self-indulgence and consumption. Human identity is no longer defined by what one does, but by what one owns. This is not a message of happiness, or reassurance, but it is the truth, and it is a warning" ("Crisis of Confidence").

The magic of the summer of '76 was shattered shortly thereafter by the Iranian Hostage Crisis in 1979. It riveted the nation's attention as we collectively snapped out of our disco-induced hypnotic trance. The United States of America, by some estimations the most powerful nation in the world, was being held hostage, and there seemed to be little that we could do about it. Our military might, our political prowess, our economic dominance seemed useless. Our neighborhoods and public spaces were filled with yellow ribbons, a hopeful, but mournful sign that we continued to live in troubled times, and that our renewed sense of security and patriotism was indeed naive. Media outlets, political pundits, and average citizens counted each passing day of the crisis, highlighting our collective angst.

All of these events flowed together in a confluence indicating that things were about to change, perhaps with more alacrity than anyone had expected. When Ronald Reagan was elected President, many people spoke of the "Reagan Revolution." It was, indeed, something very different than anything we had seen before. The Reagan Revolution was a point of departure for our country, both politically and economically. Indeed, there were some reports that Reagan emissaries had purposefully convinced the Iranians to delay the release of the hostages until Reagan had actually taken office. It was a powerful symbol that partisan politics was alive and well in our country. We had entered an age where image was, indeed, everything.

Not only had we elected a Hollywood actor as President, something that I will discuss in more depth in later chapters, but we had also entered a bizarre world where lawbreakers were worshiped as heroes. Oliver North, one of the key figures in the shameful Iran-Contra affair, became a national celebrity with many calling on him to run for president. Somehow secretly selling weapons to Iran to fund insurgency in Central America and raising additional funds by covertly smuggling drugs into the United States, actions that contravened both international and U.S. law, were transformed into the ultimate act of patriotism.

This was not the only symbolic act that signified a political break with the past. I recall that one of the first things President Reagan did when he took office was to rip out the solar panels that his predecessor, President Carter, had installed at the White House. The energy conservation that marked the Nixon, Ford, and especially Carter Presidencies was a thing of the past under the Reagan Administration. Commenting on his rejection of energy conservation policies, Reagan mused: "Energy conservation means being too hot in the summer, and too cold in the winter!" Interestingly, under the Carter Administration the United States had reduced its dependence on foreign oil to 28% (Lewis, 1990, p. 30A). By contrast, in the first year of the Obama presidency, prominent politicians and business leaders noted America's enduring foreign-oil dependency: "In 2008, the U.S. imported nearly 70% of its oil. Since 1974, every president has promised to reduce dependency—and failed" (Pickens et al., 2009, p. 25). Ironically, our increasing dependence on foreign oil first started under the Reagan Administration. Additionally, under Reagan, "[f]unds for research on energy conservation were cut toward the vanishing point. Energy efficiency standards for cars and appliances were cut back, opposed, delayed. And the Reagan Administration just about ended the search for solar and other renewable energy sources" (Lewis, p. 30A).

Assessing this shift in policy, Arthur Allen wrote in *Mother Jones* magazine:

> The budget for the solar institute—which President Jimmy Carter had created to spearhead solar innovation—was slashed from $124 million in 1980 to $59 million in 1982. Scientists who had left tenured university jobs to work under Hayes [head of the Solar Energy Research Institute] were given two weeks notice and no severance pay. The squelching of the institute—later partly re-funded and renamed the National Renewable Energy Laboratory—marked the start of Reagan's campaign against solar power. By the end of 1985, when Congress and the administration allowed tax credits for solar homes to lapse, the dream of a solar era had faded. The solar water heater President Carter had installed on the White House roof in 1979 was dismantled and junked. Solar water heating went from a billion-dollar industry to peanuts overnight; thousands of sun-minded businesses went bankrupt. (Allen, 2000)

Our political community was not the only thing that was undergoing radical reorientation, but our economic lives were changing as well. "Reaganomics," one of the many slogans associated with the newly elected President was a simple, one-word amalgamation of economics, politics, and ideology. Reaganomics was often associated with idea of the free market: "It was clear, first of all, that [Reagan] was influenced by the economic theories of Professor Milton Friedman, the Nobel laureate from the University of Chicago. ... Friedman is a true believer in free markets, that is, markets free of government regulation and interference. Ronald Reagan sympathized with these ideas" (Regan, 1988, pp. 157–158). However, as Donald Regan makes clear, it was more than simple free market economics:

> The President was, moreover, a believer in supply-side economics, a system of ideas derived from many sources, including Adam Smith. ... The mixture of the two [monetarism and supply-side economics], with some other elements added in was what the press called "Reaganomics." George Bush,

> when he was opposing Reagan in the 1980 Republican primaries, had termed this philosophy "voodoo economics." (p. 158)

Bush was not alone in his initial skepticism: "Senator Howard Baker (the Senate majority leader during the first term and White House chief of staff beginning in 1987) later described it as 'a riverboat gamble'" (Niskanen, 1988, p. 5). Nevertheless, people were enchanted with the phrase, and it immediately popularized an arena where an average citizen had previously feared to tread. Economics, formerly known as the "dismal science," was the domain of economists and technocrats. Now, it was something that everybody was persuaded that they needed to understand. After all, media outlets, leaders of industry, and politicians were all telling us that there was a buck to be made, and everyone was being promised a piece of action. The technical shroud that had previously enveloped economics had been purposefully lifted. Everyone felt like they needed to be at the table of this popular new economic game: get rich quick, no long-term commitments, no risk, and little to no work required. This shift in sentiment planted the seeds for one of the most significant economic expansions in the history of the United States. Millionaires were sprouting up as fast as sunflowers in Kansas. And like a tightly managed casino, those in power made sure that everyone knew the names of these lucky lottery winners. The losers, and assuredly there were a lot of losers in the intervening 40 years, did not seem to receive the same press. It was a little-known fact that the rich-poor gap grew significantly during the 1980s, and was by the end of the decade more pronounced than at any other point since the years leading up to the Great Depression. In a "Special Report" on American wealth inequality in 2006, *The Economist* noted, "[A]t the start of the 1980's, the gap between rich and poor began to widen" ("Inequality," 2006, p. 29). By the end of Reagan's two terms in office, the rich-poor gap was at a record high: "By 1989, the richest two-fifths of families had the highest share of the national income (67.8 percent) and the poorest two-fifths the lowest share (15.4 percent) in the forty years the Census Bureau had been compiling such statistics" (footnote omitted) (Cannon, 2000/1991, p. 9).

One of the key elements of Reaganomics was the appropriately maligned theory of "trickle-down economics." The idea, of course, was simple: steal from the poor to give to the rich. For someone who had visited Sherwood Forest in England as a young child, and was drawn to the noble, even if mythical, cause of Robin Hood, this seemed to me to be precisely backward. Still, the ballyhooed tax cuts during the Reagan years quite unabashedly made the rich even richer. Congress enacted two significant tax cut policies during the Reagan Administration: the Economic Recovery Tax Act (ERTA) of 1981, and the Tax Reform Act of 1986. These policies shifted the tax burden away from the wealthiest people and the largest businesses. While some conservative politicians and economists point out that the share of the tax burden by the wealthiest taxpayers actually increased during the Reagan years in percentage terms, there is no question that the most significant tax cuts were enjoyed by the richest Americans. Indeed, it was the top marginal tax rate that was cut the most under these policies, cut from 70% to 28%, as was the capital gains rate, a rate that affects those with significant disposable income for investments. Additionally, the corporate tax rate was reduced from 48% to 34%. These were the first significant steps that put us on the path of the indefensible and morally bankrupt income inequality that we see today. Importantly, it was not just a simple modification of the U.S. tax laws, it was instead a complete overhaul: "Counting weekends and holidays, the President had given Treasury 310 days to revolutionize the American tax system. … *Revolutionize* was the operative word: we did not aim to plug loopholes and plaster over tax breaks, but to tear down the ramparts of the old tax system, level it to the ground, and start over again" (Regan, p. 204) (Fig. 4.1).

The theory that underpinned Reaganomics was that if the rich got richer, then their excess wealth would trickle down to those less fortunate. Not only would it trickle down through increased investments in business, and corporate expansion, but it would also trickle down through increased philanthropy. The problem was any money that did filter down was, quite literally, only a trickle. Even though this economic theory has been systematically discredited with the benefit of historical hindsight, it continues to reassert itself in our current political arenas. Indeed, I watched with dismay as the former chair of the Federal Reserve Bank, Ben Bernanke, appeared on *60 Minutes* in 2010, the first time a Fed chair had done so, to defend his massive bailout of Wall Street, and even non-banking entities, in favor of helping average citizens. "Main Street," he claimed, was entirely dependent upon the fiscal and monetary health of "Wall Street." Therefore, his oft-quoted conclusion: "What's good for Wall Street is good for Main Street," was a simple permutation of the trickle-down economics of the Reagan Administration: help big corporations and the rich first, and this would eventually trickle down to those who are less fortunate.

Fig. 4.1 In his first economic address to the nation, February 5, 1981, President Ronald W. Reagan explains how the U.S. dollar lost most of its value due to government regulation and rising tax rates. (Keystone Press/Alamy Stock Photo)

It is with great regret that I watched the same trope play out in my home state of Indiana. Some years ago, Indiana homeowners were confronted with massive property tax increases. Governor Mitch Daniels, who worked as a political adviser to President Reagan in 1985, immediately called for property tax relief. Of course, it does not take an economist to realize that those who stood to benefit the most from property tax relief were those with the largest properties and most expensive homes. To make up for the anticipated tax revenue shortfall, Governor Daniels proposed an increase in the sales tax that, of course, is a regressive tax, because it takes a bigger percentage of a poor person's, or family's income, compared to their rich counterparts. It was a classic case of shifting the tax burden from the rich to the poor. Given its success and lack of resistance, Governor Daniels subsequently did the same thing with Indiana's educational system, plundering rural and inner-city school budgets to give even more funding to affluent suburban schools and newly created charter schools, effectively taking money away from schools that needed it the most.

Those with wealth, it seems, have a vested interest in advancing this agenda, and they have the economic and political power to make it so. The extent to which many from the middle and lower classes accept and support these unsettling public policy initiatives illustrates the power of those with money. Greed and the blind pursuit of wealth had taken over, and everyone was seduced into believing that they could be the next person to strike it rich. Reagan had set the stage, and his followers seemed only too willing to advance the cause. When everybody is of the same mind, it becomes remarkably easy to make a lot of money. The stock market in particular demonstrated how people could make outrageous sums with little to no commitment to actual companies. Speculation had trumped sound investment, and it led to an incredible accumulation of wealth for many of those who agreed to play along.

The difficult thing with this mob mentality, though, is that it works both ways, as we have recently come to realize. Outrageous returns for little to no risk created an increasingly vulnerable situation. One thing we learn from the history of capitalism is that unlimited progress and expansion do not last forever. It tends to exist in natural boom to bust cycles. From 1980 onward, though, we acted as if we were in denial about this fundamental fact. At some point, though, a day of reckoning arrives, and those who left their money on the table for too long, blinded by greed, carelessness, and ignorance, would suffer tremendous losses. The number of people affected both directly and indirectly by the most recent economic downturn, dubbed the Great Recession of 2008, is and continues to be substantial. Significantly, the speed at which the crash happened was more accelerated and pronounced than at any other time in history. Five to ten percent swings were a daily reality in the global markets.

Capitalist self-interest was a dominant trope during the Reagan years. There was a purposeful rhetorical program designed to convince us that economics, ambition, efficiency, profit, deregulation, expansion, and growth should be the centerpiece of our lives. Put in historical perspective, the change that was underway was profound. Between the years 1933 and 1981, when Reagan took office, only three Republicans had held the White House, war hero Dwight Eisenhower, the discredited Richard Nixon, and the uninspired Gerald Ford. The Democrats, however, fielded five presidents, including four terms by Franklin Delano Roosevelt, the most ever by a U.S. President. The Roosevelt presidency alone defined the twentieth century, but put together with the others, a powerful message had emerged. In my estimation, the dominance of the Democrats was nothing less than a repudiation of the capitalist excesses of the 1920s, the laissez-faire programs of Republicans Calvin Coolidge and Herbert Hoover. The Reagan years marked a point of departure and, importantly, a point of return. The principles of laissez-faire capitalism found a new voice in a president whom some deemed "The Great Communicator." William Niskanen, a former graduate student under Milton Friedman at the University of Chicago, and one of the chief architects of President Reagan's economic program while he served on Reagan's Council of Economic Advisers from 1981 to 1985 concurs, "'Reaganomics' represents the most serious attempt to change the course of U.S. economic policy since the New Deal" (p. 3).

Importantly, Reagan did not just advance a pro-business, pro-rich, agenda, he took it upon himself to demonize those on the other side of the ideological and political fence. In his 1976 Presidential campaign, Reagan recounted the anecdote of the "welfare mother" from the south side of Chicago who had cheated the government by using 80 addresses, 30 aliases, 12 social security cards, and 4 fictional dead husbands to obtain $150,000 in inappropriate welfare disbursements, and veteran's benefits. We later discovered, though, that the account of this woman was either totally fabricated or grossly exaggerated.

Reagan also advanced his cause by demonizing government regulation. One of the famous slogans that summarized Reagan's political and economic vision was: "If it moves, tax it. If it keeps moving, regulate it. And if it stops moving, subsidize it." In a speech entitled, "Whatever Happened to Free Enterprise," delivered in 1975 to the Rotary Club of Oakland, Reagan recounted the following example: "A druggist in the Midwest complains, every time he fills a prescription the paperwork required by the government takes more time than he spends mixing the medicine. ... It's doubtful that penicillin would be licensed if it were discovered today" (Reagan, 1975, p. 5). Reagan warmly embraced deregulation in all aspects of public life. In defining Reaganomics for *The Concise Encyclopedia of Economics*, Niskanen (n.d.) observed, "Reagan eased or eliminated price controls on oil and natural gas, cable TV, long-distance telephone service, interstate bus service, and ocean shipping. Banks were allowed to invest in a somewhat broader set of assets, and the scope of the antitrust laws was reduced" ("Reaganomics"). Reagan unabashedly made the case for a return to free market principles, a corporate world unfettered by government oversight and regulation. Indeed, as I will discuss later, many of the laws put in place to check the capitalist excesses of the years leading up to the Great Depression were repealed under Reagan.

To achieve his ends, Reagan had to cast a powerful rhetorical spell. He had to convince people that the market regulations, social programs, and welfare apparatus of the post-Depression years had to be abandoned in favor of deregulation, self-interest, and allegedly smaller government. Reagan seeded the ground for these tropes to take root years before his Presidential election in 1980. A little-known fact about Reagan is that until 1962, he was a Democrat. Almost immediately after his political and ideological conversion, the Republican Party took advantage of this popular Hollywood icon. In 1964, he was asked to give a speech on national television to support Barry's Goldwater's presidential campaign, a speech that Goldwater himself called the "best speech of the campaign" (Reid & Klumpp, 2004, p. 758). This was Reagan's first political speech on national television. Reagan expanded the speech, later dubbed "A Time for Choosing," for his successful gubernatorial campaign in California the following year. In this speech, Reagan clearly outlined the "sides" as he saw them: "I would like to suggest that there is no such thing as a left or right. There is only up and down—up to man's age old dream—the ultimate individual freedom consistent with law and order—or down to the ant heap of totalitarianism" (Reid & Klumpp, p. 759). He consistently decried government involvement in the economy. He encouraged stimulation of the so-called private sector. He lamented the growth of welfare, Medicare, and social security in society. Indeed, he "criticized a wide range of federal programs, including some that were considered to be politically invulnerable—farm subsidies, TVA, urban renewal, social security, the proposed job corps, foreign aid, a variety of government regulations, and the progressive income tax" (Niskanen, p. 14). Finally, in a classic example of red baiting, he claimed that the Democratic Party had become the party of Marx, Lenin, and Stalin.

Red baiting was a common trope of the Reagan Presidency. Indeed, one of his infamous political gaffes was to jokingly "outlaw" the Soviet Union, and "authorize" the bombing of the USSR within minutes. He made these comments, of course, not realizing that he was actually on the air at the time. In his speech to the National Association of Evangelicals in 1983, Reagan called the Soviet Union an "evil empire," and contended that the struggle between the United States and the Soviet Union was a "struggle between right and wrong and good and evil" (Reid & Klumpp, p. 803). Many credit Reagan with "winning" the Cold War, and it was another place where politics and economics came together under Reagan. President Reagan aggressively increased defense spending by 35%, including untenable sums spent to develop the aforementioned "Star Wars" program, a program built upon a science-fiction induced belief that we could develop a laser-based missile defense shield that would detonate incoming nuclear missiles before they would reach their targets. For Reagan, his free market-based revolution in economics was intimately connected to his belief in expanding America's military might: "Economic decline is viewed as a very serious problem, linked to the decline of American military influence around the world. Restoration of economic power is seen as a necessary parallel to restored military and diplomatic influence" (Reagan, 1980, p. 5). Some say that this allowed Reagan to negotiate from a position of strength with the USSR. It effectively placed the Soviet Union in an economic and geo-political game that it could not win. The ensuing arms race essentially bankrupted the Soviet Union into submission. I sincerely believe, however, that not nearly enough credit is given to Mikhail Gorbachev for dismantling key economic components of the USSR. His programs of "perestroika" and "glasnost" had a far greater impact on the break up of the Soviet Union than anything that President Reagan did. Lost in the "celebration," however, was the fact that Reagan had also effectively bankrupted the United States with the combination of the aforementioned tax cuts, and massive defense spending. Budget deficits reached an all-time high under the Reagan Administration. And, of course, deficits require borrowing, and it put the American economy in a tremendously vulnerable position. Indeed, privately held federal debt increased from 22.3% of the GDP to 38.1% ("Reaganomics"). This highlights one of the deep ironies of Reagan's economic legacy stretching back to his time as Governor of California: "One intriguing dimension of Ronald Reagan and an indicator of his probable behavior as president is that he maintained his general theme about government as the problem even when serving as governor of the nation's largest state, a period which real state government spending increased at a record rate" (Niskanen, p. 14). In addition, many argue that the Savings and Loan debacle of the late 1980s and early 1990s, something I will turn my attention to later, can be directly linked to the historic budget deficits of the Reagan Administration.

Reagan's rhetoric remained remarkably consistent over the years. At the Reagan Presidential library, I unearthed a little-known untitled handwritten speech that Reagan delivered at the Indiana State Fair in 1968. Reagan wrote many of his speeches by hand. When Donald Regan tried to demonstrate the benefits of writing with a computer, Reagan reportedly replied, "I was born into the age of pencil and pen, and I'm too old to change over to one of those things" (p. 276). In this particular speech, Reagan employed his usual trope of demonizing government regulation and government assistance programs to build his case for the merits of the free market:

> Is our failure to eradicate poverty and human misery the result of our callousness on our part or indifference to human suffering as some would have us believe? I doubt that any people in all the history of mankind have shared so generously in this effort to end poverty. The Zeitgeist—the wind of the times is against us. The new social philosophy has all the answers and they make no provision for self reliance and independence. Never mind a hand up, and hand out is everyones [sic.] just due and no need to work in the vast Fed. plantation … now almost 8 mil. are on the dole in one or the other of some 450 programs. I think most of the 8 mil. would rather be out on their own with jobs but they are caught up and bound to a giant bureaucracy that thinks of them as clients to be served until the 4th generation. Eight cabinet depts. and 12 so called independent agencies administer to their health. There are 35 separate housing programs, community assistance facilities are provided by 62 agencies, 33 Fed. agencies meddle in nearly 300 consumer protection activities and in just on medium size city [,] 140 separate urban projects have been found administered by 7 Fed. depts. Thirty six mil. Am's. share in in assorted govt. food programs & 6 mil. more get surplus food packages or help through the food stamp program. (Reagan, 1968, p. 10)

In the aforementioned speech to the Rotary Club in Oakland, Reagan made clear his unwavering faith in the free market, and his intention to fight for it: "The time has come to fight back against those who would throw aside the free market system. Truth is our sword and our shield, and we must bring it to our customers and workers and, above all, to our sons and daughters who have heard too much political and economic mythology in too many classrooms" ("Whatever happened," p. 7). Reagan, of course, was not the only person who was engaged in this rhetorical campaign to recover key aspects of laissez-faire capitalism, but he was perhaps the chief image and voice for a growing conservative movement. As is the case with almost any historical figure deemed "revolutionary," there are widely diverging opinions assessing the Reagan Presidency. Chester Pach (n.d.) has commented:

> Historians have had difficulty assessing Reagan's contradictory record. The most recent poll of scholars, completed three years ago, placed Reagan in the "average" category, far below the greatness of Washington and Lincoln but comfortably above the failures of Harding and Buchanan. Yet this composite ranking is misleading, since many members of the panel thought that Reagan was anything but average. Seven of the thirty-two jurors considered Reagan's record "near great," but nine thought he was a "below average" chief executive. Four consigned his presidency to "failure." ("Assess Reagan")

Still, Ronald Reagan seems to be fondly remembered by those in power. Indeed, perhaps appropriately, a video tribute to Reagan aired right before the kickoff of Super Bowl XLV in 2011. The date coincided with the 100th anniversary of Reagan's birth. During recent Republican presidential primary debates, candidates vying to be the Republican nominee for president in both 2012 and 2016 were falling all over themselves trying to convince those watching the debate that they were more like Ronald Reagan than their opponents. This recent glorification of Ronald Reagan is not even confined to the United States. On June 29, 2011, a life-size statue of Reagan was unveiled in Budapest on Freedom Square in front of the U.S. Embassy. On June 30, 2011, Prague renamed the street in front of the U.S. Ambassador's office the Czech equivalent of "Ronald Reagan Street." On July 4, 2011, the British government unveiled a statue on Reagan in London on Grosvenor Square. Indeed, in my home state of Indiana, we recently built the Ronald Reagan Parkway as the main road to the new Indianapolis Airport despite the fact that Reagan had no formal connection with this state. He did briefly tour the state on campaign visits, and apparently a Hendricks County Commissioner was so moved by Reagan's visit and speech in Danville, Indiana, in 1987, that he advocated for Reagan's name to be attached to the first part of the parkway project. Not to be outdone, local officials in Allen County renamed Interstate 469, a 31 miles bypass of Fort Wayne, the Ronald Reagan Expressway in 2004.

There is an organization called the Ronald Reagan Legacy Project founded in 1997 by Americans for Tax Reform President Grover Norquist. His stated objective is to have at least one notable public landmark named after Reagan in each state, and all 3067 counties in the United States.

Norquist once remarked that the motivation for the project was to create "teachable moments." He explained, "The reason we do this is so we have children turn to their parents ... and have conversations about who Reagan was and why he was important" (Lackey, 2011). Some educators have been moved by this initiative. In Brownsburg, Indiana, also in Hendricks County, there is a public school named Reagan Elementary. To create these teachable moments, "teachers weave information about Reagan into class projects" (Lackey). The school principal, Carla Hubbard, contends, "It doesn't have anything to do with political viewpoints. It is more about the model he set as a good American, and so we try to emphasize that in the curriculum" (Lackey). That certainly begs the questions of what precisely constitutes "political," and why Ronald Reagan is any "better" an American than his predecessor, Jimmy Carter. Surely there is more to being "good" than simply being popular. This also raises the issue of what we are teaching our children. I had a recent epiphany in the classroom the other day. I casually referenced Ronald Reagan assuming that my students had the same lived experience that I had with him during his time as President. After all, it seemed like only yesterday. But one student remarked, "We weren't even alive when Reagan was president!" It dawned on me that the only understanding this generation of young people have of Ronald Reagan was the mythos that surrounds him. That realization hit home when Jordin Sparks, the youngest winner of "American Idol," remarked, "I just thought [Reagan] was really, really amazing" (Page, 2011). Of course, Sparks was born after Reagan left office, but "heard her parents talk with admiration about the former president" (Page). In 2010, Sparks and Nick Jonas, another pop star who was born years after Reagan had left office, were named Co-Chairs of the National Youth Leadership Committee for the Ronald Reagan Centennial Celebration. Together they led a committee of 38 young people under the age of 25 who claimed to be inspired by Ronald Reagan even though nearly all of them were born after the Reagan presidency. This illustrates both the power of myth in our culture and how irrelevant direct experience with "reality" can be in sustaining and nurturing this myth.

Bracketing the question about which assessment holds the most merit, one thing is certain: Reagan changed the political and economic landscape of the United States more than any president since, perhaps, Franklin Delano Roosevelt. A new ideology had taken root, and it set the tone for life in the coming years. This ideology promulgated the virtues of big business, deregulation, the free market, individualism, and personal wealth. The Reagan Revolution was not so much a "revolution" as it was a recapitulation of the principles of free market capitalism that had been summarily rejected because of their contributions to the Great Depression. Indeed, the parallels are unmistakable: "[In the years leading up to the Great Depression], Republicans devised tax credits, refunds and abatements to benefit private corporations, and they enacted four major reductions in income-tax rates, purposely skewed to benefit the upper-income brackets" (Greider, 1987, p. 294). In short, Reagan's economic policies were more a "devolution" than a "revolution." It is not surprising that the band Devo was receiving critical acclaim around the same time from the mid-1970s to mid-1980s. Their band name, of course, was drawn from their concept of "de-evolution," the belief that human society was actually regressing in many ways, contrary to what most people have been led to believe. Perhaps too many people were dancing rather than paying attention to what these artists, and others like them, were really trying to tell us about the economic and political "de-evolution" underway in the United States at that time.

Many of those who had experienced the Great Depression first hand, however, were no longer in a position to challenge this unsettling return to these discredited principles for economic and political life. As such, as it has often been said, those who do not learn from history are doomed to repeat it. And while much ado is made about the longest peacetime expansion of economic activity under Reagan, recent events remind us that unchecked capitalist excess creates incredibly fragile and vulnerable economic situations.

My favorite band growing up was The Police, a band that was ahead of its time, and a band that helped me get through the 1970s and 1980s. The lead singer of the band, the world-renowned songwriter Sting, released a book entitled, *Lyrics*, in 2007. In it, he reflected on the motivating influences behind all of his music, commenting on each song in its turn. The Police's final album, the critically acclaimed and intellectually complex *Synchronicity*, was recorded on the island Montserrat in 1983. It was perhaps most remembered for the song, "Every Breath You Take." I remember seeing The Police perform the song live during their *Synchronicity* tour. It was the last song of the regular set before the encore. Briefly introducing the song before performing it, I remember Sting commented, "This is not a love song," to counter the popular perception of the same. Instead, it was an unsettling song about surveillance and control. Years later, writing about the song in *Lyrics*, he reflects:

> [There is] no release of emotions or change in the point of view of the protagonist. He is trapped in his circular obsessions. Of course, I wasn't aware of any of this. I thought I was just writing a hit song, and indeed it became one of the songs that defined the 80's, and by accident was the perfect sound track for Reagan's Star Wars fantasy of control and seduction. (Sting, 2007, p. 84)

Living through the 1970s and 1980s was an interesting and instructive experience. Some of us remember this time differently than those who celebrate the countervailing popular myth surrounding the legacy of the Reagan Administration. To be sure, Reagan helped define the end of the twentieth century, and he continues to have a lasting impact on American politics and economics. In that sense, I concur with Donald Regan, who observed, "Ronald Reagan was proposing to revolve the economic turntable of the nation by 180 degrees" (p. 158). The Reagan Presidency, however, had some darker and less palatable moments that are regretfully glossed over in recounting his time in office. Among those in my estimation was Reaganomics, a political and economic program that put us on a path of growing income inequality, increasing federal deficits, a demonization of government regulation, a pro-business bias, an aggressive foreign policy, a glorification of self-interest, and a dangerous new embrace of the free market.

References

Allen, A. (2000). Prodigal sun. *Mother Jones*. Retrieved July 21, 2021, from https://www.motherjones.com/politics/2000/03/prodigal-sun/

Benne, R. (2001). *Quality with soul: How six premier colleges and universities keep faith with their religious traditions*. William B. Eerdmans Publishing.

Brinkley, D. (1998). *The unfinished presidency: Jimmy Carter's journey beyond the White House*. Penguin.

Cannon, L. (2000/1991). *President Reagan: The role of a lifetime*. Public Affairs.

Carter, J. (1979, July 15). Crisis of confidence. *PBS*. Retrieved July 21, 2021, from https://www.pbs.org/wgbh/americanexperience/features/carter-crisis

Greider, W. (1987). *Secrets of the temple: How the federal reserve runs the country*. Simon & Schuster.

Haimerl, A. (2010, October 26). Banks spend big to sell credit cards to students. *CNNMoney*. Retrieved July 21, 2021, from https://money.cnn.com/2010/10/26/pf/college/college_credit_cards/index.htm

Inequality in America: The rich, the poor and the growing gap between them. (2006, June 15). *The Economist*, 28–30.
Lackey, K. (2011, January 24). In Reagan's name, "teaching moments." *USA Today*. Retrieved July 21, 2021, from https://usatoday30.usatoday.com/news/washington/2011-01-24-ronald-reagan-names_N.htm
Lewis, A. (1990, October 8). Paying for Reagan. *Baltimore Sun*, 30A.
Mitchell, G. (2000). *Strategic deception: Rhetoric, science, and politics in missile defense advocacy*. Michigan State University Press.
Niskanen, W. A. (1988). *Reaganomics: An insider's account of the policies and the people*. Oxford University Press.
Niskanen, W. A. (n.d.). Reaganomics. *The concise encyclopedia of economics*. Library of Economics and Liberty. Retrieved July 21, 2021, from https://www.econlib.org/library/Enc/Reaganomics.html
Pach, C. (n.d.). How do historians assess Ronald Reagan? *History News Network*. Retrieved July 21, 2021, from https://historynewsnetwork.org/article/341
Page, S. (2011, January 20). Ronald Reagan: A "folklore" president who led a revolution. *USA Today*. Retrieved July 21, 2021, from https://usatoday30.usatoday.com/news/washington/2011-01-19-ronald-reagan-legacy_N.htm
Pickens, T. B., Podesta, J. D., & Reid, H. (2009, February 24). Solving our nation's energy problems. *Chicago Tribune*, 25.
Reagan, R. (1968). Untitled speech at the Indiana state fair. Hannaford/CA HQ-Ronald Reagan Speeches-6/13/1980. 1980 Presidential Campaign Papers, Box 20, Speeches. Handwritten Drafts.
Reagan, R. (1975, March 6). Whatever happened to free enterprise? An address by Ronald Reagan, Governor of California, 1967–1974 to the rotary club of Oakland. Hannaford/CA HQ-Ronald Reagan Speeches-3/16/1975.
Reagan, R. (1980, April 28). Economic policy statement for governor Ronald Reagan: Richard J. Whalen draft (4/28/80). Hannaford/CA HQ-Ronald Reagan-Speeches.
Regan, D. T. (1988). *For the record: From Wall Street to Washington*. Harcourt.
Reid, R. F., & Klumpp, J. F. (2004). *American rhetorical discourse* (3rd ed.). Waveland Press.
Sting. (2007). *Lyrics*. The Dial Press.
Zetter, K. (2010, September 2). Sept. 2, 1969: First ATM starts doling out dollars. *Wired*. Retrieved July 21, 2021, from https://www.wired.com/2010/09/0902first-us-atm

CHAPTER 5

Spirits in the Material World: Alan Greenspan and the Newspeak Economy

In George Orwell's unsettling dystopian classic *1984*, the main character, Winston Smith, worked for the government's Ministry of Truth. His primary job was in the Records Department, adjusting statistics provided by the Ministry of Plenty. Citizens in Orwell's dystopia had a hard time distinguishing fact from fiction because government claims and evidence were constantly being manipulated. And without access to the past, or objective records to assess government claims and evidence, the government could quite literally advance whatever arguments they wished, and people had no choice but to accept it. In Orwell's words, "[All government pronouncements had] to be accepted, because they did not exist, and never again could exist, any standard against which [they] could be tested" (2003, p. 96). For example, the government of Oceania constantly revised war and alliance initiatives, one week declaring a state of war with Eurasia, and a state of peace with Eastasia, only to claim the situation reversed the following week. Significantly, the public could not perceive, nor evaluate this inconsistent turnabout because, in Orwell's words, "to trace out the history of the whole period, to say who was fighting whom at any particular moment, would have been utterly impossible, since no written record, and no spoken word, ever made mention of any other alignment than the existing one" (pp. 34–35). The Government dubbed this "Reality Control," or "Doublethink," in Newspeak, the officially sanctioned government language.

G. D. Klinger et al., *Money Talks*,
https://doi.org/10.1007/978-3-031-00816-0_5

Another illustration of Doublethink, and one more on point for the purposes of this chapter, was the constant revision of rationed commodities by the government. For example, chocolate rations were constantly revised upward, or downward, depending on the mood and effect that the government wanted to create. Ration decreases were typically coupled with good news to temper an unwanted reaction from the people. In one instance, when the government announced a successful battle campaign against Eurasia, it coupled this good news with the bad news that "chocolate rations would be reduced from thirty grams to twenty" (p. 26). A short time earlier, though, the Ministry of Plenty had issued a "categorical pledge" that "there would be no reduction in chocolate rations during 1984" (p. 40). More often than not, the Ministry of Plenty would underestimate the actual output of a particular product, say, boots, to advance the argument that the government had once again exceeded its expected quota (p. 42). A typical government announcement designed to spark public jubilation sounded like this: "Attention comrades! We have good news for you. We have won the battle for production! Returns now completed on the output of all classes of consumer goods show that the standard of living has risen by no less than twenty percent over the past year" (p. 59). Perhaps not surprisingly, the announcement continued; "All over Oceania this morning there were irrepressible spontaneous demonstrations when workers marched out of factory offices and paraded through the streets with banners voicing their gratitude to Big Brother for the new, happy life which his wise leadership has bestowed on us" (pp. 59–60). Concurrently, there was a celebration that the government had raised the chocolate ration to 20 grams, despite the fact, as noted above, "it had been announced that the ration was to be *reduced* to twenty grams a week" (p. 60). "Was this possible," Winston wondered, "that they could swallow that, after only twenty-four hours? Yes, they swallowed it" (p. 60).

The use and misuse of government statistics to manipulate public opinion forced Winston to reflect on the job he performed at the Ministry of Truth:

> But actually, he thought as he readjusted the Ministry of Plenty's figures, it was not even forgery. It was merely the substitution of one piece of nonsense for another. Most of the material that you were dealing with had no connection with anything in the real world, not even the kind of connection that is contained in a direct lie. Statistics were just as much a fantasy in their original

> version as in their rectified version. A great deal of the time you were expected to make them up out of your head. (p. 42)

He continued, "And so it was with every class of recorded fact, great or small. Everything faded away into a shadow-world in which, finally, even the date of the year had become uncertain" (p. 42). The use of numbers and statistics creates the impression of neutrality and scientific objectivity, but this was and is merely an illusion, a cloak to hide the fact that statistics can be used to support wildly varying interpretations of reality. Take, for example, the fact that the U.S. Federal Government constantly revises GDP and inflation figures after they are officially announced. The revisions typically garner less critical scrutiny than the original announcements. Such revisions assuredly have an Orwellian feel to them.

Importantly, since the government controlled the media in *1984*, the messages emanating from the various mediums of communication simply reinforced the messages advanced by the government. "[T]he telescreens bruised your ears with statistics proving that people had more food, more clothes, better houses, better recreations—that they lived longer, worked shorter hours, were bigger, healthier, stronger, happier, more intelligent, better educated, than people of fifty years ago" (pp. 76–77). Moreover, "Not a word of it could ever be proved or disproved. ... Everything faded into mist. The past was erased, the erasure was forgotten, the lie became the truth" (p. 77). The government control of all communication was complete: "This process of continuous alteration was applied not only to newspapers, but to books, periodicals, pamphlets, posters, leaflets, films, sound tracks, cartoons, photographs—to every kind of literature or documentation which might conceivably hold any political or ideological significance" (p. 41).

The government controlled not only the mediums of communication, but they attempted to control the substance of it as well. They did this by developing and mandating an official language. As noted above, this language was dubbed "Newspeak." The idea was that if the government could control language, they could literally control every person's mind. As British social psychologist Michael Billig (1987) contends in *Arguing and Thinking*, the process of thinking is fundamentally rhetorical. People think by using symbols, or signs. Subsequently, language is the primary determinant of human thought. By controlling language, the government sought to control every thought of the citizens of Oceania. The project was ambitious. Winston talked with his friend, Syme, who was ironically a philologist, and who worked for the Research Department of Ministry of Truth, about that department's progress on creating the 11th Edition of the Newspeak Dictionary. Syme boasted, "We're destroying words—scores of them, hundreds of them, every day. We're cutting them down to the bone. … It's a beautiful thing, the destruction of words" (p. 52). It seemed that too many words were difficult to control, both in terms of sheer quantity and in terms of their nature. Particularly troublesome were classes of words like metaphors that had no obvious, or direct, connection with some underlying reality. Consequently, one of the characteristics of each new edition of the Newspeak dictionary was that they contained fewer and fewer officially sanctioned words. The dictionary kept getting smaller, and the reason for this was obvious: "Newspeak was designed not to extend, but *diminish* the range of thought" (p. 310). The ultimate goal of Newspeak was for words to "issue from the larynx, without involving the higher brain centers at all" (p. 319).

Orwell's account, of course, is fictional, but there are several unnerving parallels to current times. Indeed, if people were asked to identify the individual who performed the same job as Winston Smith in our society, many would point their finger at the Chair of the Federal Reserve Bank. While Ronald Reagan was able to set the stage for the reintroduction of free market capitalism through the use of his popular slogan, "Reaganomics," he needed an architect to implement his ambitious economic agenda, and assure its continued vitality even years after he left office. To that end, he appointed Alan Greenspan chair of the Federal Reserve toward the end of his two-term presidency. He had the chance to do so earlier, in July 1983, but he reappointed Paul Volcker instead. According to Niskanen (1988), "Reagan strongly opposed Volcker's reappointment but had no viable substitute" (p. 171). By waiting to appoint Greenspan when he did, Reagan ensured that his free market-based economic agenda would live beyond his presidency. Alan Greenspan was chair of the Federal Reserve from 1987 to 2006. He held his position under four different presidents. Greenspan is especially interesting because his discourse negotiated the relationship between government monetary policy and public disclosures of the same. Thus, Greenspan personified the economic and rhetorical "artist" described in the introduction, and each picture that he painted was one to which many turned an attentive eye.

On June 2, 1987, President Ronald Reagan announced that the chair of the Fed, Paul Volcker, was resigning. Reagan moved quickly to appoint the former chair of the Council of Economic Advisers under President

Ford, Alan Greenspan, to fill the vacancy. Greenspan was both an immediately popular, yet curious choice. He was consistently the first, or second, choice for the job among the financial community,[1] and had a distinguished career as a government servant and economic consultant.[2] But his choice is also curious given his somewhat outspoken views as a student of, and lecturer for, Ayn Rand. Rand once said of Greenspan, he is "my disciple philosophically, but his career as an economic analyst is his own achievement. He is an advocate of full laissez-faire capitalism" (Nash, 1987, p. D27). Among the strongest connection to Rand's philosophy was Greenspan's belief in an unregulated economy, which makes his appointment to the chief interventionist branch of government in the regulation of monetary policy an especially interesting one to study discursively given such ideological commitments.

For years, Greenspan worked in the private sector, most notably, the economic consulting firm, Townsend-Greenspan & Company. He was also chair of the Council of Economic Advisers under President Ford. He was actually appointed by President Nixon, but by the time the Senate took up his nomination, President Nixon had resigned. He accepted the government position with reluctance, but it was his Mentor, Arthur Burns, who finally convinced him to take the job. "Burns appealed to Greenspan's sense of patriotism and suggested that it was his duty to go to Washington and fight inflation" (Martin, 2001, p. 90).

Greenspan was quickly confirmed in the Senate by a vote of 91–2. Bill Bradley voted against him because of his views on bank deregulation. Sen. William Proxmire almost voted against him for the same reason, and the fact that he had a "dismal forecasting record" for inflation and economic growth (Uchitelle, 1987, p. D1). Townsend-Greenspan had overestimated inflation by 1.2% to 2.4% each of the prior four years. In fact, Greenspan's firm was ranked dead last in its forecasting record among the eight firms studied by the Federal Reserve (Uchitelle, p. D1). Proxmire was previously Greenspan's biggest detractor during his confirmation hearing to chair the Council of Economic Advisers.

During that hearing before a branch of the Senate Banking Committee, Greenspan was taken to task by Proxmire. He had obviously done his

[1] According to a poll conducted by Richard Hoey of Drexel, Burnham, Lambert, Inc. (Blustein, 1987, p. 1).

[2] Since his government service in 1977, he helped run the economic consulting firm Townsend-Greenspan and Co.

homework on Greenspan, calling attention to his writings for *The Objectivist*, which I discuss below. In particular, Proxmire quizzed Greenspan on his intellectual resistance to consumer protection laws that, on face, seemed to benefit consumers from unscrupulous market participants. Greenspan explained that these laws were an inexpedient and cumbersome way to protect consumers. The free market, he contended, provided adequate protection to consumers because companies have an incentive to provide quality products for consumers. This argument, of course, assumes consumers have constant access to a free flow of information, which is assuredly not always the case, and that consumers will always make rational choices, an assumption that I challenged in the introduction. All one has to do is check the current collective waistline of the United States to realize that consumers, especially American consumers, do not always make healthy choices. Further, marketing and advertising by fast food companies often takes the ability to make good decisions out of the hands of consumers in a barrage of ideologically driven propaganda blitzes aimed at beguiling consumers for the sake of boosting profits. Proxmire was skeptical, as well. In his concluding remarks at the confirmation hearings, he stated, "I have great, great difficulty with the fact that you are a free enterprise man who does not believe in antitrust, does not believe in consumer protection, does not believe in progressive income tax. … [Y]ou seem to be opposed to many of the social programs that we have been able to achieve" (Nominations, 1974, p. 52). Nevertheless, Greenspan was confirmed by the Senate to lead the Council of Economic Advisers on August 19 without a record vote.

As noted above, it was Arthur Burns who finally convinced Greenspan to accept the position as chair of the Council of Economic Advisers. Burns and Ayn Rand were perhaps the two most significant intellectual influences on Greenspan in his formative years. Greenspan took a seminar on business cycles at Columbia University from Arthur Burns.[3] Burns, like Greenspan, later became chair of the President's Council of Economic Advisers and, ultimately, chair of the Fed. He had an early and decisive impact on Greenspan's approach to monetary policy. Burns was an

[3]Another student of Arthur Burns was Milton Friedman. Friedman is a critic of monetary policy and the Fed's undue influence over the economy. Importantly, he is especially critical of restrictive Fed policy that he felt contributed significantly to economic downturns. In *A Monetary History of the United States, 1867–1960*, Friedman and co-author Anna Schwartz (1971) conclude that monetary policy was the primary determinant for the Great Depression.

outspoken critic of Keynes, who was the dominant influence in macroeconomics at the time. One central theme of Burns' empirical approach to the economy was that "government policy might actually be counterproductive to the economy" (Martin, p. 29). Excessive government spending, in Burns' estimation, was the primary cause of inflation. Importantly, "[u]nder Burns's tutelage, Greenspan would do an about-face. He'd start moving away from the benevolent-government perspective advocated by Roosevelt, Keynes, and his own father. He would grow to be a staunch supporter of laissez-faire and limited government" (p. 29).

One of the central positions in Greenspan's approach to monetary policy, reinforced by his time as a student with Arthur Burns, was his resistance to inflation. Countervailing economic theory during that time contended that inflation and unemployment tended to move in opposite directions. Fed policy in the past had tried to seek a delicate balance. On the one hand, it attempted to tame inflation through restrictive monetary policy, but on the other hand, it did not want to impede growth to the extent that it created substantial unemployment. This was the central dilemma in Fed policy, the Scylla, and Charybdis of Keynesian economic theory.

Greenspan substantially altered the nature of that balance. He did not cloak the fact that his primary role as Chair of the Fed prioritized fighting inflation first (Hershey, 1987). While still important, unemployment and related statistics became a peripheral concern. Every discussion, every policy move, seemed to be directed toward fighting inflation. At his confirmation hearing to be chair of the Fed, Greenspan noted, "[I]t is absolutely essential that [the Fed's] central focus be on restraining inflation because if that fails, then we have very little opportunity for sustained long-term economic growth" (Nominations, p. 29). Indeed, many of the restrictive moves taken by the Greenspan Fed were not even a response to actual inflation, but the fear of inflation in the future. At one point, Greenspan quipped, "If you wait to see the eyes of inflation, then it's too late" (Beckner, 1996, p. 68). In short, over the course of a few years, Greenspan had shifted not only the nature of Fed policy but also an entire economic culture. Now, monetary policy's primary responsibility was to fight inflation first. While subtle, this was one of Greenspan's proudest accomplishments. Initially, he claimed that "arguments in favor of price stability as the main goal of monetary policy were 'at the cutting edge ... Now, they are boilerplate'" (Beckner, p. 349).

Fighting inflation was a common trope in Greenspan's rhetorical arsenal. And it was nearly a constant one, as well. While his more recent views about fighting inflation as the primary focus of the Federal Reserve are well known, this is a policy line that he held throughout his career. In 1974, in the midst of growing stagflation, a term that combines economic "stagnation" with high "inflation," Greenspan commented, "If inflation continues, our system will not hold together in its present form" (Schoenebaum, 1979, p. 252). Greenspan's views about fighting inflation were widely popularized. In 1977, he published a piece with Arthur Okun in *Fortune* magazine entitled "Debate: How to Stop Inflation" (Greenspan & Okun, 1977, pp. 116–120). And in 1979, he wrote, "Inflation's Effect on Investment" in the *New York Times* (Greenspan, 1979, p. D2). Fighting inflation first was a policy priority that Greenspan shared with Reagan: "During the Reagan-Volcker years the control of inflation became the Holy Grail of monetary policy, and it remains enshrined under Greenspan and President Clinton at century's end. This policy is the most enduring of Reagan's economic legacies" (Cannon, 2000, p. 238).

Not everyone agreed with this shift in economic priorities. The goal of fighting inflation first, often at the cost of greater unemployment, led to several public clashes between Greenspan and Henry Gonzalez in Congress, President George H. W. Bush, and eventual Fed vice-chair, Alan Blinder, among others.

One of the chief conundrums of Greenspan's private and public commitments involves his extensive interactions with Ayn Rand and Objectivism. While Greenspan's approach to economic theory was shaped in a large part by his work at Columbia with Arthur Burns, he was perhaps even more influenced by Ayn Rand. Indeed, Martin observes, "If Burns can be credited with pushing Greenspan in a free-market direction, it's Rand who finished the job" (p. 41).

Rand had a remarkable influence on Greenspan in his formative years. "[F]rom Greenspan's late twenties to his early forties[,] objectivism played a major role in his life, and he spent countless hours in the company of Rand and her circle" (p. 35).[4] Significantly, Rand was not initially drawn

[4]It is important to note that Greenspan found Rand to be a "devoted Aristotelian—the central idea being that there exists an objective reality that is separate from consciousness and capable of being known. Thus she called her philosophy objectivism" (Greenspan 51). A close reading of Aristotle's *Politics*, *Ethics*, and *Rhetoric*, however, demonstrates that this is a vast oversimplification of his writing.

to Greenspan. After an early meeting with him, she remarked, "He looks like an undertaker" (Branden, 1999, p. 113). But eventually, Rand welcomed Greenspan to "the Collective," the ironic name loosely assigned to her reading and discussion group. Discussion topics of the Collective were wide-ranging: "politics, current events, philosophy, literature, movies, and painting" (Martin, p. 41). Rand was an unabashed supporter of the laissez-faire capitalism, and the important role of the individual in that system:

> Rand made her case for laissez-faire vehemently, incisively, passionately. A frequent topic of discussion—irony of ironies—was the futility and destructiveness of central banks. ... During these discussions, the Fed was often taken to task for making mistakes that brought on the Great Depression. Errant Fed policies could also lead to inflation, in turn making citizens' money worth less. The Objectivist party line held that inflation was an insidious form of taxation. (Martin, p. 43)

Greenspan was a strong supporter of Rand and her philosophy (Rubin, 2007). He came to the defense of Rand's book, *Atlas Shrugged*, which had publicly received more criticism than acclaim. In a 1957 *New York Times* "Letter to the Editor," published in the *New York Times Book Review*, Greenspan wrote, "*Atlas Shrugged* is a celebration of life and happiness. Justice is unrelenting. Creative individuals and undeviating purpose and rationality achieve joy and fulfillment. Parasites who persistently avoid either purpose or reason perish as they should" (Greenspan, 1957, p. 283). The influence of Rand on Greenspan's approach to economics was unmistakable. In the February 24, 1975, issue of *Newsweek*, Greenspan, who graced the cover of this issue, commented, "When I first met Ayn Rand, I was a free enterpriser in the Adam Smith sense ... impressed with the theoretical structure and efficiency of markets. What she did was to make me see that capitalism is not only efficient and practical, but also moral" (Mayer et al., 1975, p. 61).

Ayn Rand and her first lieutenant, Nathaniel Braden, published a newsletter called *The Objectivist*. As noted above, Greenspan often wrote articles for this publication. In some of those essays, Greenspan attacked both antitrust regulations and consumer protection laws because they represented government intervention in the exercise of the free market (Rand, 1967, p. 63, 118). In short, Greenspan's positions regarding the free market were becoming solidified long before he became chair of the Fed.

A term that is often used to describe the mysterious statements that emanate from Fed officials is called "Fedspeak." Of course, it smacks in many ways of Orwell's "Newspeak" language where the government controlled every aspect of acceptable and unacceptable discourse in his famous novel, *1984*. But it recognizes an important point about the discourse of the Federal Reserve generally, and Greenspan specifically.

Some might argue that the discourse of the Fed should not matter, that their true power comes from their control of the economy. The Fed should be nothing more than a neutral conveyor of monetary policy, and that the Fed is and should be "apolitical" at all times. These beliefs fail to recognize at least two things. First, as I argue throughout this book, there is no facile distinction between politics and economics. Second, it underestimates the rhetorical power of the Fed. It takes about one year for changes in monetary policy to have an impact on the economy. The impact of the discourse announcing that policy is immediate. Macroeconomic and market fluctuations are tied to the discourse, not the underlying policy initiative. As Martin observes, "Regardless of his intent, the reality was that stocks bobbed and wove on his every word" (p. 222).

When people cast economics as a neutral "science" rather than an art, they lose important elements that a more holistic view of the enterprise would bring forth. While this might be news to some neo-classical economists, "[m]ost Fed officials frankly admit conducting monetary policy is an imprecise exercise—more of an art than a science" (Beckner, p. 100). Indeed, Gerald Corrigan, president of the New York Fed, recognized the power of rhetoric during the Crash of 1987: "There is a real art to this. … It's all in code. Bankers all know the code" (Corrigan, 2000). The discourse of the Fed is rhetoric dressed up to look like science—that is the essence of Fedspeak.

Greenspan has demonstrated that he is a master of Fedspeak, a subject we will revisit in later chapters. Martin notes, "Greenspan has attained a remarkable level of power and mystique. The world hangs on his every word" (Martin, p. xx). Others concur: "[P]eople could listen to Alan comfortably. Alan's role, in my view, was to come in and offer reasoned argument. He was able to be a dispassionate advocate when it was important to talk quietly, intelligently, and thoughtfully in order to bring people together" (Herbits, 2000). More than one commentator has drawn a parallel between Greenspan's work on the Fed and his love of music,[5] especially Jazz: "Adaptability is Greenspan's hallmark. … For a Fed

[5] Greenspan studied at the Julliard School of Music and is an accomplished clarinet player (Tuccille, 2002).

chairman, he has a rare ability to improvise. There's a parallel between that and his stint as a professional musician" (Jones, 2000).

Greenspan was well aware that the unpredictability of the economy required the chair of the Fed to be flexible. He was also well aware that even his individual word choices had significant consequences. "On at least one occasion, Greenspan actually assigned an aide to follow the markets in real time during his testimony. That way, if a particular speaking point seemed to be having a deleterious effect on stocks, he could change course in midstream" (Martin, p. 222).

Greenspan was on his way to becoming the ultimate rhetorical artist. He had to paint a picture of a relatively stable and healthy economy amidst growing dysfunction in the economic markets and growing pessimism amongst his relevant audience: business leaders, government officials, and consumers. This, it seems, is the point of Samuels when he urges readers to view economics as a collection of "modes of discourse" giving effect to particular "systems of belief" for relevant audiences. In this case, Greenspan had to boldly cross Galbraith's cultural divide between "transmission and reception" with a rhetoric of reassurance.

We learn a lot by studying the rhetorical artistry of Alan Greenspan. First, as noted above, it is interesting to study the evolution of Greenspan's discourse away from his publicly pronounced views of an unregulated economy, a monetary policy that prioritized fighting inflation, and a policy that urged the deregulation of the nation's banks. The demands of several economic crises during his tenure as chair of the Fed created constrained rhetorical situations that forced Greenspan to modify his views, and consequently, his public discourse.

Second, Greenspan's discourse is an appropriate object of study because of his "institutional" position, a role uniquely vested with a "performative power." During times of economic uncertainty, this power must be used prudently in order to assuage consumer fears. Indeed, the chair of the Fed is often the most important figure speaking to the economic health of the United States. Thus, during the economic crises that we will study in more detail in subsequent chapters, Greenspan's rhetoric became both increasingly more important and simultaneously more constrained.[6] At first, Greenspan seemed to misunderstand his unique position in this regard,

[6] See, for example, some reports suggesting that Greenspan's rhetorical position was even more important than President Reagan's regarding the economy because of a perception of Reagan's growing political ineffectiveness. One analyst argued, "Greenspan is the only candidate for restoring confidence in the markets. It's the chairman of the Fed, when it comes down to it, that pulls the levers" (Murray, "Market's Frenzy" 26).

but his discourse shifted indicating that he became increasingly more aware of the rhetorical power with which he was vested and he later came to exercise it more prudently.

Finally, the rhetoric of Alan Greenspan is interesting to study in that it offers a fine case study for examining the material impact of economic rhetoric; it is in this sense that Greenspan's rhetoric is normative. There was an intellectual gap between the economic "object" of Greenspan's discourse, the language he uses, and the impact of his language. Greenspan's position was a unique one in that he could quite literally make something the case by saying it was so. As analysis of his rhetoric will later demonstrate, consumer confidence, the stock market, foreign markets, indeed, the very perception of the relative strength in the U.S. economy hinges on the words and actions of Greenspan and the Fed. Critics bear an important duty to carefully study the rhetoric of Alan Greenspan given his unique rhetorical position, and the enormous political potential and consequences of his discourse.

Critics who examine Alan Greenspan's discourse during his tenure as chair of the Fed will find recognizable patterns, and a few anomalies. The ways in which Greenspan responded during a series of economic crises share similarities and suggest that there may be certain tropes and themes to which he was particularly attentive. These similarities seem to fall into four categories: immediate reassurances, critical reassessment at a later time, a general pattern of qualified optimism, and indications of a split intellectual allegiance. While these categories overlap significantly, each can be discussed in turn.

The first of the methods to which Greenspan turned was the use of rhetorical reassurances. Immediately after a crisis, or other negative economic reports, Greenspan attempted to create a picture of unambiguous stability and a Fed ready to take any measure to check future uncertainty. These reassurances took three forms: the promise of monetary liquidity, the movement of key interest rates, and the pledge of better regulation. Greenspan turned to various combinations of these tropes in handling each of the economic crises in order to assuage investor and consumer fears, and assure them that they were still sailing upon safe economic waters. They emphasized, more than anything, continuity in Fed policy, stability in the U.S. economy, and confidence that Fed policy had the crisis under control. Rarely, though, did these immediate responses of virtually unlimited positive action lock the Fed into later policy commitments.

Rather, Greenspan turned to a second method to supplement the above: a cautious reassessment of the strength of the U.S. economy, but with some distance from the heat of the particular crisis. The unguarded optimism cited above did much to prevent panic reactions from the public, but it often did not accurately assess the underlying economic problems. Thus, Greenspan reassessed the situation, but from a position that would not worsen consumer and investor fears. And it was with this critical distance that Greenspan discussed actual Fed policy in what seemed more realistic terms when compared to the promise of unlimited monetary support in the days that immediately followed the crisis.

But while Greenspan did seem to reassess crisis situations in more realistic terms, he was careful never to paint a picture of total pessimism, even when it became obvious that the situation was much worse than he had anticipated. Thus, the worst that one heard from Greenspan was a reluctant admission of a problem, immediate moves to downplay the seriousness of the problem, and a guarded optimism about the future. Indeed, as the problems seemed to grow worse, Greenspan's rhetoric evolved in order to diminish any increased concern. He seemed to learn later in his tenure to rhetorically "hedge his bets," especially in handling the recession, so as not to be later blamed for incorrect analysis or response. Thus, one finds the use of qualifiers (e.g., "probably," "might," "may," "possibility," or "relatively"), and qualified statements (e.g., "slightly tip the scales," "soft landing," "temporary hesitation," "pause," "cautious optimism," or "not without risks") commonplace in his discourse.[7]

Finally, one issue that was highlighted at the outset was the irony of Greenspan being appointed to the chief interventionist branch in regulating the nation's economy given his intellectual commitment to the principles of laissez-faire capitalism. This was not a new tension for Greenspan. The same one played out in the 1970s, as well, during his previous work for the government: "Like Rand, Greenspan believes that government has no business meddling with free enterprise—yet here he is helping make policy for an American government that intervenes in nearly every aspect of the economy" (Mayer et al., p. 60). This continuing irony was especially acute during Greenspan's tenure as Chair of the Fed given that he constantly had to engage economic crises that required interventionist

[7] For more background on the use of qualifiers in public arguments, see Stephen Toulmin's, *The Uses of Argument* (1958).

policy and rhetorical responses from the Fed. The tension played itself out in the discourse of Greenspan; indeed, at times it seemed like Greenspan had a split monetary personality. It often seemed a struggle for him to call for increased monetary intervention, the manipulation of interest rates, and stricter regulation given his faith in the "self-correcting" tendencies of the market; it was a struggle between his private intellectual commitments and the growing need for public reassurances during times of crisis, and strands of both tendencies are found throughout his discourse which often created the impression of a mixed, or contradictory message. No place is this clearer than in the conclusions of the two reports issued just months apart from two independent committees appointed by President Reagan to study the reason for the stock market collapse in 1987. In one, Greenspan called for a radical overhaul in the regulation of the nation's capital markets; in the other, Greenspan expressed a renewed faith in the self-corrective tendency of the markets, and increased self, not federal, regulation of the same.

Overall, the discourse of Alan Greenspan indicated that he increasingly became aware both of the special performative power with which he was vested and of the fact that his words had enormous political and economic consequences. With this realization came the maturation of his rhetoric: one which sought to reassure at the right time, but one which did not just paint over existing problems; one which tended toward guarded optimism, but one which would adapt as the situation merited; one which revealed his private intellectual commitments, but one which embraced the political requirements of a job which often clashed with those commitments. He was becoming the conservative voice of capital, a quiet, but strong source of stability and credibility grounded in an unshakeable belief in the free market. It proved, time and again, to be just what the public wanted, or so they believed. As John Adams once observed, "[The public] instantly give away their liberties into the hand of grandees, or kings, idols of their own creation" (2000, p. 244).

One of the more significant points of Orwell, and this chapter, generally, is that words function largely as spirits in the material world. They do not have any fixed ontological status, but are rhetorical constructions designed to create purposive psychological effects upon a particular audience. Words are not real, in the traditional sense of the word, but they are material, and they have material consequences. The words used by scientists or economists are no more real, authentic, or objective, than the words used by poets, priests, or politicians, despite the fact that they claim otherwise.

There were three categories of words in Newspeak. The economic rhetoric of Alan Greenspan would most likely be classed in the B Category, a category that consisted of words that had been "deliberately constructed for a political purpose" (Orwell, p. 313). Despite their outward appearance of neutrality, these ideologically loaded words were "intended to impose a desirable mental attitude upon the person using them" (p. 313). Many of these words "had highly stylized meanings, barely intelligible to anyone who had not mastered the language as a whole" (p. 315). Historically, economics has been a field shrouded in technical jargon and expertise. Greenspan used this characteristic of economic discourse to advance his free market agenda, and disarm those who stood in his way. He subsequently enjoyed nearly unchecked economic and political power for 20 years, more than doubling the direct impact that President Reagan, who first appointed Greenspan, had during his two terms of office. This appointment assured Reagan's free market legacy would survive well past his presidency.

When Federalist John Adams was voted out of office in favor of Republican Thomas Jefferson, and the Federalists lost both houses of Congress in the same election during what was called the "Revolution of 1800," President Adams did his best to ensure that the Federalist ideology still played a significant part in the Federal Government going forward. Since the Federalists had lost both the Executive and Legislative branches, Adams set his sights on the judicial branch. Adams significantly expanded the number of judges, and made several last-minute judicial appointments, entrenching Federalist influence in the Judiciary. Indeed, he was signing new appointments up until the very last day, and very last minute, of his time in the White House. When Jefferson arrived for his first day of work as the new President, he found a stack of unsigned appointments still on his desk. These "Midnight Appointments" provided the cause of action in the infamous *Marbury v. Madison* case.

Judicial appointments are especially significant because judges are often appointed for life, and not subject to the same term limits as politicians. Indeed, many say this must be done to ensure that judges are insulated from political pressures. Through his numerous judicial appointments, Adams had secured a Federalist legacy in the Federal Government for years to come.

Like Adams, toward the end of his presidency, Ronald Reagan wanted to secure his legacy, especially the main components of Reaganomics. Among other things, Reagan had a decisive influence on the make-up of the Federal Courts for many years. These Reagan appointees to the Federal bench enforced anti-labor, anti-consumer, pro-industry, pro-free market, and deregulatory policies. Reagan, however, had a weapon in his quiver that Adams did not possess given that there was no national bank at the time; he had the power to appoint the new chair of the Federal Reserve toward the end of his second term, and he was well aware of this power. Appointing a free market apologist to chair the Federal Reserve was a goal of his presidency stretching back to the 1980 presidential campaign:

> The Federal Reserve System is, much like the Supreme Court, wisely independent of the Congress and the Executive Branch of government. This independence must be preserved. But the President has the responsibility of nominating the members who serve as the Governors of the Federal Reserve. I will make every effort to ensure that those I nominate are committed to sound, responsible monetary policies. (Reagan, 1980, p. 15)

The chair of the Federal Reserve is more like a judge than a politician in that they are theoretically insulated from political pressures, as I note above, and they are also not subject to term limits. They do need to be reappointed, but that did not seem to be a problem in Greenspan's case. He made himself irreplaceable to four different Presidents during his 20-year tenure at the Fed. Greenspan became the key mouthpiece for advancing the deregulatory, free market-oriented approach of Reagan. While Greenspan seemed to have a mixed personal and professional relationship with Reagan, they shared key sentiments regarding the merits of laissez-faire capitalism. In his autobiography, Greenspan had this to say about Reagan: "Though his grasp of economics wasn't very deep or sophisticated, he understood the tendency of free markets to self-correct, and the fundamental wealth-creating power of capitalism. He trusted Adam Smith's invisible hand to … produce outcomes that he generally perceived as fair" (Greenspan, 2007, p. 89). Ironically, of course, Reagan was an economics major as an undergraduate at Eureka College. Still, given their common commitment to the free market, Greenspan ensured that Reagan's economic legacy was secure years after Reagan had left office.

The main point that I want to contend about Greenspan is that his power during his long tenure as chair of the Fed was more rhetorical than it was economic. While his monetary policy was significant, to be sure, it is not what moved markets and shaped economic conditions with immediacy. Instead, the public and the markets, not only in the United States but also around the world, turned on Greenspan's every word. Significantly, Martin has recognized, "Monetary policy works with a time lag, anywhere from three months to two years" (Martin, p. 205). Beckner concurred with this assessment when he cited the "Fed's oft-stated belief that the effects of its actions are not fully felt for at least a year or a year and a half" (p. 225). So it was not the actual economic impact of a change in monetary policy that moved markets almost immediately, but the discourse surrounding that change. Greenspan seemed to later recognize and embrace this fact as his experience grew. In his biography, he openly admits that a good part of what he had to do as Fed chair was public posturing, and using rhetoric judiciously to achieve a particular effect. As Martin postulated, "A considerable portion of market behavior is driven by human psychology" (p. 173). And as social psychologist Michael Billig, whom I cite above, recognizes, rhetoric is the key to understanding the inner workings of social psychology. From a macroeconomic perspective, rhetoric drives both market and consumer fear, and it can assuage the same.

One of the most cherished institutions among the citizens in George Orwell's *1984* was the lottery. Orwell sadly reflected, "The Lottery, with its weekly pay-out of enormous prizes, was the one public event to which the proles paid serious attention. It was probable that there were some millions of proles for whom the Lottery was the principal if not the only reason for remaining alive" (p. 88). The Lottery spawned a whole secondary market, or, in Orwell's words, "a tribe of men who made a living selling systems, forecasts, and lucky numbers" (p. 88). One interesting fact about the Lottery that Winston observed given his position in the Ministry of Truth, "[T]he prizes were largely imaginary. Only small sums were actually paid out, the winners of big prizes being nonexistent persons" (p. 88).

The point of the lottery was not to increase wealth; it was actually designed to control wealth while at the same time giving the appearance that collective wealth was increasing, much like casinos and state lotteries do, as we observed earlier. The underlying concern for the government in *1984* was "[a]n all around increase in wealth threatened the destruction ... of hierarchical society" (p. 194). The belief was that "[i]n the long run, a hierarchical society was only possible on a basis of poverty and ignorance" (p. 194). Importantly for Orwell: "*Who* wields the power is not important, provided the hierarchical structure always remains the same" (p. 215). Alan Greenspan himself was not as important as the role that he was playing, a role that called for a particular actor during a transformative economic and political juncture in the history of the United States. His character was pre-scripted for an actor who was supposed to grease the wheels of capitalism, and advance the cause of the free market. Greenspan seemed to slip quite comfortably into his role that encouraged him to use Fedspeak in order to manufacture free market consent just as Winston used Newspeak to reinforce the power of the government in *1984*.

References

Adams, J. (2000). A defence of the constitutions: 22 March 1778. In G. W. Carey (Ed.), *The political writings of John Adams* (pp. 105–303). Regnery Publishing.

Beckner, S. K. (1996). *Back from the brink: The Greenspan years.* John Wiley & Sons.

Billig, M. (1987). *Arguing and thinking: A rhetorical approach to social psychology.* Cambridge University Press.

Blustein, P. (1987, June 3). Fed jolt: Nominee Greenspan shares Volcker's goals but not his clout. *Wall Street Journal*, A1.

Branden, N. (1999). *My years with Ayn Rand.* Jossey-Bass Publishers.

Cannon, L. (2000/1991). *President Reagan: The role of a lifetime.* Public Affairs.

Corrigan, G. (2000). Interview with Justin Martin. 21 January 2000. Excerpts reprinted in Martin, J. (2001). *Greenspan: The man behind money.* Perseus.

Friedman, M., & Schwartz, A. J. (1971). *A monetary history of the United States, 1867–1960.* Princeton University Press.

Greenspan, A. (1957, November 3). Letter to the editor. *New York Times Book Review, 283.*

Greenspan, A. (1979, August 8). Inflation's effect on investment. *New York Times*, D2.

Greenspan, A. (2007). *The age of turbulence: Adventures in a new world.* Penguin.

Greenspan, A., & Okun, A. (1977). Debate: How to stop inflation. *Fortune, 95*, 116–120.

Herbits, S. (2000). Interview with Justin Martin. 22 February 2000. Excerpts reprinted in Martin, J. (2001). *Greenspan: The man behind money.* Perseus.

Hershey, R. D. Jr. (1987, July 22). Passing of the guard at fed: Greenspan's inflation vow. *New York Times*, D1.

Jones, D. (2000). Interview with Justin Martin. 19 January 2000. Excerpts reprinted in Martin, J. (2001). *Greenspan: The man behind money.* Perseus.

Martin, J. (2001). *Greenspan: The man behind the money.* Perseus.

Mayer, A., Whitmore, J., & Abraham, P. L. (1975, February 24). Greenspan – Atlas jogs. *Newsweek*, 60–61.

Nash, N. C. (1987, June 3). A laissez faire pragmatist: Alan Greenspan. *New York Times*, D27.
Niskanen, W. A. (1988). Reaganomics. *The concise encyclopedia of economics.* Library of Economics and Liberty. Retrieved November 1, 2021, from https://www.econlib.org/library/Enc1/Reaganomics.html
Nominations of Philip A. Loomis and Alan Greenspan. Hearing before the Committee on Banking, Housing and Urban Affairs. United States Senate. (1974, August 7).
Orwell, G. (2003/1949). *1984.* Centennial Edition. Harcourt Brace.
Rand, A. (1967). *Capitalism: The unknown ideal.* Signet.
Reagan, R. (1980, April 28). Economic policy statement for Governor Ronald Reagan: Richard J. Whalen draft (4/28/80). Hannaford/CA HQ-Ronald Reagan-Speeches.
Rubin, H. (2007, September 15). Ayn Rand's literature of capitalism. *New York Times*, C1.
Schoenebaum, E. (1979). *Political profiles: The Nixon/Ford years.* Facts on File.
Tuccille, J. (2002). *Alan shrugged: Alan Greenspan, the world's most powerful banker.* Wiley.
Uchitelle, L. (1987, June 24). Forecasts: Greenspan's grades. *New York Times*, D1.

CHAPTER 6

(Misery at the) Funplex: From Ideology to Imagology

According to German folklore, during the Middle Ages, the village of Hamelin, Germany, was dealing with a rat infestation in their town. A man dressed in pied or multi-colored clothing appeared and offered to solve the town's problem by luring the rats away with a magical song played on his pipe in exchange for a certain sum of money. Even though the piper kept his end of the bargain and successfully lured the rats away from the town, the townspeople did not give the piper the full amount they had promised. Enraged by this, the piper left the town, but threatened to return to make the townspeople pay for what they had done. Subsequently, the piper did return, this time dressed in green, and played his pipe again, this time to lure away the children of the town. Enchanted by this music, all of the children, save three, followed the piper to a cave and were never seen again.

If there is a contemporary equivalent to the Pied Piper, shrouded in green, luring the children of the revolution away from the safety of their village, Alan Greenspan seems to fit the bill. Disappointed by broken promises on multiple levels, Greenspan led the children of our community to embrace the merits of the free market, dismantling years of government safeguards that had been put in place to ensure that we would never again repeat the macroeconomic errors that led to the Great Depression.

One of the more interesting aspects of Alan Greenspan's life is the relationship that he had with his father. Greenspan's father left his family when

G. D. Klinger et al., *Money Talks*,
https://doi.org/10.1007/978-3-031-00816-0_6

Alan was a young child, presumably to chase elusive profits as a broker on Wall Street. He had planned to take advantage of the free market, and to catch the wave of profiteering at the tail end of the roaring 1920s. It seems, though, that Greenspan's father joined the party too late, and he eventually came to question the merits of the free market. In fact, he later wrote a book called *Recovery Ahead!*, a book that called for increased government intervention in the market to address the lingering effects of the Great Depression. Significantly, he dedicated the volume to his son, Alan. The inscription read: "May this my initial effort with constant thought of you branch out into an endless chain of similar efforts so that at your maturity you may look back and endeavor to interpret the reasoning behind these logical forecasts and begin a like work of your own" (Greenspan, 2007, p. 21). Greenspan noted that he merely "looked at the book, read a few pages, and put it aside" (p. 21).[1] The ardent wish of his father fell on deaf ears, and the younger Greenspan spent his whole life moving in the opposite direction. While I am not a psychologist, I believe it is very telling that Greenspan's intellectual and political commitments to the free market ostensibly ran counter to what his father had concluded years earlier, a father who had largely abandoned him at a young age. Greenspan admitted, "[N]ot having a dad left a big hole in my life" (p. 20).

While Greenspan mostly upheld the secrecy that surrounded the inner workings of the Fed, he unquestionably changed the role the Fed chair played in society. In his autobiography, Greenspan claimed, "I've never been entirely comfortable being cast as the person who calls the shots," and that "I feel ill at ease in the spotlight. Extrovert, I am not" (p. 9). Greenspan's public record, however, seems to suggest a contrary conclusion. His personal sentiments aside, Greenspan significantly transformed the role of the Federal Reserve in the public sphere.

If economics is a science, a field that theoretically should work like a well-oiled machine based on "universal" commitments and beliefs, then all it needed was somebody with the right skill set to run the machine, and to simultaneously reassure the public that things were in good hands. To be sure, Greenspan knew what he was doing, and he invited people to

[1] *Recovery Ahead!* was not the only book that Greenspan set aside. Greenspan also left his personal copy of William Niskanen's 1988 book, *Reaganomics* at the Federal Reserve Library. I found it on the shelves there while I was conducting research for this book. On the title page is the following dedication: "To Alan Greenspan. May I wish you, in the words of Adam Smith, 'peace, easy taxes, and a tolerable administration of justice.'"

participate in his economic vision, one that trumpeted the cause of Reaganomics, specifically, and the free market, generally. Early in his autobiography, he reflects, "If the story of the past quarter century has a one-line plot summary, it is the rediscovery of the power of market capitalism. After being forced into retreat by the failures of the 1930s and the subsequent expansion of state intervention through the 1960s, market capitalism slowly reemerged as a potent force" (p. 14). Embedded in this, of course, is a concurrent move toward deregulation of economic life. He continues, "[T]he forces of the marketplace have gradually displaced some significant powers of the state. Much regulation promulgating limits to commercial life has been dismantled" (p. 15). While perhaps not as pronounced in the years before his appointment to the Federal Reserve, Greenspan has always held strong ideological commitments to the principles of laissez-faire capitalism, and he ensured that these commitments guided monetary policy during his tenure as chair of the Fed.

Commenting on the nature of charismatic leaders, German sociologist Max Weber (1969) has this to say about the nature of charisma:

> The term "charisma" will be applied to a certain quality of an individual personality by virtue of which he is set apart from ordinary men and treated as endowed with supernatural, superhuman, or at least specifically exceptional powers or qualities. These are such as are not accessible to the ordinary person, but are regarded as of divine origin or as exemplary, and on the basis of them the individual concerned is treated as a leader. (pp. 358–359)

In the Taoist model of leadership, Greenspan found his parade, and he led it. Like a great conductor, he made sure that both the orchestra and the audience were in sync and following his lead. Indeed, more than one commentator dubbed him "The Maestro" of the economy. His performance was very effective, and inspired tremendous public and market confidence. In many ways, he was the perfect choice to continue the economic and political revolution that Reagan had started. To this end, Weber continues, "In traditionally stereotyped periods, charisma is the greatest revolutionary force. ... It may then result in a radical alternation of the central system of attitudes and directions with a completely new orientation of all attitudes toward the different problems and structures of the 'world'" (p. 363). Charisma has, according to Weber, a direct relationship with economic priorities and organization: "The immediate effect of charisma in economic as in other connexions is usually strongly revolutionary;

indeed, often destructive, because it means new modes of orientation" (p. 373). Once the "creative destruction" of the previous economic system was undertaken, including but not limited to a complete overhaul of the tax code and the deregulation of industry and financial markets, and the free market had been thrust back into place, both Reagan and Greenspan made sure that all of the "true believers" fell into line. One lesson to be learned from this is that it becomes very easy to make a lot of money when nearly all concerned parties are of the same mind. When a community places almost blind faith in such leaders, though, it often leads to unrealistic expectations and an incredibly vulnerable economic situation. It also opens such leaders up to demanding public scrutiny, since not everyone is a true believer.

Greenspan seemed to recognize this fact and always attempted to curb the tendency to excess, setting an overall conservative tone for the economy and markets. Indeed, one did not want to over-stimulate the economy because that would release Greenspan's "White Whale," inflation. So even though deregulation, mergers, and monopolization were the direct results of a return to free market principles, Greenspan did his best to communicate to the public and the markets, that this was not a "free-for-all." Instead, as we know now, it was really only a "free-for-a few." His infamous comments demonizing "irrational exuberance" were one example of this. In what I consider to be a powerful symbolic gesture, one of Greenspan's first acts upon arriving at the Fed was to increase the wine budget by $1 a bottle. The message it sent, of course, was that everyone was going to have a good time, but things were not going to get out of control.

He realized that people and the media were paying attention, and he wanted to sell the right package, the right choice of words, and the right image. This, of course, raises an important point. Earlier, I discussed how Greenspan's power was more rhetorical than it was economic. This observation comes into play again here. One thing that changed about the chair of the Fed during Greenspan's tenure was the importance of his image. The Fed, long cloaked in secrecy, was now starting to attract more public attention. According to Carl Moore, the 1960s were the turning point when the media and the public started paying more attention to the Fed: "[From 1960–69] [m]ore and more people were now aware that there was a Federal Reserve System. Even the evening news might include an item about the Fed—a short item, but it was getting attention" (1990, p. 134). Historically, communication scholars have seemed more interested in studying actual text-based arguments, rather than other significant nonverbal elements of persuasion. More recently, however, several writers have turned their attention to non-discourse-based artifacts to help us develop a more all-encompassing view of rhetorical theory and practice. Some authors study nonverbal aspects of movements, others study images in the media, and still others study public monuments. The ascendancy of the image in our society seems to have only accelerated in recent years. In 1991, tennis star Andre Agassi boasted in an advertisement for the Canon Rebel camera that "Image is everything." Although this provided fodder for pundits and critics alike, it seemed to capture a snapshot of American life at this time. Like it or not, Greenspan was thrust onto the public stage, and everyone in the world seemed to be watching.

In his *New York Times* Best Seller, *Immortality*, Czech writer Milan Kundera (1999) reflects:

> All ideologies have been defeated: in the end their dogmas were unmasked as illusions and people stopped taking them seriously. For example, communists used to believe that in the course of capitalist development the proletariat would grow poorer and poorer, but when it finally became clear that all over Europe workers were driving to work in their own cars, they felt like shouting that reality was deceiving them. Reality was stronger than ideology. And it is in this sense that imagology has surpassed it: imagology is stronger than reality. (p. 114)

Kundera is significant because he writes in the midst of one of the more remarkable events in recent political history, the dismantling of the Iron Curtain. That event is important not just because of the more obvious political repercussions, but because it has irretrievably altered the working assumptions of modern political order. As writers such as Foucault, Baudrillard, Lyotard, and Habermas have demonstrated, the structural conditions of contemporary society have irrevocably changed. We live in a world where images define important elements of our political community. Commenting on these structural changes, French philosopher Michel Foucault (1994) writes:

> The space of order, which served as a common place for representation and for things, for empirical visibility and for the essential rules, which united the regularities of nature and the resemblances of imagination in the grid of identities and differences, which displayed the empirical sequence of representations in a simultaneous table, and made it possible to scan step by step,

> in accordance with logical sequence, the totality of nature's elements thus rendered contemporaneous with one another--this place of order is from now on shattered. (p. 239)

Many have identified Reagan as an important turning point in the nature of the Presidency and politics, generally. He in many ways symbolized the rise of the imagological president. On this point, Donald Regan (1988) writes:

> No American President of the television age has combined the common touch with the unique ability to be everywhere at once in electronic form so successfully as Ronald Reagan. To a degree, this triumph was forced on Reagan by the times in which he lived—times for which he was superbly equipped by his physical appearance, his personality, and his long experience in front of the camera. (He made his first movie in 1937). (p. 243)

Bob Schieffer and Gary Paul Gates (1989) called Reagan "The Acting President" in their book entitled the same. In his sweeping biography, *President Reagan: The Role of a Lifetime*, Lou Cannon (1991/2000) comments, "Hollywood had been the center of Reagan's life from the time he was twenty-six years old until after he turned fifty. Even when he was gone from Hollywood, Hollywood was never gone from him. … He was an actor, in the White House and out of it. Acting was what he did best" (pp. 43–44). Not only was Reagan an actor by profession, but he also set the stage for other figures of popular culture to rise to positions of political prominence, such as Clint Eastwood who served as the Mayor of Carmel, California, Sonny Bono who served as the Mayor of Palm Springs, California, and served in the United States Congress, Jesse "The Body" Ventura who was elected Governor of Minnesota, and Arnold Schwarzenegger who was elected Governor of California. Schwarzenegger in particular merits some special attention.

While President Reagan assuredly set the stage, Arnold Schwarzenegger represented another significant turning point in American Politics. While Reagan had experience in politics in addition to his Hollywood background, Schwarzenegger was purely a celebrity built upon a background in bodybuilding, and no formal experience in politics. It was during his Gubernatorial campaign in California's recall election in 2003 when the line between political "reality" and Hollywood "fiction" dissolved. Schwarzenegger's campaign and subsequent rise to power illustrates the broader theoretical argument at work here: Image *became* everything. In his book, *Ideology and the Image*, Bill Nichols (1981) observes, "[C]inema, like theater, allows characters to be inhabited 'in the flesh' by actors, although cinema, unlike theater, is marked by the presence of the actors where he/she is absent—by the image, and the 'image' (icon, idol) thereby established" (p. 90). Importantly, he continues in a footnote here: "Contrariwise, this very play across boundaries (actor/character/actor-star—and the 'image' thereby fixed in place) allows for an ambiguity, a hide-and-seek play of referrals from one level to another" (fn 24; p. 318). Image had surpassed reality because the reality was that Arnold Schwarzenegger was in no way qualified to run the state of California given his limited educational background (he graduated, by correspondence, with a degree in international fitness marketing from the University of Wisconsin-Superior), and his lack of meaningful political experience.

Schwarzenegger used what Kenneth Burke called "strategic ambiguity" to both remake politics and fuel his rise to power. He used tropes from his Hollywood films to edify and justify his political agenda, and he used dramatic and visually powerful campaign tactics to further conflate Schwarzenegger the politician, and Schwarzenegger the actor. The media followed his lead, playing re-runs of his Hollywood films leading up to the election, and coined amalgams like "The Governator" to further reinforce the imagological construct at work.

When he announced his candidacy for the election on August 6, 2003, on the *Tonight Show*, he gave what amounted to his first political speech, generously sprinkling references from his aforementioned films. In many of his campaign commercials, Schwarzenegger consciously uses infamous lines from his *Terminator* films: "I'll be back" and "hasta la vista, baby." Just days before the election, on Friday, October 3, the Schwarzenegger campaign launched a small plane with the banner "Hasta La Vista, Davis!" en route to a campaign rally just outside of Los Angeles. The day before, his campaign dropped a wrecking ball on a car that had "Davis Car Tax" painted on the side. From a nearby stage, the audience listened to Schwarzenegger proclaim, "Hasta la vista, car tax!"

No stranger to drama, after becoming governor Schwarzenegger only strengthened the linkage between his mediated image and political persona: "To promote tourism, he recently spoke to a group of travel agents—preceded by a stunt double zooming through the audience on a motorcycle and dressed like a leather-jacket-clad Terminator" (Grover & Palmeri, 1994, p. 44). In his first "State of the State Address," delivered on January

6, 2004, Governor Schwarzenegger (2004a) begins his speech by saying, "OK, I changed my mind, I want to go back to acting." Later in that speech, he posits, "I am a salesman by nature. And now most of my energies will go into selling California. If I can sell tickets to my movies like *Red Sonia* or *Last Action Hero*, you know I can sell just about anything." In his "Remarks at the Republican National Convention" on August 31, 2004, Schwarzenegger (2004b) begins his speech, "Thank you. What a greeting! This is like winning an Oscar! … As if I would know! Speaking of acting, one of my movies was called *True Lies*. And that's what the Democrats should have called their convention." In that same speech, Schwarzenegger, again borrowing a reference to his mediated image, claims, "[I]f you believe we must be fierce and relentless and *terminate* terrorism … then you are a Republican!" (emphasis added). He also recounts the story of a young soldier going to Iraq, who leaves Schwarzenegger by saying "Arnold … I'll be back." This final reference illustrates the aforementioned impact of image politics on the public, namely, that since the public has no direct access to "the person," they use the image as a substitute for that person. Based on the evidence, I sincerely believe that in this recall election many people felt like they were quite literally electing the "Terminator" to office, and anecdotal stories seem to validate this conclusion.

The issue of access and image management deserves more attention here. The Schwarzenegger campaign was meticulous about leaving Schwarzenegger's political persona at the level of superficial image. Indeed, Liz Marlantes of the *Christian Science Monitor* noted:

> In the two weeks since announcing his candidacy on the *Tonight Show*, the actor has offered no policy proposals—or even much in the way of opinions on issues facing the state. He's given no in-depth interviews, and has rarely appeared in public. This unique position as the recall's best-known and least-defined major candidate is in many ways proving to be Mr. Schwarzenegger's primary source of strength—and weakness. (Marlantes, 2003, p. 1)

The weakness suggested by the Marlantes stems from the fact that a poorly defined political identity can open candidates to the criticism that they lack "substance" on "the issues." Despite efforts to that end, the image of Schwarzenegger, even if superficial, proved too powerful to overcome.

The campaign seemed to thrive on restricting access to the candidate. Journalists constantly expressed their frustration at the fact that Schwarzenegger spoke from scripted speeches, and that he rarely made himself available to the press corps, which is the norm for most political candidates. In one case where he did do this, he read a brief message to the reporters, and handled only two questions before abruptly cutting off the interview (Hertzberg, 2003). Daniel Wood (2003) of the *Christian Science Monitor* observed the same phenomenon: "With national, state, and local press in tow, he puts in an appearance at an elementary school, a factory plant, and a popular retail mall, tossing out just enough kernels of information to entice followers, but not enough substance to anger or galvanize opposition" (p. 1). He skipped the campaign's first three televised debates, participating in only one, a "debate" where all the candidates saw the 12 questions in advance of the debate. His only detailed interviews were granted to his longtime friends in the entertainment-news media, talk show host Oprah Winfrey, self-proclaimed "shock-jock," Howard Stern, and political pundit, Larry King. Raphael Sonenshein, a political scientist at California State University-Fullerton, recognized, "He's running his campaign like a movie premiere" ("Debate no-show," 2003). Indeed, there was even a temporal connection between the two: *Terminator 3: Rise of the Machines* had widely opened in theaters only two days before he declared his candidacy on the Jay Leno's *Tonight Show*.

In both words and actions, Schwarzenegger strived to ensure that the image for which most people would vote would be the image of the "hero" from so many of his films. And while some people expressed frustration with that, others, including one-time gubernatorial rival, Arianna Huffington, called Schwarzenegger a "charming man," adding that voters find him appealing because they are "longing for something different, for an outsider" (Booth & Sanchez, 2003). Huffington identifies a recurrent trope of the Schwarzenegger campaign: present the candidate as a political outsider, one who serves as the voice of "the people." Indeed, at one rally, screaming supporters chased his campaign bus around while "We're Not Gonna Take It" from Twisted Sister blared from loudspeakers. Despite his attempt to cast himself as a political outsider, Schwarzenegger immediately surrounded himself with political insiders during his campaign, a fact that was largely ignored by the media, and the public. Instead, he relied on his image as a good-hearted renegade outsider who had come to save the day by striking at the heart of what he contended was a dysfunctional political and economic system.

While assuredly there was an ideology attached to Schwarzenegger's personal and political agenda, that ideology was simply a convenient construct to advance this broader imagological program. The ideology behind Schwarzenegger's political images, of course, was unnerving in its own right. His father was a member of the Nazi Party in Austria, and Schwarzenegger was quoted in a 1990 *U.S. News and World Report* article as saying, "People need somebody to watch over them. … Ninety-five percent of the people in the world need to be told what to do and how to behave" (Rosellini, 1990, p. 62). When one believes this, it justifies extraordinary authoritarian action, and Schwarzenegger made it clear that he would destroy and rebuild government according to his view of the world. In his aforementioned 2004 "State of the State Address" Schwarzenegger proudly proclaimed, "Every governor proposes moving boxes around to reorganize government. I don't want to move boxes around; I want to blow them up." Ironically, given his dim views on the ability of people to govern themselves, Schwarzenegger claimed in the same speech: "I love working for the people of California. It is better than being a movie star. It gives me great joy and satisfaction. I am honored to do this work for the people" (Schwarzenegger, 2004a). This is another revealing example of the Orwellian doublespeak that I discussed earlier.

When image is used as a vehicle for masking while simultaneously covertly enacting deeply disturbing ideological predispositions, it has significant implications for the theory and practice of politics, and it outlines the urgent need to more vigorously engage some of the traditional assumptions about image-oriented politics. In many ways Schwarzenegger's campaign laid the basic groundwork for the tremendously popular presidential campaign of Donald Trump in 2016. Schwarzenegger made it acceptable to seek political office solely on image not experience, to skip debates and say very little about specific policy proposals, and to run campaigns based on spectacle rather than substance.

Kundera's earlier point is that images have become the primary loci of meaning for our political communities. Reagan understood this point, and played his part well. Indeed, many deemed him the "Teflon President." It should perhaps come as no surprise, then, that the person he appointed to be his chief economic architect of free market principles embraced this realization, as well. Although tentative at first, Greenspan steadily became more attentive to the imagological power that he held. He was chair of the Federal Reserve at the confluence of two structural changes in politics and economics. This was a time when "image politics" ruled the day, and economics was popularized like never before. It created a unique rhetorical opportunity for the right person, and Alan Greenspan fit the bill, so to speak, for that occasion.

Greenspan's "ethos," or credibility, steadily climbed during his tenure. Justin Martin writes, "By the dawn of the new millennium, it was nearly impossible to find anyone who wasn't gaga over Greenspan. Democrats and Republicans, Wall Street and Main Street, dogs and cats—all were high on the Fed chairman" (Martin, 2001, p. 226). Greenspan was rising to celebrity status. He appeared on the cover of several news magazines, he was frequently covered on the front page of both financial and world news sections of major newspapers, he was constantly caricatured in political cartoons, he was the subject of a game show on *The Motley Fool*, and he even made an "appearance" on *The Simpsons.*

As Martin notes, the magazine coverage alone, even before he took the reins at the Fed, was significant: "[Greenspan was] featured on the cover of *Newsweek*—unprecedented for an economist. Fellow 1975 cover subjects included Bruce Springsteen, Nolan Ryan, Patty Hearst, Mel Brooks, Christina Onassis, and Jimmy Hoffa" (Martin, p. 127). In 1985, two years before his appointment to chair of the Fed, Greenspan appeared in magazine advertisements for the Apple IIc computer. The ad claimed that this was the computer Greenspan used to organize his finances. Greenspan, it seemed, was no stranger to the media, a relationship that would only continue to expand upon his appointment to the Fed. When he left the Council of Economic Advisers in the 1970s, he made concerted efforts to stay in the limelight. He "made about a speech a week, hoping to stay in the public eye and elevate his profile. Greenspan also began to court the press more assiduously" (Martin, p. 139). During the 1970s, Greenspan had dated Barbara Walters whose "social network extended to Hollywood" (Greenspan, p. 81). During the 1980s, Greenspan dated Susan Mills, a producer for the MacNeil-Lehrer NewsHour. In 1997, he married Andrea Mitchell, a noted political correspondent for NBC. Greenspan also admits that he "learned a bit about the media industry doing work for the William Morris Agency," which was a client for Townsend-Greenspan (p. 81).

On the cover of the February 15, 1999, issue, while he was Chair of the Fed, *Time* magazine "appointed" Greenspan to the three-person "Committee to Save the World." Significantly, his reach extended beyond the economic and political boundaries of the United States. Indeed, Greenspan became a global image for the international economy. He was named Commander of the Légion d'honneur (Legion of Honor) in 2000, and Queen Elizabeth II of Great Britain knighted Greenspan in 2002. Not to be outdone, of course, George W. Bush awarded Greenspan the presidential "Medal of Freedom" in 2005.

In one of my favorite political cartoons, elementary school children returning to school were comparing their new lunch boxes in the lunchroom. While most had the usual pop culture stars, or super-heroes, one serious young girl had a lunch box with a picture of Alan Greenspan emblazoned on the side. For better or worse, Greenspan had achieved mythological status. Martin concurs, "The Fed chairman was promoted to iconic status and joined the ranks of Harry Houdini, General Douglas MacArthur, and Madonna" (p. 221) (Fig. 6.1).

One of the more telling examples of the growing power of Greenspan's image was the oft-noted "Briefcase Indicator." CNBC invented a tool to

Fig. 6.1 Fed Chair Alan Greenspan delivers the keynote address at the World Bank/International Monetary Fund in 1999. (REUTERS/Alamy Stock Photo)

predict forthcoming actions of the Federal Reserve based on the size of Greenspan's briefcase on his way to a Federal Open Market Committee (FOMC) meeting. The theory was that if Greenspan had a thick briefcase, it was a sign that Greenspan had a lot on his mind, and a lot of evidence to share with the Committee, and that pointed to a probable change in interest rates. On the other hand, if Greenspan's briefcase was thin, it indicated that he had a clear mind and not much to discuss, and that no change in interest rates was likely. Interestingly, the Briefcase Indicator was correct 17 of the first 20 times it was used. Some, such as Mark Haines, anchor of CNBC's morning finance program, *Squawk Box*, believed that Greenspan became aware of the "Indicator" and adjusted his behavior accordingly, presumably to keep people guessing. To this end, he posited, "It was right 17 out of the first 20 times, but has a built-in destruct mechanism, because Greenspan packs his briefcase. He can make it wrong or right. He has never publicly acknowledged the Indicator, but we have reason to believe that he knows about it. We have to consider the fact that he wants us to stop doing it because the last two times, the briefcase has been wrong, and that's disturbing" (Frank, 1999, Section 6, p. 35).

The power of Greenspan's image was growing, and he seemed to grow increasingly aware of it. About this aspect of Greenspan's legacy, Martin writes,

> In every way, his tenure was to be a challenging one. Ahead lay stock-market crashes and global meltdowns. He'd battle Congress, battle the press, battle presidents. He'd be caricatured and lampooned, at times even demonized. Yet he'd also manage to rise above all the rabble for a spell, catching a wave of cultural zeitgeist to become an American first—a celebrity Fed chairman. (p. 158)

Greenspan was not only becoming a figure of popular culture, but his power as the international voice of capital was growing as well. He carefully managed his image, and used its power to effect purposeful change in the American and world economic and financial markets. His words, of course, were a part of that imagological package, and I will turn my attention to that aspect of Greenspan's rhetorical power in the next chapter. In assessing Greenspan's growing power, Martin concludes, "Even if it was unclear what the Fed did—or perhaps precisely because of that—he captured the popular imagination. … Greenspan managed to achieve a level of acclaim never before bestowed on a Fed chairman and probably never to be bestowed again" (pp. 221–222). Greenspan simultaneously elevated the public status of the Fed while at the same time maintaining its carefully guarded secrecy and independence. In short, he cemented the place of the image in monetary policy:

> As things stand now, the discussion of monetary policy in the media is, purely and simply, show business. There is little attempt to educate the investor or the general public on the subject. The media focus on official statements and speeches and dissect the information presented by the Fed and government agencies in excruciating detail. A word change here, a word change there or a slight turn of a phrase, and it is headline information. (Santow, 2009, p. 226)

Given the worldwide respect and international accolades Greenspan enjoyed during his tenure as chair of the Fed, it must have been quite a shock to find himself on CNN's "Ten Most Wanted: Culprits of the Collapse" list after the financial and economic collapse of 2008. The power he wielded, and the reputation he enjoyed, like most things in life, was contingent upon a particular situation: the booming excess of the capitalist business cycle. When things went sour, however, the public and the media searched for scapegoats and placed them in a "rogue's gallery of Wall Street executives, politicians, and government officials who did not do their jobs" ("Culprits," 2008). As any celebrity or public figure knows, fame is often a fleeting thing.

In their highly regarded book, *The Power of Myth*, Joseph Campbell and Bill Moyers (1988) observed, "Myths are clues to the spiritual potentialities of human life" (p. 5). We began this chapter by reconsidering the contemporary relevance of the Pied Piper myth. There is a similar instructive myth that comes from ancient Greek mythology. Depending on your source material, the myth roughly goes like this. Orpheus of Thrace, son of Apollo and the muse Calliope, was given a llyre or harp by his father, and he played it so beautifully that no one could resist the allure of his music. He fell in love with Eurydice who met a tragic fate. Heartbroken, Orpheus descended to Hades to see Eurydice again where he charmed the guardian Cerberus, and eventually Hades himself. Hades agreed to allow Eurydice to accompany Orpheus back to the living world on one condition: he was not allowed to turn to see if Eurydice was following behind him until they reached the light. Orpheus agreed, but being skeptical of Hades' promise, he turned back to see if Eurydice was really following him. Since Orpheus broke his part of the bargain, Eurydice's shadow was whisked back to Hades. Engulfed with melancholy, Orpheus played his lyre with renewed angst, and openly longed for his own death. Soon thereafter, Orpheus was granted his wish, but the muses decided to keep his head amongst the living so that his music could continue to enchant the multitudes.

Ronald Reagan and Alan Greenspan achieved mythological status in their time. They played a song of greed and self-interest that transformed political and economic culture. They certainly did not invent these ideas that are as old as humanity itself, but they gave them new life and vitality. Reagan and Greenspan's fates waxed and waned throughout and immediately following their tenure, but just as Orpheus' head was preserved by the muses, so too do their tropes remain just below the surface waiting for a new actor to reanimate them for a new generation.

As I noted at the outset in recounting the story of the Pied Piper, there were three children who escaped the lure of the piper's music. The first child was lame, and simply could not keep up, the second child was deaf and followed the other children merely out of curiosity, and the third child was blind and could not see where they were going. It is certainly an overstatement to claim that all of the children of the Reagan Revolution followed the alluring song on the Piper. As was the case in the fairy tale, there were some who did not hear the song, some who did not see where the piper was leading the others, and some who simply could not, or did not want to keep up. Although minority voices, their stories are slowly starting to be told, and it is critically important for the townspeople to listen carefully to better understand what happened to the other children, the children who followed the piper down the path of the free market.

References

Booth, W., & Sanchez, R. (2003, October 2). Actor leads race as an outsider. *Washington Post*, A1.

Campbell, J., & Moyers, B. (1988). *The power of myth*. Doubleday.

Cannon, L. (1991/2000). *President Reagan: The role of a lifetime*. Public Affairs.

Debate no-show. (2003, September 5). Schwarzenegger's debate no-show may hurt his chances, experts say. *Baltimore Sun*. Retrieved July 21, 2021, from https://www.baltimoresun.com/bal-te.recall05sep05-story.html?coll=bal-nationworld-headlines.

Foucault, M. (1994). *The order of things: An archeology of the human sciences*. Vintage.

Frank, R. H. (1999). Safety in numbers. *New York Times, 6*, 35–37.
Greenspan, A. (2007). *The age of turbulence: Adventures in a new world*. Penguin.
Grover, R., & Palmeri, C. (1994). Arnold is hitting his marks. *Business Week*, 42-44.
Hertzberg, H. (2003, September 3). Strongman. *New Yorker*. Retrieved July 21, 2016, from https://www.newyorker.com/magazine/2003/09/29/strongman.
Kundera, M. (1999). *Immortality*. Harper Perennial.
Marlantes, L. (2003). His image is Herculean, but is he's wispy on issues. *Christian Science Monitor*, p. 1.
Martin, J. (2001). *Greenspan: The man behind the money*. Perseus.
Moore, C. H. (1990). *The federal reserve system: A history of the first 75 years*. McFarland.
Nichols, B. (1981). *Ideology and the image: Social representation in the cinema and other media*. Indiana University Press.
Regan, D. T. (1988). *For the record: From Wall Street to Washington*. Harcourt Brace.
Rosellini, L. (1990, November 26). Pumping the political persona. *US News and World Report*, 62.
Santow, L. J. (2009). *Do they walk on water? Federal reserve chairmen and the Fed*. Praeger.
Schieffer, B., & Gates, G. P. (1989). *The acting president*. E.P. Dutton.
Schwarzenegger, A. (2004a, January 6). State of the state address [Speech Transcript]. California Governors" Library. Retrieved July 21, 2016, from https://governors.library.ca.gov/addresses/s_38-schwarzenegger1.html.
Schwarzenegger, A. (2004b, August 31). Remarks at the republican national convention [Speech video recording]. American Rhetoric. Retrieved July 21, 2016, from https://www.americanrhetoric.com/speeches/convention2004/arnold-schwarzenegger2004rnc.htm.
Ten most wanted: Culprits of the collapse. (2008, October 23). *CNN*. Retrieved July 21, 2016, from http://www.cnn.com/2008/US/10/17/most.wanted.culprits/index.html.
Weber, M. (1969). In T. Parsons (Ed.), *The theory of social and economic organization*. The Free Press. (Original work published 1947).
Wood, D. (2003, September 7). Even on stump, Schwarzenegger follows script. *Christian Science Monitor*, p. 1.

CHAPTER 7

Public Image Limited, or He Blind(er)ed Me with Silence

When Alice tumbled down the rabbit hole in Lewis Carroll's *Alice in Wonderland*, she tumbled into a "curious" world where things were not always as they were expected to be. From the Mad-Hatter's Tea Party to the trial to determine "who stole the tarts," rules and conventions were turned on their head. It was a topsy-turvy world where readers were invited to reflect on the socially constructed nature of rules, laws, facts, evidence, statistics, mores, customs, education, politics, things so often taken for granted and considered "universal," and immutable. In quizzing Alice about her schooling, the Mock Turtle asked Alice about her education, specifically, the "different branches of Arithmetic—Ambition, Distraction, Uglification, and Derision." Assuredly, this is a different take on the study of numbers than we see in today's society, although one does not have to do a tremendous amount of work to see the satirical point Carroll is making about the often-dire consequences that can result from the blind worship of numbers. In his book, *The Ethics of Rhetoric*, Richard Weaver (2009) notes that terms like "science," "progress," and "fact" have tended to be "God terms" in our contemporary systems of discourse and belief. In other words, they have positive connotations, and they have reached nearly "unquestioned" status. The study of numbers, whether in mathematics, physics, logic, computer science, engineering, accounting, or economics, often engenders a particular approach to human understanding, one that is influenced by a Cartesian, Newtonian, and Baconian

G. D. Klinger et al., *Money Talks*,
https://doi.org/10.1007/978-3-031-00816-0_7

worldview. For Descartes, the world was best viewed as a grand machine, a clock of sorts. Newton and Bacon helped Descartes realize his dream by using mathematics and science to unravel the mysteries of the world *qua* machine. It is important to note, despite the ascendency of mathematics and science both in education and in life, they represent only two of multifarious ways to view the world. Seeing the world mathematically, or scientifically, engenders a remarkably different worldview than seeing the world artistically, or spiritually, for example. Perhaps not surprisingly, given its bias toward a particular vision of economics and the enormity of all the variables involved in an ever-changing economy, Alan Greenspan (2007) reported in his autobiography that Cathy Minehan, president of the Federal Reserve Bank of Boston, remarked in January 2000 meeting that "I feel kind of like Alice in Wonderland" (p. 214).

In an effort to cement their domain and mission in the foundation of science, several academic and professional disciplines reconfigured the orientation of their fields. Political science, sociology, law, and economics all claimed to have some sort of scientific basis in a newly created intellectual domain: the social sciences. The first book that mentions the term "social science" was *An Inquiry into the Principles of the Distribution of Wealth Most Conducive to Human Happiness*, written by William Thompson (2005) in 1824. While the creation and evolution of each of the social sciences has a unique history, there seem to be points of common interest, especially in terms of their commitment to study the world scientifically. In his book, *An Essay on the Nature and Significance of Economic Science*, London School of Economics Professor Lionel Robbins (2007) defined economics as "the science which studies human behavior as a relation between scarce means having alternative uses," in 1932.

Ironically, around the same time, the validity of that new scientific grounding for economics received a significant challenge as some of the best economic minds and models available could not solve the economic conundrums created by the Great Depression. Indeed, economics was supposed to be Herbert Hoover's forte. Still, there continues to be a countervailing belief that numbers and free markets will solve all of our problems. Greenspan took advantage of this bias toward science in economics. He fully embraced science and mathematics as the only legitimate foundation for the theory and practice of economics. He praised his mentor, Arthur Burns, for his "devotion to empirical evidence and deductive logic" (Greenspan, 2007, p. 35). And he hopefully reflected, "I immediately saw the power of these new tools: if the economy could be accurately modeled using empirical facts and math, then large-scale forecasts could be derived methodically, without the quasi-scientific intuition employed by so many economic forecasters" (pp. 35–36). The scientific bias was not unique to Greenspan; it permeated every aspect of the Federal Reserve: "Officials of the Federal Reserve were themselves the ultimate rationalists—economists who analyzed numbers, constructed scientific theories to explain economic behavior and tested the theories against reality" (Greider, 1987, p. 54).

Casting economics as science engenders an additional benefit: it reinforces the power of technocrats who claim to be experts in the science. Laypersons who want to understand the science of economics have to rely on self-proclaimed technical experts to explain economic events: "The public's confusion over money and its ignorance of money politics were heightened by the scientific pretensions of economics. Average citizens simply could not understand the language, and most of the economists made no effort to translate it for them" (p. 55). Greenspan used this cult of expertise to his advantage, and the rhetoric that he deployed only reinforced the power that attended it. As we noted in previous chapters, Greenspan had to negotiate at least two significant tensions during his tenure as Chair of the Fed. First, he had to try and reconcile his own intellectual commitment to an unregulated free market while serving as the chief interventionist in U.S. monetary policy. Second, he had to struggle with his claim to be an introvert while serving in position that demanded ever-increasing public scrutiny. He resolved the first tension by always falling back on the rhetoric of the free market after intervening in the marketplace, a telling illustration of Orwellian "newspeak." He attempted to manage the second tension by reluctantly embracing the limelight while still maintaining a veil of secrecy, strategic ambiguity, and mystique. That veil, though, was increasingly challenged during his time as Chair of the Fed.

Greenspan had a long history of limiting his public exposure, so he was well-practiced in the art of secrecy and ambiguity. When he was a member of President Ford's Council of Economic Advisers in the 1970s, Greenspan noted, "I used to joke that I had to put on my bulletproof vest and armor when I'd go up to the Hill to testify" (p. 70). One of the things that Greenspan did while he was chair of the Council of Economic Advisers was that he reduced the number of this agency's press releases. In 1997, although Greenspan never completed his dissertation, NYU chose to award him a Ph.D. based on articles that he had published in a variety of places. While graduate schools have done this in the past, especially with those who have achieved notoriety in their careers, it happens only rarely. Some questioned whether the award of this degree in Greenspan's case was legitimate. Further, "Greenspan didn't help matters by requesting that NYU withhold from public view the collection of articles that comprised his Ph.D. work" (Martin, 2001, p. 138). Typically, such work is open to all and housed at least in the library of the degree-granting institution. Greenspan, though, continued his pattern of restricting communication, unless it suited his purposes.

That pattern continued during his time as Chair of the Fed. Five weeks after he took office in 1987, Greenspan remarked to an audience: "Since I've become a central banker I've learned to mumble with great incoherence. If I seem unduly clear to you, you must have misunderstood what I said" (Beckner, 1996, p. 18). This rhetorical strategy was not something that he did "off the cuff"; it was well planned and rehearsed. For example, he would often practice his testimony before the staff of the Council of Economic Advisers: "To prepare for public appearances, he used to try and say something and make it take the longest possible way to parse it out" (MacAvoy as cited in Martin, 2001, p. 127). Such a strategy seemed to be intentional, and it served Greenspan's purposes well. Importantly, his use of Fedspeak stretched back years before he became Chair of the Fed, and it even had a unique name: "[His] complex thoughts spill forth in that special language insiders have dubbed 'Greenspanease'" (Mayer et al., 1975, p. 60).

Renowned University of Minnesota economist G. Edward Schuh observed, "[Greenspan]'s great at obfuscating. He'd do it in such a way that he'd say his piece and they wouldn't ask any questions" (as cited in Martin, p. 127). While this strategy frustrated several observers, others seemed to delight in the game of secrecy that Greenspan played. Indeed, Greenspan was sometimes so hard to understand that the *Motley Fool* radio show started a game called "What Did the Fed Chief Say?" where contestants were challenged to interpret confusing passages from Greenspan's speeches. Not everyone was equally amused, though. Senator Paul Sarbanes gave Greenspan "the obfuscation award of the month" for his answer about future Fed policy in the wake of the growing Gulf Crisis. The statement that led an exasperated Sarbanes to give Greenspan this fictitious award was: "Whether an efficacious policy response to current developments would seek higher, lower or unchanged interest rates will depend on the specifics of the situation, which are shifting day to day" (Wessel, 1990, p. A2). U.S. House Representative Jim Cooper similarly quipped, "I don't know whether you took lessons in Delphic utterances, but I think you've passed the boards" (p. A2).

Despite their misgivings, politicians had to tolerate this strategy of obfuscation. The U.S. Federal Government has little to no authority over the Fed, so there was not much they could do to compel more clarity. The strategy of strategic ambiguity was not unique to Greenspan, although he seemed to perfect it. In dealing with Congress, economic advisers can be open and honest, or they can choose to equivocate, or "say something without saying anything—to deftly dodge, evade, or sidestep the query" (Martin, p. 127). And, as Martin continues, "muddle and mystification are hallowed Fed strategies for keeping critics at bay" (p. 159). A good part of this strategy emanates from the nature of the institution itself, and that deserves some additional scrutiny.

The Federal Reserve Bank is a powerful and fascinating institution. Like Greenspan, it has its own internal and operational contradictions. The fact that it is called "Federal" is misleading. Despite the fact that it is the primary entity for managing U.S. monetary policy, and it works closely with several branches of the U.S. Federal Government, it is not actually part of the Federal Government. The Federal Reserve Bank is a private institution: "Philip E. Coldwell, who served nearly thirty years in the System, as president of the Dallas Reserve Bank and on the Board of Governors, observed, 'To some extent, the Federal Reserve considers itself government. Other times, when it serves, it considers itself not government" (Greider, p. 49). Its unusual quasi-government status is without precedent, or analog:

> [A] new "creature" was born. A unique creature, it was neither government nor private but part of both. Created by Congress, organized with private capital, most of its employees would not be considered "government" employees, but the system would set up its own salary schedules and retirement plan. ... Required to earn their own funds to cover expenses (no appropriation from Congress), the Fed banks had to be profitable. Yet they were to be not-for-profit organizations operating in the public interest. (Moore, 1990, p. 8)

In one of the more amusing exchanges in the history of the Fed, one that highlighted the fact that while the Fed operated as a quasi-political agency, it was still not technically a part of the government and therefore not tax-exempt, the District of Columbia sent a tax bill to the Federal Reserve's

Board of Governor for property taxes due on the Fed's new home office building on Constitution Avenue, opened in 1937. When the Fed declined to pay, "In December 1941, four days before Pearl Harbor, the District of Columbia government published a notice of delinquent taxes and scheduled a public auction. It would sell the Federal Reserve's marble temple to the highest bidder" (Greider, p. 49). The auction never happened after the Fed agreed to essentially cede the building to the U.S. government by executing a quitclaim deed.

Its unusual position as a quasi-government agency, simultaneously enjoying the benefits of a de facto government agency while still maintaining its independence, illustrated the fact that by since its inception, the Fed has operated as an inherently anti-democratic institution: "When the Federal Reserve was created in 1913, purposely insulated from the hot breath of politics, the new institution effectively defined the permanent limits of American democracy" (Greider, p. 267). Monetary policy, once an important matter of public concern, was ceded to a group of technocratic "experts." In the great compromise that led to the creation of the Fed, it was decided that "[d]ecisions on great public issues that were once left to politics should be consigned to disinterested experts, bureaucratic technicians who had specialized training" (Greider, p. 284). Significantly, the Fed is subject to very little Congressional oversight: "The Fed enjoyed privileges extended to no other agency in Washington—it raised its own revenue, drafted its own operating budget and submitted neither to Congress for approval" (Greider, p. 50).

The Federal Reserve was crafted in the years leading up to the Great Depression. Up until that point, banks were largely controlled by individual states. The central banking concept had been tried and discarded earlier in the nineteenth century. The First Bank of the United States operated for only 20 years, from 1791 to 1811, and the Second Bank of the United States also remained open for only 20 years, from 1816 to 1836. There was strong populist resistance to the theory and practice of consolidating monetary policy on a federal level. Because of this resistance, the dominant banking interests of the time created an economic crisis to weaken political opposition to a central bank. There is some evidence that J.P. Morgan circulated a rumor that several major banks were on the brink of insolvency. This led to a massive spike in insolvency and bankruptcies. U.S. Representative Charles A. Lindbergh astutely recognized what was happening in his 1913 book *Banking and Currency and The Money Trust*. He contended,

> [T]he king bankers put in motion, in 1907, a great scheme, they had gambled and speculated on Wall Street until so many watered stocks and bonds had been manufactured on speculation, that numberless speculators, big and small, sprang up all over the country and stocks, bonds, and credits were pyramided, re-pyramided, and re-re-pyramided. Of course such a condition could not last and a crash was inevitable, because it was not natural for such gambling to continue. ... The king bankers knew the condition and informed the favored of their friends what was to come. There was to be a panic in the fall of 1907 that would be advertised as the result of our bad banking and currency laws. (Lindbergh, 1913a, pp. 34–35)

The plan was to blame banking regulations and oversight to create a perceived need for deregulation of the banking industry, and the creation of a strong central bank. The panic of 1907 led to congressional investigation headed by Senator Nelson Aldrich, who had ties to bankers, and eventually became part of the Rockefeller family through marriage. Perhaps not surprisingly, the outcome of the investigation was a recommendation for a central bank.

Consequently, banking leaders held a secret meeting in 1910 on Jekyll Island off the coast of Georgia. The Island was part of the Rockefeller Estate. The meeting was shrouded in secrecy and participants shielded their identities and participation from public view. It was at this meeting that the Federal Reserve Act was written. Importantly, it was bankers, not Congress, who penned this important legislation. Senator Aldrich pushed the legislation through Congress, and President Wilson agreed to sign it in exchange for campaign support. Representative Charles Lindbergh warned, "[T]his act establishes the most gigantic trust on earth ... when the president signs this act, the invisible government by the money power ... will be legalized" (Lindbergh, 1913b, p. 1446). He was not alone in his criticism and concern.

Congressman John G. McHenry (D-PA) was even more vigorous in his comments:

> The bill enables Wall Street to turn panics off and on at will. The Secretary of the Treasury would become the "hired man" of Wall Street. Shall we close, as a fitting climax to the billion-dollar Republican Congress, by crowning our masters, King Morgan and King Rockefeller, the heroes of the last panic, or shall it be King Taft, Wall Street's hired man? (Moore, p. 6)

Interestingly, the Fed first began its operations on November 16, 1914, less than a year after J. P. Morgan passed away. Up until his passing, Morgan had operated as the *de facto* central bank: "[J. P.] Morgan and his men made choices about which banks would be saved and which ones allowed to fail" (Greider, p. 269). The Fed was largely created to fill the vacuum created by Morgan's death. I previously noted that the Federal Reserve is inherently anti-democratic. That aspect stretches back to the very passage of the Federal Reserve Act that was pushed through Congress on December 23, 1913, when most members of Congress had already left for the holidays. The Act passed a nearly empty Senate by a vote of 3–0.

What Lindbergh feared was that the creation of a central bank would create a streamlined machine for economic manipulation. His worries proved well-founded. The first initiative of the Federal Reserve Bank was to steadily increase the money supply from 1914 to 1919, a move that created massive indebtedness. Then, in 1920, the Fed abruptly reversed course and contracted credit. This led to bank runs as people sought to cover their indebtedness, and numerous banks failed as a result. Importantly, the vast majority of bank failures were banks outside of the Federal Reserve System. This allowed the Banking Industry to further consolidate its growing monopolistic power. Representative Lindbergh was not surprised by the early results of the Federal Reserve Act: "Under the Federal Reserve Act, panics are scientifically created. The present panic is the first scientifically created one, worked out as we figure a mathematical equation" (Lindbergh, 1923, p. 95).

Perhaps emboldened by their success, the Fed again expanded the money supply from 1920 to 1929, and this once again, predictably, created another vulnerable situation of ballooning commercial and private debt. To compound the vulnerability, a new type of loan was created: the "banker call loan." Investors could control 100% of the underlying stock with only 10% of money down to cover the underlying investment. This type of loan was the forerunner for the options market, hedge funds, and the derivatives market. This new type of loan was very popular during the roaring 1920s. While the markets soared upward, there seemed to be little downside risk to this investment, but it created an incredibly vulnerable situation insofar as the loans could be called in at any time within 24 hours. This is precisely what unfolded in the Crash of 1929. Major players in the banking industry, such as J. D. Rockefeller and Bernard Baruch, quietly exited the market, and they then called in these banker loans creating yet another run on banks, and the collapse of even more banks. This allowed the Banking Industry to further consolidate its power, and gobble up its failed competitors for pennies on the dollar.

This banker created crash and crisis moved Representative Louis McFadden, Chair of the House Banking Committee, to file a petition for impeachment against the Federal Reserve Board. In introducing the petition, McFadden argued:

> Mr. Chairman, we have in this country one of the most corrupt institutions the world has ever known. I refer to the Federal Reserve Board and the Federal Reserve Banks. This evil institution has impoverished and ruined the people of the United States ... and has practically bankrupted our government. It has done this through the defects of the law under which it operates, through the maladministration of that law by the Federal Reserve Board, and through the corrupt practices of the moneyed vultures who control it. (Jones, 2018)

The petition failed, and the power of the Federal Reserve Bank continued to grow through the years. In the past 40 years, we have witnessed continued bank consolidation through several additional crises in the Banking Industry, something I will discuss in more detail later in the book. The point that I want to make here is that since its inception, the Federal Reserve System has been enveloped in a shroud of secrecy. And that shroud has effectively cloaked the fact that those who created the Federal Reserve System stood to benefit the most from its existence. Despite claims to the contrary, the Federal Reserve System does not exist to benefit the public; it exists to maintain and strengthen the Banking Industry. In an effort to push the Federal Reserve Act through Congress, U.S. Representative Carter Glass promised that the Fed would always operate in the public interest: "No financial interest can pervert or control the Board. It is an altruistic institution, a part of government itself, representing the American people, with such powers as no man would dare misuse" (Moore, p. 6). Further, Glass contended that the Fed would always be subject to full public accountability and oversight:

> Carter Glass assured his congressional colleagues that the Federal Reserve Board would operate under "the x-ray of publicity" so there "can be nothing sinister about its transactions." Instead the money question receded from political debate and became submerged in a new managerial complexity. When the Federal Reserve was crated, the realm of acceptable political discourse shrank. (Greider, p. 281)

As social theorist Max Weber observes, "All economic activity in a market economy is undertaken and carried through by individuals to make provision for their own ideal or material interests" (1969, p. 319). While sometimes it is in the interest of the Banking Industry to enrich particular segments of the public, that is not always the case. Sometimes, as history has taught us, the Banking Industry actually grows stronger during times of economic and political crises.

Given this, it is perhaps not surprising that the Federal Reserve Bank and those who run it have continued to operate under a veil of secrecy. Some contend that one of the more significant powers of the President is the power to appoint Justices to the Supreme Court insofar as these judges are both insulated from the political process and appointed for life. In the twentieth century, a new Presidential appointment rivaled the power to appoint Supreme Court Justices, the power to appoint the chair of the Federal Reserve. Like the Supreme Court, the chair of the Fed is at least theoretically insulated from the political process, and the appointment can continue *ad infinitum* as long as the chair is reappointed by a sitting President. While we have term limits on the President to prevent a monopolization of power by one person, or political party, no such term limits exist for the chair of the Fed. And while board members do have term limits, 14 years to be precise, this is longer than any other Federal appointment, save justices of the Supreme Court.

The Board of Governors of the Federal Reserve System is one of the more powerful institutions in our society. To maintain this power, and the hegemony of its preferred economic ideology, the Fed employs a powerful brain trust: "The Fed has hundreds of Ph.D. economists in Washington alone—one of the largest concentrations anywhere in the world—and many more were scattered among the twelve regional banks" (Martin, p. 171). Overall, it has 2000 employees and an annual budget of $300 million (Greenspan, 2007, p. 101). The *Huffington Post* reports that the number of professional and academic economists on the Fed payroll creates an inherent conflict of interest in the field of economics, stifling dissent at all levels, including the Academy:

> The Fed keeps many of the influential editors of prominent academic journals on its payroll. It is common for a journal editor to review submissions dealing with Fed policy while also taking the bank's money. A *HuffPost* review of seven top journals found that 84 of the 190 editorial board

members were affiliated with the Federal Reserve in one way or another. (Grim, 2009)

The concern that emerges from this state of affairs is echoed by unlikely sources, as well. Milton Friedman, for example, warned of the potential for groupthink involved in the Fed's domination of the economic landscape:

> I cannot disagree with you that having something like 500 economists is extremely unhealthy. As you say, it is not conducive to independent, objective research. You and I know there has been censorship of the material published. Equally important, the location of the economists in the Federal Reserve has had a significant influence on the kind of research they do, biasing that research toward noncontroversial technical papers on method as opposed to substantive paper on policy and results. (Grim)

While the Fed is required to report to Congress twice a year, it has its own budget, funded from the value of its own investments. Aside from its semi-annual testimony before Congress, the U.S. Federal Government has no additional political or economic control over the Fed. Indeed, the requirement for semi-annual testimony before Congress itself was a relativity recent development. In 1978, Congress passed the Full Employment and Balanced Growth Act, also known as the Humphrey-Hawkins Act. Among other things, it now required the Fed to make its target ranges for monetary growth public, and also required the Chair of the Fed to appear before Congress twice a year in what is often called the chair's "Humphrey-Hawkins testimony." As I noted earlier, despite its name, the Fed is essentially a private corporation. It has two different deliberating bodies: the Board of Governors and the Federal Open Market Committee (FOMC). Both bodies make decisions based on majority rule, but until only recently, they withheld the results of their votes from public view (Fig. 7.1).

Perhaps because of its unsettling origins, or perhaps because the control of communication is one of the simplest ways to maintain power, the veil of secrecy that envelops the Federal Reserve System permeates all aspects of the institution. For over 60 years, the Fed's deliberations and decision-making were conducted in almost total secrecy. As Martin has observed, "Traditionally, the Fed has adhered to the notion that the less that is known about its inner workings the better" (Martin, p. 206). William Greider's 1987 book, *The Secrets of the Temple*, is one of the more

Fig. 7.1 Longtime chairman of the Federal Reserve, Alan Greenspan, waiting to testify before the US Senate Banking Committee in February 2005. (REUTERS/ Alamy Stock Photo)

compelling accounts of the many different dimensions of Fed secrecy. Greider likens the economic, political, and rhetorical power of the Fed to the mystical role that religion has played historically in society:

> The central bank, notwithstanding its claims to rational method, enfolded itself in the same protective trappings that adorned the temple—secrecy, mystique, an awesome authority that was neither visible nor legible to mere mortals. Like the temple, the Fed did not answer to the people, it spoke for them. Its decrees were cast in a mysterious language people could not understand, but its voice, they knew, was powerful and important. (p. 240)

Perhaps appropriately, the Second Bank of the United States was actually housed in a Greek temple in Philadelphia. When I visited the Fed to do research in the Fed library in 2013, its centennial year, it seemed to be a heavily guarded, lavishly appointed temple. I could not move anywhere within its confines without an armed security escort. My request to see the boardroom was summarily denied even though I could see that it was empty from the bottom of the stairs. Works of art by 34 Fed staff members adorned the halls as part of the sixth annual Staff Art Show. Perhaps my favorite feature of the Fed, though, was a display of "Volcker Bricks" by the library. These were small pieces of 2 x 4's that had been mailed to Volcker while he was chair as a form of protest by unemployed construction workers and were meant to represent buildings that we not being built because of Volcker's tight monetary policy.

The FOMC is composed of 12 voting members: the 7 members of the Board of Governors, and a rotation of 5 of the 12 district Federal Reserve Bank presidents, save the New York Fed that maintains constant voting membership. The FOMC meets eight times a year behind closed doors. The idea, as part of the great compromise that led to President Wilson signing the Federal Reserve Act, was that the Board of Governors would serve as a public check on the power of the commercial banking industry that was represented by the bank presidents. In practice, though, we know that the members of Board of Governors historically have come from a close-knit circle of economists that tend to support the interests of the banking and financial industries. The end result, of course, has been largely a self-fulfilling prophesy when it comes to decision-making at the Fed.

Before each FOMC meeting, the staff economists at the Fed prepare two highly confidential documents: the greenbook and the bluebook. The former presents an economic forecast for the upcoming two years, while the latter presents the committee with a different set of short-term policy alternatives given the aforementioned economic assumptions. These documents are not available to the public and are not subject to any type of Congressional oversight. Greider (1987) comments on the culture of control of all decision-making and communication at the Fed:

> The institution's official secrecy naturally enhanced the mystique. The Federal Open Market Committee met to deliberate on the money supply eight to ten times a year, but its decisions were made in secrecy. Only six or eight weeks later, after the FOMC had held its next meeting, would the Fed release a brief report on what the previous meeting had decided. Internal reports and memos, the economic analysis that supported the decisions, were kept confidential for five years. A full transcript of the committee deliberations was never available, because it was no longer kept. (p. 54)

Whenever Congress passed legislation to democratize and open up the Fed, officials at the Fed always found way to circumvent these new requirements. For example, the Fed used to keep a transcript of its deliberations; however, "When Congress was enacting the Freedom of Information Act, Federal Reserve Chairman Arthur Burns decided to abolish the full transcript, lest litigation force it into public view prematurely and embarrass Fed officials. No other agency of government, not even the Central Intelligence Agency, enjoyed such privacy" (Greider, p. 55). Burns, as I noted earlier, was one of Greenspan's more important mentors and their management styles had a lot in common, especially in terms of the culture of control.

Like the Fed itself, the staff economists operate in near seclusion, and they all tend to be of one mind in terms of the job they are supposed to perform: "The System's many research departments did not, as a rule, hire eccentric thinkers who produced grand new theories of economics that might disrupt conventional thinking" (Greider 265). This was another way that the culture of control permeated all aspects of decision-making and communication at the Fed. The staff economists prepare a series of policy alternatives and there are purportedly significant differences of opinion and vigorous debate about these alternatives. But, in the end, the staff prepares its forecast as if it is one, unified voice, sublimating any difference of opinion. As Beckner notes, "uncertainties and exigencies are kept secret" (p. 374). The forecast is based off a single countervailing assumption regarding economic activity, and it is based almost solely on assumptions about movement in short-term interest rates. Dissent is not tolerated at the Fed on any level, and where it does exist, such dissent is carefully managed before it reaches the public:

> "Arthur [Burns] just hated dissents," Governor Philip Coldwell said. "I guess it wasn't three months after I came on board, I threw him a dissent along with Alfred Hayes, president of the New York bank. For the next five meetings, Al Hayes and I would be brought into Arthur's office beforehand for little prep sessions—a lecture from Arthur on the importance of consensus." (Beckner, p. 341)

One of the more telling examples of the Fed's culture of control during Greenspan's tenure occurred in 1989. On Friday, October 13 of that year, the Dow Jones Industrial Average plunged 190 points. On Sunday, both the *New York Times* and the *Washington Post* quoted an "anonymous Fed official" that the Fed was prepared to create liquidity in the market to "prevent financial crisis." Greenspan and the President of the Federal

Reserve Bank of New York, E. Gerald Corrigan, discovered it was Manley Johnson who had made the statement, and they were reportedly "furious" over the breach in communication. Corrigan reflected, "It was the absolute, classic worst case moral hazard. ... One of the things you learn with these things is you never, ever, ever, ever, ever tip your hand in advance as to what you'll do or what you won't do" (Beckner, p. 148). Greenspan said that the "unauthorized" pledge of emergency liquidity had "severely restricted our options" and he implored other members to "stay away from the press" (p. 148). The Fed controlled not only what was said but how it was said, as well. As I noted earlier, Fedspeak is typically vague and technical, characteristics that tend to insulate the Fed from public scrutiny while simultaneously reinforcing its authority. Greider observes, "The Federal Reserve, in this setting, established another precedent for the future—its ability to obfuscate and confuse when under attack. Public discontent was blunted by long and complicated technical answers that diverted attention from the Fed's own role in economic distress" (p. 295). In the following years, however, there were rumblings of change both inside and outside of the Fed.

These calls for change tended to wax and wane over the years. U.S. Representative Wright Patman was one of the more outspoken critics of the Fed: "Year after year, as Chairman of the House Banking Committee [from 1965–75], Patman held meticulous hearings and introduced reform legislation to make the Fed more democratic and less subject to the influence of major banks" (Greider, p. 51). During Greenspan's tenure, as early as 1991, Representatives Lee Hamilton and Bryon Dorgan introduced legislation that would have required more openness from the Fed, but the measure never passed. The next year, however, a new and more determined voice challenged the Fed's culture of secrecy. On November 19, 1992, Henry Gonzalez announced that he would submit legislation to require more openness and accountability at the Fed. Among other things, the legislation was aimed at requiring the Fed to immediately release the FOMC minutes, and it called for the Fed presidents to be appointed by the President. He "vowed to force 'an end to the aura of secrecy and confusion' by requiring the Fed to videotape its closed meetings and make it public" (Beckner, p. 295). He also called for more clarity in the statements issued by the Fed. At the same time, Lee Hamilton was introducing legislation in the House of Representatives regarding voting rights and term limits for Fed officials. Congress subsequently started a series of hearings regarding the Fed's accountability.

On March 4, 1993, Gonzalez introduced new legislation directed toward decreasing the regulatory authority of the Fed. On March 10, Donald Riegle requested that all 12 Fed presidents appear before Congress. This, of course, was a peculiar request because the Fed presidents, unlike their counterparts on the Fed's Board of Governors, were not appointed by the President, nor confirmed by the Senate. The move indicated that the probe into the secrecy surrounding the Fed was broadening. At the hearings, Riegle complained, "Maybe there ought to be Senate confirmation [of the Fed presidents] and maybe your minutes ought to be made public" (Beckner, p. 302). President Clinton wrote a letter to Henry Gonzalez on September 20 that year. In it, he claimed, "On balance, I am disinclined to seek a change in the Federal Reserve Act at this juncture. There are several reasons. Perhaps the main one is a general feeling that the System is functioning well and does not need an overhaul right now" (Beckner, p. 313). Nevertheless, Gonzalez held his own hearings shortly thereafter and they involved appearances by Greenspan, the Board of Governors, and the Fed presidents. On October 13, Greenspan spoke out against the bill mostly because it ran the risk of politicizing the Fed. On October 19, Greenspan defended the closed nature of FOMC discussions and the announcement of policy directives. He contended that in comparison to other central banks, the U.S. Federal Reserve was a fairly transparent system. He also warned that the immediate disclosure of Fed minutes would "tend to produce increased volatility in financial markets, as market participants reacted not only to actual Federal Reserve actions but also to possible Federal Reserve actions … [and the release of transcripts] would so seriously constrain the process of formulating policy as to render those meetings nearly unproductive" (Beckner, pp. 316–317).

When pressed about the nature of the records at Fed meetings, Greenspan said that he kept rough notes, and that the meetings were audiotaped to assist the staff in preparing the written minutes. This admission was significant. "For the first time Greenspan had revealed to stunned FOMC members that the Fed had been secretly keeping verbatim transcripts of FOMC meetings since 1976" (Beckner, p. 316). Shocked, some officials called for the secretly recorded transcripts to be destroyed. In the end, though, Greenspan relented and on November 17, he authorized the release of these transcripts with a five-year delay. Gonzalez was dissatisfied with the lengthy delay, but Greenspan said any earlier release would "succeed only in stifling originality, new ideas and the give and take debate that so often open up new insights for the FOMC as a whole" (Beckner,

p. 320). In the meantime, Gonzalez accused Greenspan of "lying" and "stonewalling" by attempting to cover up the existence of these transcripts because FOMC members had previously claimed in earlier hearings that no formal notes or records were kept of the meetings other than their own personal notes (Beckner, p. 317). Further, Gonzalez felt that the proposed five-year delay was "arbitrary and without any rational basis" (Wessel, 1993, p. A10).

At this point, the Clinton Administration decided to join the chorus. Treasury Secretary Lloyd Bentsen advanced a plan for a Federal Banking Commission that significantly reduced the regulatory authority of the Fed. The President would appoint all five members of this new regulatory commission. As expected, Greenspan vigorously opposed this proposal. Eventually, the idea just withered away. But it was yet another way to place political pressure on the Fed, especially in terms of its secret deliberations and carefully controlled communication. At the same time, Gonzalez was widening his probe of the Fed. Now he was criticizing the Fed's commitment to diversity in employment practices, their extravagant spending on entertainment, and their acceptance of gifts from private bankers. Robert Auerbach's 2008 book, *Deception and Abuse at the Fed: Henry B. Gonzalez Battles Alan Greenspan's Bank*, offers a full account of Gonzalez' challenge to the nearly unchecked economic and political power of the Fed.

In addition to his attempts to change the culture of secrecy that dominated the decision-making and communication at the Fed, in 1994, President Clinton also took steps to change the culture from within. That year, Clinton had the opportunity to appoint the Vice-Chair of the Fed. On April 22, he appointed Princeton economist Alan Blinder to that post. He appointed University of California at Berkeley economist Janet Yellen to the Board of Governors at the same time. Blinder and Yellen tried mightily to change the Fed culture, but they purportedly found tremendous institutional and personal resistance. People with power tend to give up that power only grudgingly, if at all.

Blinder commented on the "cultural bias" against dissenting at the Fed: "Dissenting around here, any dissenting vote, is a big deal" (Uchitelle, 1995, p. 49). He was also concerned about the power of the Fed's staff of economists. Among other things, he found them tremendously inaccessible. He was worried that the staff writers had an undue influence over Fed discussions and policy making. New appointee Janet Yellen, who was appointed chair of the Fed in 2014, concurred: "The ethos behind what the staff does is that the governors, the Chairman, nobody is supposed to mess with them. Early on, I asked if I could go to the room where the forecast was prepared, and I was told that I could not" (Beckner, pp. 371–372). Significantly, "Greenspan became concerned when he saw Yellen talking to the staff, fearing that she might 'impurify' the staff forecast" (p. 372). In addition to a lack of intellectual diversity, the Fed has also historically lacked other forms of diversity, as well, a point raised by Henry Gonzalez. Indeed, Yellen is the first woman to ever serve as chair of the Fed.

Blinder, in particular, felt that the power of the Fed demanded more openness and public accountability. He argued, "I think [the fact that our policies cannot be reversed] gives us a tremendous obligation to explain what we're up to, why we're up to doing it, and why we think it is the right thing" (Bradsher, 1994, p. D5). He continued, "My biggest disagreement with my colleagues at the Fed is over openness. I believe we should talk to society more. … But the position of this institution has always been to be extremely tight-lipped" (Uchitelle, p. 37). Further, Blinder challenged the grounding assumption at the Fed, the need to fight inflation first: "Blinder indicated that he felt the Fed should make unemployment a priority, alongside inflation" (Martin, p. 209). At one point, Blinder "argued for an essay-style communiqué to accompany announcements of rate changes, instead of the two-sentence releases that are now standard. Under current practice, the heavily edited minutes are only issued six weeks after each meeting" (Uchitelle, p. 49). In part frustrated by the intransigence of his colleagues, and their resistance to change, Blinder left the Fed in January 1996 to return to Princeton. His tenure lasted less than two years. Rob Johnson, who was one of the leading economists on the Senate banking committee for many years, believes, "Blinder made the mistake of behaving as if the Fed was a place where competing ideas and assumptions were debated. … In closed-door meetings, Blinder did what so few do: challenged assumptions" (Grim). This upended the accepted ritual of Greenspan essentially telling the Fed staff "what to conclude and they [would] produce studies in which they conclude this. … [I]t just created a stir inside—it was sort of like the whole pipeline of Greenspan-arriving-at-decisions was disrupted" (Grim).

Acutely aware of the challenges to his authority, Greenspan made internal changes to decision-making and communication at the Fed, perhaps in an effort to stave off stronger legislation that sought to completely overhaul, or even eliminate the Fed. The Fed revisited the idea of releasing transcripts and announcing policy changes the day after an FOMC meeting at their March 22, 1994, gathering. This seemed like an appropriate time to revisit the subject because the Fed had just tried out the new mechanism for announcements the previous month. The consensus was that

> a useful purpose would be served in reducing or eliminating potential misrepresentation of the committee's decision and the related risk of overreactions in the financial markets. ... The news of the committee's action would be conveyed unambiguously to the entire public at once and not filtered through the financial markets' interpretation of open market operations. (Beckner, p. 357)

Part of the shift in policy meant that the Fed would change rates immediately after the FOMC meeting rather enacting moves in between meetings at the chair's discretion. In addition, policy directives now came with a bias statement, a future-oriented, *de facto* early warning radar system of sorts so that the markets and the public were not caught off guard if and when the changes actually came. David Wessel of the *Wall Street Journal* reported in 1993, "The Federal Reserve, under pressure from Congress, said it will release edited transcripts of past monetary-policy discussions after a five-year delay, but hasn't decided whether to do the same for future meetings" (Wessel, p. A2). Representative Henry Gonzalez "called yesterday's action 'a positive development but 'wholly inadequate'" (p. A10). In addition, as I noted earlier, Gonzalez also found the five-year time lag completely arbitrary. In 1994, the Fed agreed to disclose the results of meetings on the day they took place at 2:15 p.m. Previously, the Fed did not announce interest rate decisions until at least six weeks after the Federal Open Market Committee meetings. Tellingly, Owen Ullmann of *Business Week* noted in 1994, "[T]he glare of openness is unnerving financial-market players used to being kept in the dark. The Fed's unprecedented announcement of a policy change in February sent Wall Street into a tizzy" (1994, p. 73). Apparently, the move to make the Fed more open and accountable undermined Wall Street's authority over interpreting the cryptic actions and pronouncements from the Fed. In 2011, again facing public and government pressure, Fed chair Ben Bernanke agreed to meet with the press four times a year ("Fed plans," 2011, p. 3B).

Despite these changes, enacted to stave off further reform and criticism, the culture of secrecy and control is still alive and well in the Fed, and its power over both economics and politics has expanded over the years. Indeed, Niskanen (1988) writes, "Over its history the Federal Reserve Board ... has developed an aura, influence, and independence that go far beyond the intentions of its creators" (p. 156). The consequences of this largely unchecked, anti-democratic power and authority cannot be underestimated:

> Citizens were taught that [the Fed's] activities were mechanical and nonpolitical, unaffected by the self-interested pressures of competing economic groups, and its pervasive influence over American life was largely ignored by the continuing political debate. Its decisions and internal disputes and the large consequences that flowed form them remained remote and indistinct, submerged beneath the visible politics of the nation. The details of its actions were presumed to be too esoteric for ordinary citizens to understand. (Greider, pp. 11–12)

Importantly, the culture of secrecy was not limited to the Fed; it has become an unsettling role model for corporate crisis communication. For example, when workers were trying to execute a "top kill" on the damaged oil well from the Deepwater Horizon eco-catastrophe in 2010, the largest oil spill in the history of the United States, British Petroleum released a statement saying that it would only provide updates on the operation in "formal settings" because such information was considered "stock-market sensitive" (Nuckols & Bluestein, 2010). When we tolerate anti-democratic institutions, or initiatives in our society, they tend to spread like a disease until they create a debilitating miasma, and our economic and political rights as citizens suffer irreparable damage as a result. In his book, *End the Fed*, Ron Paul (2009), warns, "[I]t is irresponsible, ineffective, and ultimately useless to have a serious economic debate without considering fundamental issues about money and its quality, as well as the Fed's massive role in manipulating money to our economic ruin" (p. 1).

In the Epilogue to his companion volume to *Alice in Wonderland*, Lewis Carroll (1946) concludes *Through the Looking Glass* with a poem. The first letters of each line spell out the name of the original "Alice," Alice Pleasance Liddell:

> A boat, beneath a sunny sky
> Lingering onward dreamily
> In an evening in July—

Children three that nestle near,
Eager eye and willing ear
Pleased a simple tale to hear—

Long has paled that sunny sky:
Echoes fade and memories die:
Autumn frosts have slain July.

Still, she haunts me, phantomwise
Alice moving under skies
Never seen by waking eyes.

Children yet, the tale to hear
Eager eye and willing ear
Lovingly shall nestle near.

In a Wonderland they lie,
Dreaming as the days go by,
Dreaming as the summers die.

Ever drifting down the stream—
Lingering in the golden gleam—
Life, what is it but a dream? (p. 307)

The turn to "Alice" here is purposeful. Alice is also an acronym for the Alice Project conducted by the United Way, studying those who are "asset limited, income constrained, employed." The 2018 data indicate that 43% of households in the United States did not earn enough to fund basic living expenses, and consequently find it difficult to "survive in the modern economy" (Luhby, 2018). Despite years of economic expansion, nearly half of households in the United States have been left behind, another manifestation of the disappearing middle class.

From 1987 to 2006, the world took part in the lifelong dream of Alan Greenspan, quietly consenting to the return of free market capitalism. Dreams, however, are delicate and ever-changing things, and can quickly become nightmares given a particular set of circumstances, and those circumstances were soon to follow. One suspects Greenspan called his autobiography *The Age of Turbulence* for a very good reason.

References

Auerbach, R. D. (2008). *Deception and abuse at the fed: Henry B. Gonzalez battles Alan Greenspan's bank*. University of Texas Press.

Beckner, S. K. (1996). *Back from the brink: The Greenspan years*. John Wiley & Sons.

Bradsher, K. (1994, September 26). New vice chairman stirs the board's pot. *New York Times*, D1, D5.

Carroll, L. (1946). *Alice in wonderland and through the looking glass*. Grosset and Dunlap.

Fed plans to meet with press four times a year. (2011, March 25). *USA Today*, 3B.

Greenspan, A. (2007). *The age of turbulence: Adventures in a new world*. Penguin.

Greider, W. (1987). *Secrets of the temple: How the federal reserve runs the country*. Simon and Schuster.

Grim, R. (2009, October 23). Priceless: How the federal reserve bought the economics profession. *Huffington Post*. Retrieved June 15, 2014, from https://www.huffpost.com/entry/priceless-how-the-federal_n_278805

Jones, S. (2018, January 1). A historical perspective: The banking monopoly. *The Banking Swindle*. Retrieved June 21, 2021, from https://criminalbankingmonopoly.wordpress.com/

Lindbergh, C. A. (1913a). *Banking and currency and the money trust*. Omni Publications.

Lindbergh, C. A. (1913b, December 22). *Congressional record* 51, p. 1446.

Lindbergh, C. A. (1968). *The economic pinch*. Noontide Press. (Original work published in 1923).

Luhby, T. (2018, May 18). Almost half of U.S. families cannot afford basics like rent and food. *CNNMoney*. Retrieved June 21, 2021, from https://money.cnn.com/2018/05/17/news/economy/us-middle-class-basics-study/index.html

Martin, J. (2001). *Greenspan: The man behind money*. Perseus Publishing.

Mayer, A. J., Whitmore, J., & Abraham, P. L. (1975, February 24). Greenspan—Atlas jogs. *Newsweek*, 60–61.

Moore, C. H. (1990). *The Federal reserve system: A history of the first 75 years*. McFarland.

Niskanen, W. A. (1988). *Reaganomics: An insider's account of the policies and the people*. Oxford University Press.

Nuckols, B., & Bluestein, G. (2010, May 28). Live camera showing oil spill becomes an internet sensation. *St. Louis Post-Dispatch*. Retrieved June 2, 2010, from https://www.stltoday.com/news/national/live-camera-showing-oil-spill-becomes-an-internet-sensation/article_022fca2c-e449-50ed-b732-7dc0bd3c5fa7.html

Paul, R. (2009). *End the fed*. Grand Central Publishing.

Robbins, L. (2007). *An essay on the nature and significance of economic science.* Mises Institute. (Original work published in 1932).

Thompson, W. (2005). *An inquiry into the principles of the distribution of wealth most conducive to human happiness.* Elibron Press. (Original work published in 1824).

Uchitelle, L. (1995, March 18). Opening the fed's doors from inside: Alan Binder preaches communication at tight-lipped central bank. *New York Times*, 37, 49.

Ullmann, O. (1994, September 26). At the fed, silence isn't golden anymore. *Business Week*, 73.

Weaver, R. (2009). *The ethics of rhetoric.* Routledge.

Weber, M. (1969). *The theory of social and economic organization* (T. Parsons, Ed.). The Free Press. (Original work published 1947)

Wessel, D. (1990, September 20). Greenspan says oil prices curb fed moves; Poll finds Mideast crisis slowing economy. *Wall Street Journal*, A2.

Wessel, D. (1993, November 18). Federal reserve to release transcripts of past sessions after five-year delay. *Wall Street Journal*, p. A2, A10.

CHAPTER 8

(Tell Me Why) I Don't Like Mondays: The Crash of 1987

In the midst of writing this chapter, my daughter was reading John Steinbeck's (1947/1994) timeless classic, *The Pearl*, in her 7th Grade English class. The central theme of that book, Kino's discovery of the "Pearl of the World," summarizes succinctly what I want to communicate here. Steinbeck writes that the discovery of this massive Pearl infected everyone in the town with a venom, as they dreamt about the economic impact Kino's sale of the pearl would have on their lives. The priest, the doctor, the pearl dealers, indeed, everyone, imagined how they would spend their fortunes. Even the beggars of the town were given hope because, they realized, "there is no almsgiver in the world like a poor man who is suddenly lucky" (p. 28). This chapter tells a cautionary tale about the dire consequences when an entire community is infected by unexpected wealth and, consequently, the miasma of greed.

In order to better understand the causes and repercussions of the stock market crash of 1987, it is important to first consider its closest analog: the stock market crash of 1929. As tempting as it is to identify a single cause for that historic market collapse, it is nearly impossible to do so in isolation. Instead, a confluence of factors flowed together to create a market level that was simply unsustainable. In one of the more compelling accounts that examines this market implosion, *The Great Crash: 1929*, John Kenneth Galbraith (1955) admitted as much: "No one was responsible for the great Wall Street crash. No one engineered the speculation

G. D. Klinger et al., *Money Talks*,
https://doi.org/10.1007/978-3-031-00816-0_8

that preceded it. Both were the product of the free choice and decision of hundreds of thousands of individuals. The latter were not led to the slaughter. They were impelled to it by the seminal lunacy which has always seized people who are seized in turn with the notion that they can become very rich" (p. 4). In the years leading up to the stock market crash, a time often referred to as the "Roaring Twenties," greed had infected nearly everyone. Although the 1920s were a time of "vision, boundless hope, and optimism," the American people "were also displaying an inordinate desire to get rich quickly with a minimum of physical effort" (p. 8). Galbraith recounted the bursting of the Florida real estate bubble as a revealing example of this speculative fever. The most notorious of the figures involved in the Florida real estate scam was none other than Charles Ponzi, the namesake for what is today called a "Ponzi Scheme."

Ponzi, however, was just a symptom of a system that was powering a speculative fervor in all aspects of life. The government, for one, was complicit in fueling this "get rich quick" mentality. Indeed, the Federal Reserve adopted an easy money policy beginning in 1927, effectively lowering the discount rate, and aggressively purchasing government securities. Adolph Miller, a dissenter on the Fed, described it as "the greatest and boldest operation ever undertaken by the Federal Reserve System ... [it] resulted in one of the most costly errors committed by it or any other banking system in the last 75 years" ("Testimony before Senate Committee," quoted in Robbins, 1934, p. 53; in Galbraith, p. 15). This simple single cause explanation, however, overlooks important elements of the larger picture. Easy money alone does not cause wild speculation; it also requires that people in the economic system to be motivated by greed.

The economic infrastructure that developed during the years leading up to the Great Depression stimulated that greed, and provided the mechanisms for people to assume even more market risk based on the belief that there was money to be made. Two things in particular developed during these years: the rise of the margin account, and the development of investment trusts. On the first front, Galbraith observed, "[T]here was still another and even more significant index of what was happening in the market. That was the phenomenal increase in trading on margin" (pp. 22–23). It first manifested itself in the Florida real estate boom. Traders did not deal with the actual land, but in "binders," or the right to buy the land at a fixed price with only 10% down. This had a multiplier effect and encouraged massive speculation. Now you did not have to pay the full purchase price for the land and this encouraged speculators to buy even more binders on the margin. "Margin trading must be defended not on the grounds that it efficiently and ingeniously assists the speculator, but that it encourages the extra trading which changes a thin and anemic market into a thick and healthy one" (p. 25). In the early 1920s the "call loan" market was only $1 to $1.5 billion. By 1928, that amount had ballooned to $6 billion (p. 26). "People were swarming to buy stocks on margin" (p. 26). The interest on call margins consequently increased from its norm of 5% to a high of 12%. In other words, banks could borrow money from the Fed at 5% interest, and resell it as a call loan for 12% interest. According to Galbraith, "This was, possibly, the most profitable arbitrage operation of all time" (p. 27).

On the second front, Galbraith commented, "The most notable piece of speculative architecture of the late twenties, and the one by which more than any other device, the public demand for common stocks was satisfied, was the investment trust or company" (p. 51). He continued, "The investment trust did not promote new enterprises or enlarge old ones. It merely arranged that people could own stock in old companies through the medium of new ones. … The virtue of the investment trust was that it brought about an almost complete divorce of the volume of corporate securities outstanding from the volume of corporate assets in existence" (p. 52). Before 1921 there were only a few small companies engaged in this business, but that number swelled to 160 by 1927, and another 140 formed the same year, effectively doubling the number of investment trusts in a single year. In 1928, another 186 were added, and 265 new investment trusts were started in 1929 (pp. 53–54). The amount of money that flowed into these newly created investment trusts was staggering: "In 1927 the trusts sold to the public about $400,000,000 worth of securities; in 1929 they marketed an estimated three billions worth …; by the autumn of 1929 the total assets of the investment trusts were estimated to exceed eight billions of dollars. They had increased approximately elevenfold since the beginning of 1927" (reference omitted) (p. 55). Because of their popularity, shares in these trusts were often priced substantially higher than the underlying holdings of the company were worth. People paid this premium because of the hype, but also because of an underlying belief in the fundamentals of leverage.

These factors alone did not cause the stock market to crash, but they were part and parcel of a speculative mentality that had gripped the nation at that time. The market, and the returns promised by participating in it, had become a centerpiece of popular culture. It is important to note, however, that only a small percentage of the overall population was actually seduced into playing this game. As Galbraith concluded, "[O]nly one and half million people, out of a population of approximately 120 million … had an active association of any sort with the stock market" (p. 83). Everyone was impacted by the greed of a few. In his book, *The Great Depression: America, 1929–1941*, Historian Robert McElvaine (1984) noted, "From the top of prosperity in 1929 to the bottom of depression in 1933, GNP dropped by a total of 29 percent, consumption expenditures by 18 percent, construction by 78 percent, and investment by an incredible 98 percent. Unemployment rose from 3.2 to 24.9 percent" (p. 75).

Leading up to the crash, the Fed realized it faced a painful conundrum: should it support a lagging economy by continuing its easy money policy, or should it attempt to burst the speculative market bubble by increasing rates? It chose the latter course, raising the discount rate from 3.5% to 5%. The market barely reacted since, as we noted at the outset, the market seems to be influenced more by rhetoric than by fundamentals, and the rhetoric of greed had permeated all aspects of life, and people were reluctant to give it up. The rate increase did, however, hit the economy hard with industrial production "falling at an annualized rate of 45%" ("Slumps that shaped," 2014, p. 54). Eventually, though, the stock market did reverse course, and with unprecedented alacrity. In the course of "two days, October 28 and 29th, the Dow lost close to 25%. By November 13th, it was at 198, down 45% in two months" (p. 54).

Some have called the years of the Reagan administration the "Reagan Revolution." While it was, indeed, a revolution of sorts on many fronts, one of the lesser-known revolutions occurred within the realm of economics. While "Reaganomics" was one of the familiar tag lines often associated with Reagan's economic policy, Reagan also achieved a quieter revolution in monetary policy. He was the first President to appoint the entire seven-member board of the Federal Reserve. While Greenspan assuredly had difficulties in joining the Fed as Chair, the stage was set for him to succeed. While he had his detractors, even on the Fed, he was, in many ways, preaching to the choir. He was set to lead a group of Reagan appointees, many of whom were washed in the spirit of conservative politics and laissez-faire economics.

Perhaps emboldened by this conservative coalition, on September 4, less than a month after taking office, Greenspan decided to raise the discount rate by a half point. Ever true to his word, and despite the appearance of actual inflation, Greenspan felt he was acting proactively to stop future inflationary pressures. Within two weeks, the market began to show its displeasure with this restrictive monetary policy. In one week, October 12–16, the Dow had lost 235 points. Aware that the market would be under intense pressure that following Monday, Greenspan decided to keep a speaking engagement in Dallas. He wanted to appear calm in the midst of the storm. He returned to a full-blown economic crisis. As we saw earlier, the Fed was turned into a crisis management headquarters. And there were heated debates about the appropriate Fed response.

The losses were stunning. The Dow had lost 508 points, or 22.6% of its value in its worst-ever single session in history. The loss was almost twice as large as the initial stock market crash of October 29, 1929. Nearly $500 billion had been lost on paper in a single day. To many, the United States was perched on the brink of another economic depression, or worse. Maybe this was the beginning of the end of the United States' economic dominance on the international scene. The markets were in turmoil, the public was in shock, and the politicians did not seem to have a clue; the world was hungry for a leader. They found one in Greenspan. With a remarkable sense of calm in the midst of near economic anarchy, Greenspan reacted with a steady and even hand. It seemed to be exactly what the market needed.

The crash came just months after Greenspan took office. It was an early test not only of his intellectual commitments but also of his ability to handle his new position. The crisis forced Greenspan into an intellectual dilemma: it forced him to immediately revisit his assumptions about the free market and "self-correcting mechanisms" of the market. While he was perhaps willing to accept some economic hardship to wage his war with inflation, he wanted any downturns in the economy carefully planned and controlled. Circumstances did not always accommodate his wishes. As we noted earlier, though, Greenspan had a well-developed ability to adapt to changing circumstances, even when they are radical and unexpected.

He publicly responded to the stock market crash in three different ways. First, he immediately sought to reassure consumers shortly after the crash that the financial systems in the United States remained "reasonably secure." Indeed, the day after the crash, Greenspan, in a one-sentence announcement, promised increased monetary liquidity for the entire U.S. financial system (Murray, 1987, p. 1). Greenspan, perhaps moved by the immediacy of the crisis, later endorsed the creation of an "umbrella agency" called the Financial Services Oversight Commission in testimony before the Senate Banking Committee on December 1. This announcement came the day after the stock market, still feeling the aftershocks of Black Monday, lost over 4% of its value in the eighth largest point loss in its history. Greenspan, in a statement seemingly inconsistent with his personal views regarding the regulation of markets, suggested, "The need for greater regulatory coordination could not have been brought out more clearly than in the recent stock market developments" (Nash, 1987, p. D1). Greenspan's ideological commitments were already being tested.

With more critical distance from the situation, Greenspan and others issued a report by the Presidential Task Force on Market Mechanisms. This five-member task force[1] was specially appointed by President Reagan to study the reasons for the stock market collapse in October 1987. The report was especially interesting in that Greenspan's rhetoric took a noted shift. Now the report admitted, unlike Greenspan in the days after the crash, that the financial system approached breakdown. And more interesting still given Greenspan's earlier professed views regarding the role for government regulation is the report's conclusion, a "radical overhaul of the government's regulation of all financial markets" (Murray & Ricks, 1988, p. 3). Greenspan, it seemed, had decided that the public and the markets both felt the need for more regulation. Without regulation and oversight, the free market could lead to disastrous consequences. So, initially, at least, Greenspan seemed to be willing to heed the call of greater regulation.

The message Greenspan was sending was mixed, however. In testimony before the Senate Banking Committee on March 31, 1988, Greenspan reiterated his earlier belief that the current structure of the financial markets remained "reasonably secure," and he now refused to endorse a new regulatory body to manage intermarket issues because the "self-correcting mechanisms of the markets and the market participants themselves were more important in reducing the likelihood of another stock market crash" (Nash, 1988, p. D1). As the United States moved further from the market crash, Greenspan had a greater ability to rhetorically migrate from his initial call for increased regulation of the markets.

Perhaps a more stark contrast with the conclusions of the report cited above, however, came from a similar report issued on May 18 of the same year by a similar Reagan committee, the Working Group on Financial

[1] It is interesting to note that soon-to-be Treasury Secretary Nicholas F. Brady, then chairman of Dillon, Read & Co., served on this committee.

Markets; Alan Greenspan was again one of five appointees. This report, however, concluded what appeared to be the converse of the earlier report. In it, Greenspan argued that "most of the crucial areas are already cured, either by the market levels, or by actions already taken by the self-regulatory organizations" (Ricks, 1988, p. 2). Analysts widely viewed the report as a victory for laissez-faire principles consistent with Greenspan's intellectual commitments, but it was widely criticized in Congress for what Rep. Jim Cooper called "almost Hooveresque reliance on the free market," and Rep. Edward Mackey called it "a giant step backwards" from the earlier report on the market breakdown (Ricks, p. 2). The inconsistencies did not escape everyone's attention, it seemed. But Greenspan read the situation correctly. The immediacy of the crisis had passed, and these concerns could be more easily dismissed. The market had survived the crisis mostly on its own, with some rhetorical and monetary help from the Fed, so the perceived need for increased regulation faded from memory.

On January 24, 1989, the Dow finally recaptured the total points it had lost from the crash of October 1987. Symbolically enough, as noted earlier, the breaching of the barrier was at least partially attributed to the House Banking Committee testimony of Alan Greenspan. And so ended the often-contradictory rhetorical response of Greenspan to his first major crisis as chair of the Fed.

Before moving on, it is important to note here that it was not simply Greenspan's rhetoric of reassurance that helped resolve this economic crisis. The rhetoric was important, especially initially, but the Fed had to back up their words with action. They could not just promise liquidity, they had to deliver on that promise. It was part of a two-step recovery plan, according to Beckner (1996): "Step one was issuing the statement about providing liquidity. Step two was actually providing the liquidity by visibility pumping reserves into the system through aggressive purchases of government securities" (p. 54). The Fed backed up its promises of liquidity with action: it bought three times the normal amount of securities in open market operations, stimulating the flow of money. They were also on the phone, cajoling banks to loosen up the flow of credit. The two-step plan seemed to be the right tonic for what was ailing the markets.

One of the more interesting subtexts involved in the Crash of '87 regards the role of the Fed in precipitating the crisis. As noted above, Greenspan made a deliberate decision to raise rates. This decision had a chilling effect on the market and the economy. Indeed, the market headed down decisively almost immediately in reaction to Greenspan's first-rate hike. Beryl Sprinkel, the chair of the President's Council of Economic advisers in the Reagan Administration, a post that Greenspan himself once filled, felt that the "Fed provoked the crash by tightening monetary policy too much" (Beckner, p. 62).

It is difficult to isolate one cause of something as complex as the stock market crash. There are assuredly many factors that contributed to the downturn. Even today, economists continue to argue about the causes of the Great Depression. The best answers that we have are competing theories based on what some writer deems compelling evidence. The explanations are as varied as the people who advance them. The same is true of the stock market crash in 1987. There are a myriad of explanations regarding causes and contributing factors. To be certain, there were certain new structural forces at play. The rise of institutional and computer program trading added to the volatility of the market in general, as was the case with the rise of margin accounts and investment trusts in the years leading up to the Great Depression. Add to that the magnifying effects of index trading and stock options, and a system that simply could not handle the volume of trades, nor respond to such a significant downturn, and the largely unregulated market was simply not prepared for what hit it that day. Nevertheless, the Fed has historically been the group that sets the tone for monetary policy and, consequently, the economy, and it was sending out strong signals that the unfettered economic growth in the market and economy would no longer be accommodated as they had in the past. For Greenspan, modest growth was okay, but any more than that raised the specter of inflation.

Further, Reaganomics had popularized economics, so the role that Greenspan was expected to play had changed. While some say that Greenspan sought celebrity, it is equally as likely that celebrity sought Greenspan. As such, even early in his tenure as chair of the Fed, more public attention was focused on him than previous Fed chairs.

The markets and the public demanded an economic leader, preferably one who moved in lockstep with the political leader. While Reagan and Greenspan were similar in many ways, they often did not move in lockstep. Greenspan and Reagan both tended toward discourse that was vague and abstract. "Like two magnets of the same valance, Greenspan and Reagan were not inclined to connect" (Martin, 2001, p. 185). One of the places where that disconnect was most pronounced was at the level of macroeconomic ambitions. Both Greenspan and Reagan desired significant economic expansion, but they disagreed about how to get there. For

Greenspan, the only way to ensure long-term economic expansion was through a conservative monetary policy aimed at price stability. The problem was that to ensure long-term economic growth, Greenspan believed that only a restrictive monetary policy that often sacrificed growth in the short term was the way forward. For a political figure, especially one who faced reelection every fourth year, sacrificing short-term growth often meant political disaster. Political leaders are always held accountable for economic troubles. Presidents have a built-in incentive to pursue policies that benefit the economy in the short term. This was a point of fundamental structural incompatibility between Presidents and the Fed. This is one of the reasons that the Fed is, in theory, insulated from political pressures and public accountability.

When Greenspan decided to raise rates, it was a signal that he was parting ways with the assumptions of Reaganomics. He was willing to inflict some economic pain on the Reagan administration in exchange for advancing his agenda regarding price stability. It is important to note, though, that it was not Reagan personally, or politically, who stood to suffer from this restrictive shift in monetary policy, he was near the end of his second term in office when the crash hit. Instead, the burden was placed on the Republican Party and their next nominee for the presidency, then Vice President George H. W. Bush. This was something that Bush seemed to recognize early in his run for president. Even on the campaign trail, Bush criticized the restrictive monetary policy adopted by the Fed. It was a point of contention throughout the Bush presidency, and it lead to several public clashes with Greenspan during Bush's four years in office.

It was almost as if Greenspan wanted to leave his mark on the Fed and the economy shortly after his arrival. He needed to set the tone that he was in charge of the Fed, and the Fed was in charge of the economy. It was a strong symbolic statement, especially given that it was coming from someone who was, despite his previous experience, fairly new on the job. The markets were uncertain how to react. On the one hand, they seemed to like the guiding principles behind the Reagan Revolution; on the other, they were receiving signals from a new Fed chair that he was not going to let the party get out of hand. In short, it appears that the earlier observation of Sprinkel has some merit. The Fed's decision to raise rates was not the only cause of the market collapse, but it was a significant contributing factor.

The next question is: to what extent did Greenspan see it coming? Some might argue that the stock market collapse caught everyone off guard and that it was completely unexpected. There were, of course, warning signs along the way. The market was already tending downward weeks before the crash. But the sheer size of the collapse caught even the most seasoned investors off guard. That does not appear to be the case with Greenspan. He seemed prepared; perhaps not for the breadth and depth of the crash, but prepared, nonetheless. On this point, Beckner writes, "Greenspan says he came into office aware the stock market was in an elevated state and soon ordered internal Fed committees to begin studying how the Fed could best respond to various exigencies, including a sharp market correction" (p. 36). That advance planning served him well. In fact, some might argue that it was perhaps planned too well. Greenspan seemed to be aware of the fact that a significant market correction was forthcoming, and perhaps he even invited it by raising rates. Now it would be difficult to prove that Greenspan planned a market correction of this magnitude, but he seemed willing to prune the excesses of the market to ensure the long-term health of the economy. It was in many ways a sneak preview of Greenspan's tenuous relationship with the market throughout his time as Fed chair, highlighted by his infamous "irrational exuberance" remark.

While it is perhaps easy to criticize the Fed, or Greenspan, in retrospect, we should also give credit where credit is due. Given the fact that the stock market crash here was twice the size of the well-known crash of 1929, the fundamentals were such that the U.S. economy could easily slip into a repeat performance. Indeed, there were theories being circulated at the time that the U.S. was due for a significant economic downturn. In 1988, Ravi Batra, a pop economist in every sense of the word, wrote a book called, *The Great Depression of 1990.* In it he warned that the United States teetered on the brink of the greatest economic depression in history. Considering anecdotal evidence, and unsettling parallels between the roaring 1920s and the 1980s, Batra had captured the popular imagination. Drawing off work in long-term social, monetary, and inflationary cycles, Batra (1987) argued that the downturn was inevitable; it was destined to happen every 60 years or so in capitalist economies. The United States was overripe for its next economic depression in his mind. Greenspan defeated the Kondratiev wave[2] championed by Batra and others, and this

[2] This is a theory that evolves from the work of noted Russian economist Nikolai Kondratiev who claimed that capitalist economies tend to move in long-term economic cycles of boom to bust in 40- to 60-year intervals.

is perhaps why Batra (2005) wrote another book called *Greenspan's Fraud*, published in 2005.

Given the enormous size of the losses, the impact of the stock market crash could have broadened to the economy, and surely some significant ripples were felt, but Greenspan helped to keep the damage contained. He seemed to make all the right moves at all the right times. And he even was able to reconcile his own ideological assumptions with some distance from the crisis. Although, as noted above, there are several theories surrounding the cause of the Great Depression, there seems to be a consensus among economists that the Fed made the problem worse by tightening credit at precisely the time that they should have been loosening it. As a result, the credit markets seized up, and the effects of the stock market crash filtered out to the banks and the economy generally. Greenspan did not repeat this mistake. He knew that what the markets needed more than anything after the crash was liquidity because, among other things, a lot of debts had to be settled given the size of losses in the equity markets. The engines that drove the capitalist machine needed to be greased, and Greenspan's two-step plan saw to that need. In short, Greenspan managed the first economic crisis on his watch with relative poise and confidence. He reassured a worried market and a worried public that there was a steady hand on the wheel. His management of this particular crisis would go far in solidifying his power on the Fed and the Fed's power over the economy. He had made it undeniably clear who was in charge. The public, it seemed, liked what they saw, and they demanded more. And more they would have.

In John Steinbeck's (1993/1940) monumental and Pulitzer Prize-winning novel, *The Grapes of Wrath*, one of the central characters, Ma Joad, along with her family, was trying to earn money to feed their family for the coming winter. They received advice that they could work at a local peach ranch where they would earn five cents for each box of peaches they picked. Upon arriving at work, they were escorted by the police to the ranch. Ma quickly discovered, however, that their wages were only given in the form of credits at the ranch store where she learned the prices were much higher, and the quality much lower. After a full day of work, their total wages barely covered the cost of a modest dinner that still left them hungry. In short, they were given just enough to keep them alive and productive, and nothing more. This state of affairs caused Ma to reflect, "I'm learning one thing good. … If you're in trouble or hurt or need—go to the poor people. They're the only ones that'll help—the only ones" (p. 479). This story serves as a powerful illustration of the complicity of corporate power and government support of the same, the pervasive and pernicious exploitation of the working class, and the inherent inequality of capitalist economics. Steinbeck, of course, spent his formative years growing up in the midst of the Great Depression. His story, rooted in real-life experiences in California during those years, is an instructive exemplar and metaphor for our unsettling economic times.

References

Batra, R. (2005). *Greenspan's fraud: How two decades of his policies have undermined the global economy*. St. Martin's.

Batra, R. (1987). *The great depression of 1990*. Simon & Schuster.

Beckner, S. K. (1996). *Back from the brink: The Greenspan years*. John Wiley & Sons.

Galbraith, J. K. (1955). *The great crash: 1929*. Houghton Mifflin.

McElvaine, R. S. (1984). *The great depression: America, 1929–1941*. Times Books.

Martin, J. (2001). *Greenspan: The man behind money*. Perseus.

Murray, A. (1987, October 21). Stock market's frenzy puts fed's Greenspan in a crucial position. *Wall Street Journal*, p. 1+.

Murray, A., & Ricks, T. E. (1988, January 7). Reagan task force on market crash to recommend limits on daily price moves and stricter management rules. *Wall Street Journal*, p. 3.

Nash, N. C. (1987, December 2). Fed backs regulatory umbrella. *New York Times*, p. D1+.

Nash, N. C. (1988, April 1). Greenspan wary of bill on market. *New York Times*, p. D1.

Ricks, T. E. (1988, May 17). U.S. proposes circuit breakers for markets. *Wall Street Journal*, p. 2+.

Robbins, L. (1934). *The great depression*. Macmillan.

Slumps that shaped modern finance. (2014, April 12). *The Economist*, pp. 49-54.

Steinbeck, J. (1993). *The grapes of wrath*. Random House. (Original work published 1940).

Steinbeck, J. (1994). *The pearl*. Penguin. (Original work published 1947).

CHAPTER 9

Vision Thing: The Savings and Loan Debacle

In 1929, a year that lives in economic infamy as the turning point between opulence and depression, the Daughters of the American Revolution opened their newly constructed annual convention space, Constitution Hall in Washington D.C. It was designated a national historic landmark in 1985 and continues to be Washington D.C.'s largest concert hall.

Comedian Chris Rock, whom *Time* magazine dubbed "the funniest man in America," performed at the DAR Constitution Hall in 2004, the first time in four years he had taken the stage (Farley, 1999). His performances were filmed for his HBO special "Never Scared" (Gallen, 2004). The DVD was released later that year, and a follow-up CD was released in 2005. The historical significance of the venue was not lost on me, nor I suspect, on Chris Rock. He showed no rust in his return to the stage. He was funny, witty, and incisive. And, as usual, he pulled no punches, nor punch lines. Christopher John Farley continued, "Rock's gift is this: he can make hard truths sound funny. It's an invaluable talent in a disinformation age in which it has become more and more difficult to talk about things as they actually are. There's a near constant rush toward metaphorization, toward transmuting events into mediagenic terms."

In a particularly poignant segment, he reflected on the place of money in American culture: "The number one reason people hate America is because of our religion: Americans worship money." He continued, "We all go to the same church: the church of ATM." As noted earlier, the

G. D. Klinger et al., *Money Talks*,
https://doi.org/10.1007/978-3-031-00816-0_9

conflation of money and religion is significant in my estimation. Greed and pursuit of money have been elevated to an almost quasi-religious status. Indeed, Rock concluded, "You know why banks are closed on Sunday? Because if they wasn't, church would be empty."

Earlier we learned that the rise of the ATM conveniently circumvented the legendary "banker's hours," and, consequently, significantly increased the velocity of money. Now you no longer had to rely on the bank being open to get money from your account; you could quite literally access it 24 hours a day. It did not matter how people spent their money, the important thing for the banks was that money was circulating more freely. As Chris Rock humorously quipped, "Have you ever taken out $300 at four o'clock in the morning for something positive?!" Banks were no longer conservative repositories that encouraged saving; they were conduits for stimulating spending and increasing the velocity of money with no regard to how that money was being spent. Further, they practiced what they preached. They not only encouraged individuals to spend more money, but they were more than happy to provide loans to finance this increased addiction to spending and to underwrite increasingly risky investments themselves. People are most familiar with the banking-fueled economic crisis of 2008, but a preview of what was to come played out earlier to much less fanfare in the mid-1980s to early 1990s.

Like many of us, I saw the winds of change in the banking industry first hand. For many years, I did my banking with the National Bank of Detroit, later named NBD bank. This bank has a long and proud history as a regional bank, and was founded in 1933 during the Great Depression under the auspices of the Reconstruction Finance Corporation while so many other banks were failing. The bank had an unusual ownership structure with half its shares owned by General Motors, and the other half owned by the U.S. government. In 1995, NBD merged with the First National Bank of Chicago and was renamed First Chicago NBD. Before I could get used to this new arrangement, in 1998, First Chicago NBD subsequently merged with Bank One, but that was still not the end of the story. In 2004, Bank One, then the sixth biggest bank in the United States, was acquired by J.P. Morgan Chase, itself a hybrid of J.P. Morgan & Co. and Chase Manhattan bank when they merged in 2000. Knowing what I did about J.P. Morgan, I ended my relationship with this new massive banking conglomerate. For me, a bank of this size had lost touch with my desire to do my banking at an institution with local and regional connections and commitments. Additionally, I was also concerned about the growing monopolistic power of certain banks in the industry. Monopolies may create certain efficiencies, but in the end, they grant a few select companies too much power in my estimation allowing them to dominate the market, and in the long run, it is always consumers and customers who suffer while these banks line their pockets with our hard-earned savings. Not only did banking deregulation allow these mega banks to eliminate, or assimilate the competition, but it created corporations that were deemed "too big to fail," the consequences of which I will discuss later.

It is not like corruption within the banking industry is anything new. As I noted earlier, it stretches back to the very beginning of the United States and early debates between Thomas Jefferson, George Washington's Secretary of State at the time, and Alexander Hamilton, Washington's Secretary of the Treasury. There was tremendous popular resistance to the idea of a central, or national bank historically, because people of conscience saw the perils of the consolidation of economic power. Jefferson, among others, saw through Hamilton's scheme and was steadfast in his belief that such consolidation would only benefit wealthy merchants and investors at the expense of the majority of the population. An additional concern, espoused more by James Madison, was that establishing such a national bank was unconstitutional insofar as the Constitution did not explicitly authorize the new Federal Government to establish such a powerful national economic institution, and the 10th Amendment said that any powers not explicitly granted the Federal Government must be reserved for the states or the people. Despite these misgivings, however, Hamilton won the argument with President Washington, at least temporarily, and the First Bank of the United States received a temporary charter in 1791 for 20 years. When the charter came up for renewal, Congress was deadlocked on this issue, and Vice President George Clinton broke the tie, voting against renewal, and the charter was allowed to expire. Five years later, the Second Bank of the United States was founded in 1816. It also received a 20-year charter that was not renewed. President Andrew Jackson, like Jefferson before him, was convinced that the consolidation of banking powers invited corruption, and undermined individual liberty, and he vetoed the re-charter bill.

President Jackson's concerns were well placed, it seems. Beckhart (1972) noted, "The Second Bank which opened for business on January 7, 1817, was at the outset under the control of directors whom Stephen Girard declared had been elected by 'intrigue and corruption.' There were several men on the board, he continued, 'whose occupations, moral characters, or pecuniary situation will not inspire that indispensable confidence which is absolutely necessary to establish and consolidate the credit of that institution" (endnote omitted) (pp. 9–10). The end result of such corruption was not surprising: "The Bank shortly began to overextend itself. Trade was active, prices were rising, and loans were granted with great liberality. ... To mismanagement were added speculation and fraud. Stock speculators gained control of the Baltimore branch, borrowed on the stock of the parent bank, overdrew their accounts, engaged in fraudulent transactions, and caused a loss to the branch of $1.5 million" (endnote omitted) (p. 10).

In the years leading up to the Great Depression, there were several other banking crises, most notably in 1893, and 1907. On these crises, Ben Bernanke (2013) commented, "You can see in the very severe financial panic of 1893, more than five hundred banks failed across the country, with significant consequences for the financial system and for the economy. Fewer banks failed in the panic of 1907, but the banks that did fail were larger" (p. 9). As I noted earlier, J. P. Morgan was intimately involved in the purposefully created banking crisis of 1907, and it eventually led to the creation of the Federal Reserve Bank in 1913 under circumstances that several noted politicians found both suspicious and unpalatable. Indeed, Representative Lindbergh warned that given its new power, the Federal Reserve could scientifically create economic crises at will.

William Greider (1987) noted, "Bank failures increased dramatically during the 1920–21 recession (from 63 in 1919 to 506 in 1921)" (p. 290). The Crash of 1929 "ultimately destroyed 9,800 U.S. commercial banks over the next five years" (p. 299). Further, "a third wave of bank failures swept the country, more severe than the first two. Another five thousand banks would close" (p. 302). Overall, more than 40% of all American banks were destroyed during the Great Depression (p. 296). And commercial banks were not alone. In an eerie foreshadowing of what was to come, the Savings and Loan Industry was hit particularly hard during those years. There were 12,000 savings and loans (then called "building and loan") in the 1920s. More than 1700 failed during the Great Depression, and depositors lost $200 million in savings (Pizzo et al., 1989, p. 9). This led to Congress passing the Federal Home Loan Bank Act in 1932, and creating the Federal Savings and Loan Insurance Corporation (FSLIC) in 1934. These were designed to add regulation, oversight, and stability to the Savings and Loan Industry in order to avoid a similar catastrophe in the future. Inexplicably, those regulations were removed during the 1980s, and to great and historically ignorant pomp.

On October 15, 1982, in a grand ceremony before 200 invited guests, President Reagan signed the Garn-St. Germain Act. It was a hallmark piece of Reagan's agenda to deregulate the banking industry. With the stroke of his pen, Reagan officially removed the regulations governing the Savings and Loan Industry that had been in place since the Great Depression. Self-satisfied with his accomplishment, Reagan tellingly commented, "I think we've hit the jackpot" (Pizzo et al., p. 2). The Garn-St. Germain Act did many things, but "[p]articularly significant was the elimination of limits on loan-to-value ratios—thus permitting 100% financing for the first time—and authority to make commercial real estate loans up to 40% of assets" (Strunk & Case, 1988, p. 56).

This, of course, was not the first piece of legislation that significantly impacted the banking industry, nor was legislation alone involved. Indeed, the Federal Home Loan Bank Board, under the so-called leadership of Richard T. Pratt, authorized Savings and Loans trading in the futures market in July 1981, and permitted financial options in August 1982, among other unfathomable deregulatory moves (Strunk & Case, pp. 55–56). Moreover, the Depository Institutions Deregulation and Monetary Control Act of 1980 required all banks, savings and loans, and credit unions to keep reserves with the Fed. The end result was "a historic consolidation of its institutional power" (Greider, p. 156). Further, "[i]n companion legislation, Congress repealed virtually all of the remaining government limits on interest rates, political regulation of lending that had existed since the New Deal. The price of money was free at last—free to seek whatever level the marketplace dictated" (p. 156). The so-called free market had come home to roost in the banking industry and the primary reason why was no surprise:

> Commercial banks and other financial institutions, ranging from the savings and loan industry to major Wall Street brokerages, contributed generously to congressional campaigns, a major source of financing for the politicians. For the 1980 elections, incumbent senators and representatives would receive $2,664,000 in donations from the financial sector. The largest share of that money, nearly $590,000, was given to the members of the House and Senate banking committees, the people who drafted bank legislation. (Greider, p. 163)

The problem only grew as the crisis deepened. Between 1983 and 1988, "more than 160 political action committees (PACs) representing savings and loans poured almost $4.5 million into House and Senate campaigns, with over $1 million going to members of the banking committees" (footnote omitted) (Calavita et al., 1997, p. 87). Overall, "[t]he Federal Elections Commission reports that 333 representatives, and 61 senators received contributions from the thrift industry in 1988" (p. 87). In short, politicians were effectively bribed to allow the industry to run wild and look the other way. Based on grant-supported research from the Department of Justice, sociologists Kitty Calavita, Henry Pontell, and Robert Tillman concluded, "Evidence suggests that political corruption was at the very heart of the thrift debacle. Sometimes, the evidence is direct and incontrovertible; sometimes the line between business-as-usual and outright corruption is blurred. But in the aggregate, the evidence points to the central role that blatant or implicit political collusion played in the S&L debacle" (p. 86).

Part of the specious legislation that was being passed at the time forced the Savings and Loan Industry to surrender the interest-rate differential they enjoyed over banks. Those who were banking at the time might recall that savings and loans always offered higher interest rates than banks, something that was codified by law, in order to encourage people to deposit their money in these institutions. However, that protection was revoked, and in exchange, the Savings and Loan Industry was allowed to expand their investments into riskier, and potentially more profitable endeavors, like commercial real estate, futures, options, credit cards, secured and unsecured commercial loans, consumer loans, and the like (White, 1991, p. 73). The end result could not have been entirely unexpected: massive failures in the Savings and Loan Industry allowing the major banking powers to acquire their weaker counterparts for pennies on the dollar, much as they had during the Great Depression. Greider continued, "As these weaker lending institutions failed, the larger banking organizations would acquire the remains—a steady consolidation of financial power that enabled Citibank, Chemical, Chase Manhattan and others to build the beginning structures of nationwide banks, preparing for the day when Congress finally would make them legal" (Greider, p. 165).

Although Alan Greenspan had a mixed, but generally supportive relationship with Ronald Reagan, his relationship with George Bush was decidedly more negative. In his autobiography, Greenspan (2007) claimed that the two "ended up with a terrible relationship" (p. 113). While the

Gulf War was great for Bush's approval ratings, "the crisis also threw the economy into recession" (p. 114). Complicating economic matters further in Greenspan's estimation was the collapse of the thrift industry. In 1987, the Savings and Loan Industry had more than 3600 institutions and $1.5 trillion in assets. The massive growth of the industry was largely driven by the deregulation of the Reagan Administration. As noted above, President Reagan led the charge to deregulate the entire industry. The end result is that while it stimulated economic activity in the Savings and Loan Industry, it also led to increased speculation and risky investments. The end result was "the biggest financial disaster since the Great Depression and the biggest heist in history" (Pizzo et al., p. 4).

The loosened regulations and restrictions also led some to commit outright fraud. Charles Keating of Lincoln Savings and Loan was perhaps most publicly noted example of this fraud. Besides defrauding investors, Keating and other Savings and Loan executives had contributed significant amounts to Congressional campaigns raising noteworthy conflict of interest issues. Greenspan was not immune. Indeed, Alan Greenspan was one of the private economists asked to assess the health of Lincoln Savings and Loan in 1985. After a careful study, he concluded that Lincoln's management was "seasoned and expert" and that they had restored "a vibrant and healthy state, with a strong net worth position, largely through the expert selection of sound and profitable direct investments" (Greenspan, 2000). Consequently, Greenspan advised that Lincoln was healthy enough to invest in real estate, which was one of many facets of its ill-advised speculative gambles. To his credit, Greenspan later came clean. In an unusually contrite statement, he told the *New York Times*, "Of course, I'm embarrassed by my failure to see what eventually transpired. I was wrong about Lincoln" (Nash, 1989a, p. D1). He was not embarrassed enough, however, to return the $40,000 he reportedly received for writing his letters of support, and testifying on behalf of Charles Keating (Mayer, 1990, p. 140). Indeed, "[Greenspan's] specialty was what he once called 'statistical espionage,' and the book on him in that capacity was that you could order the opinion you needed" (footnote omitted) (Mayer, p. 140).

Another infamous case was Empire Savings and Loan that alone cost the FSLIC $300 million, but these cases "represented just the first small hint of the financial holocaust to come" (Pizzo et al., p. 4). Besides the blatant fraud of Lincoln, Empire, and others, there were also structural forces at work that exacerbated the problem. The recession pushed up interest rates and this strained balance sheets industry wide. Dan Wall, chair of the Federal Home Loan Bank Board, a group that supervised the Savings and Loan Industry, was worried about the Fed's decision to raise interest rates. He contended that rate hikes would undermine the industry's ability to recover and make losses even worse (Beckner, p. 112). So, a good part of the story involved changes in the economic landscape. The Savings and Loan Industry premised many of their assumptions about the lucrative returns from continued speculative investment upon an economy that would continue expanding without hesitation. This is one of the costs associated with buying into the rhetoric of the free market. People began to believe that economic growth would never retreat, and it only emboldened them to make even more specious and risky investments. However, "When the economic slowdown began to bite in 1989 and worsened in 1990, real estate values collapsed, wreaking havoc with loan portfolios" (Beckner, 1996, pp. 161–162).

It is important for readers to understand that it was not simply risky or unsound investments that led to the Savings and Loan debacle, there was outright looting and collective embezzlement, as well. Depositor money went toward lavish parties, extravagant vacations, condominiums, and resort villas in exotic locations, personal automobiles, private jets, entertainment systems, televisions, elaborate holiday gifts, guns and ammunition, champagne, concerts, statues, and personal items in some especially egregious cases such as $6800 for towels, $19,775 for cashmere throws and comforters, and $18,500 for a letter opener (footnote omitted) (Calavita et al., p. 59). In short, it was not just poor investments that led to the massive losses in the Savings and Loan Industry, but it was outright greed, fraud, and criminal activity, as well.

The types of speculative investments and fraud that sank the Savings and Loan Industry were further emboldened by the continuing deregulation, and loosened restrictions of several markets, including the banking and investment industries. Of course, people and institutions felt safe to take these ill-advised risks, however, given the insurance mechanisms in place. The amount of government insurance on taxpayer-funded deposit insurance more than doubled under Reagan. Despite the appearance of safety that this insurance fund provided, it too was premised on the mistaken assumption of ever-expanding economic growth. When the trouble began, however, it quickly became obvious that the insurance funds have promised things that they could not deliver; there simply were not sufficient funds to cover the losses that emerged from the crisis. Consequently, the FSLIC, the insurance company that guaranteed investor deposits, quickly dried up. It was bailed out several times by taxpayer money, but eventually became insolvent and was abolished by the Financial Institutions Reform, Recovery, and Enforcement Act of 1989. The regulatory authority of the FSLIC was transferred to the FDIC, the government-run insurance company that covered all banks.

If the recession was not enough, the Savings and Loan Debacle put President Bush on the hot seat. While the Gulf War started under President Bush arguably tipped the economy into recession, President Bush had to pay the political price for the economic excess and deregulation of his predecessor, Ronald Reagan. He moved quickly to stop the bleeding when the signs of trouble first started to bubble up.

On February 2, 1989, President Bush first unveiled his "thrift rescue plan" in which he outlined expenditures for bailing out the troubled Savings and Loan Industry. Bush's original estimates pegged the cost of the bailout at $90 billion with, according to Bush Administration officials, the taxpayers being responsible for only 25% of the costs, and the Savings and Loan Industry picking up the remaining 75% (Duke & Seib, 1989, p. A5). That same day, President Bush appointed a committee to oversee the cleanup called the Resolution Trust Corporation. The committee eventually comprised Alan Greenspan, Nicholas Brady, the then-Treasury Secretary, Jack Kemp, the then-Housing and Urban Development Secretary, and two other economists from the private sector.

Within three weeks, Brady significantly revised the original Bush estimate for the bailout upward to $157.6 billion over the next ten years (Nash, 1989b, D5). That same date, in a move similar to the one made the day after the stock market crash, Greenspan promised cash liquidity to any insolvent thrifts short of money, a timely rhetorical message of reassurance (Nash, 1989a, p. A1). He made this claim especially, it seems, to calm depositor anxieties and to prevent a run on these troubled savings and loans which had already seen $15 billion in depositor accounts leave these institutions in the previous two months. Thus, the bad news of Brady was immediately countered by the rhetorical reassurances of Greenspan, reassurances that were by now falling into a discursive pattern. Indeed, one banking analyst suggested, "Greenspan is doing exactly what he did during the stock market crash. He is saying that no one will lack liquidity" (p. A1).

On August 9, 1989, President Bush finally signed legislation authorizing the largest Federal fiscal rescue in U.S. history (Hershey, 1989, p. A1). The cost was now estimated at $166 billion over the next 10 years, and

$300 billion over the next 30 with taxpayers now responsible for over 75% of the costs.[1] Nevertheless, President Bush proclaimed, "This legislation will safeguard and stabilize America's financial system and put in place permanent reforms so these problems will never happen again" (Hershey, p. D2). Ironically, the last time words like this were spoken was in the years following the financial collapse during the Great Depression, yet in later efforts to stimulate the economy, President Bush urged *repeal* of much of the legislation put in place during those years to ensure that the U.S. banking system would remain stable in the future.[2] So, while much of the blame can be placed on Reagan for the deregulation of this and other industries, it seems that President Bush encouraged action that would only exacerbate, rather than ameliorate the fundamental problem at work.

On May 25, 1990, the Bush Administration, in spite of earlier revisions, admitted for the first time that it had "badly underestimated" the cost of the Savings and Loan bailout. The cost was now estimated at more than triple the original Bush figure and stood at $300 billion over the next ten years, and $500 billion over the next 30 years; further, this new estimate only represented costs to the taxpayers and excluded interest payments (Murray & Wessel, 1990, p. A2). That comes to approximately $2000 for every man, woman, and child in the United States by the year 2020 (Mayer, p. 2). There is no hiding behind the misleading veil of "insured" deposits; that money was effectively stolen from every person in the United States. Greenspan, in surprisingly pessimistic tones, suggested that the "size of the hole is astronomical". The tenor of these words was later modified for on September 13, Greenspan, in a statement seemingly antithetical to his aforementioned views on bank deregulation, and perhaps moved again by the perception of a growing banking crisis, suggested that "even more vigilant bank regulation and still higher standards for capital levels could improve the industry's financial security" (Labaton, 1990, p. A1).

Only seven days later, however, in what seems to be a move inconsistent with these words, the Federal Reserve ended the long time ban for

[1] Perhaps the evolution of the Bush Administration's economic rhetoric during these crises is an even more interesting object of study than Greenspan's, but that remains for another day.

[2] Specifically, Bush's "recovery" plan urged the repeal of the Glass-Steagall Act (1933), the McFadden Act (1927), and the Bank Holding Act (1956). The Bush plan received high praise from none other than Alan Greenspan whose sentiments regarding bank deregulation were well-known.

commercial banks to trade in securities, previously enforced under the Glass-Steagall Act of 1933, something that was formalized by the U.S. Congress under the Clinton Administration. The original purpose of this act was to put an end to banks engaging in the often shaky and speculative securities market, actions that were cited as reasons for the unstable conditions of the U.S. banking industry during the Great Depression. Interestingly and symbolically, J.P. Morgan & Co. was the only bank chosen among the five major banks that applied for the right to underwrite securities; Greenspan had previously served as director of J.P. Morgan, a conflict of issue that was raised during his confirmation hearings. Whatever the implications of this observation, it was widely reported that such a "deregulatory move was in sharp contrast to testimony by Federal Reserve Chairman calling for tighter supervision of the largely troubled banking industry" (Duke & Smith, 1990, p. C1). Greenspan's message had become even more complicated, but seemed to be falling into more predictable patterns of response, patterns that negotiated the private intellectual commitments of Greenspan and the need for public reassurances of Fed action.

The Resolution Trust Corporation had been created to clean up the mess, as I note above. The job they had to do, however, was overwhelming given the magnitude of the problem. They essentially had to try and recoup some money from all of these ill-advised real estate investments. Further, they had to act with some alacrity insofar as "vast numbers of uninhabited properties [the RTC] managed were deteriorating rapidly from lack of maintenance" (Greenspan, 2007, p. 116). Writing in retrospect, Greenspan admitted that the situation and the price tag were "not a pretty thought." Bill Seidman, who chaired both the RTC and the FDIC, "calculated that if the RTC sold off $1 million of assets a day, it would need three hundred years to sell them all" (p. 116). Since this seemed an untenable timeline, the RTC decided to sell off huge blocks of real estate for pennies on the dollar. Further, instead of adding legitimacy to the process, the fire sale of assets took the U.S. Federal Government to a new low: they solicited bids from buyers who, in Greenspan's estimation, were less than "savory" and included "so-called vulture funds and speculators whose reputations could have used a face-lift" (p. 117).

Importantly, Martin (2001) observes, "To this day, no one has a clue as to the actual price tag. Estimates range anywhere from $500 billion to $1 trillion" (p. 192). While the amounts are staggering, and the economy still feels the shock from this massive bailout, the lessons from the Savings and Loan debacle were quickly forgotten. If the public and the U.S. Federal Government had pressed harder for more answers, and more accountability, if there has been a more serious inquiry into the root causes of the collapse of the Savings and Loan Industry, perhaps later crises could have been avoided. Despite its size and magnitude, however, the nation quickly returned to business as usual, choosing not to abide by and learn from the lessons the debacle, let alone take any corrective action. It was viewed as an anomaly, a blip on the radar of a continuing economic expansion. It was, in many ways, a dress rehearsal for the economic collapse of 2008 that was similarly linked to banking and investment deregulation, a rise in risky investments coupled especially to untenable positions in a vulnerable and over-extended real estate market. To Greenspan, the "deal looked like a giveaway," and "greedy investors rushed to get in on the action" (2007, p. 117). For those who were outraged by the government bailouts of banks, brokerages, and other companies in 2008, the government liquidation of the Savings and Loan Industry provides an unnerving and instructive analog:

> Deregulation of savings and loans sparked a period of waste and corruption, excess and debauchery the likes of which the nation had not seen since the roaring twenties. The ink wasn't dry on the Garn-St. Germain legislation deregulating the thrift industry, before high-stakes investors, swindlers, and mobsters lined up to loot S & Ls. They immediately seized the opportunity created by careless deregulation of thrifts and gambled, stole, and embezzled away billions in an orgy of greed and excess. (Pizzo et al., p. 4)

While the Savings and Loan debacle was monumental, the real concern was that the crisis would spill over into the banking industry generally. And there were signs that began to raise serious concerns. In the four years of the Bush presidency, nearly 900 banks failed, the highest number since the Great Depression. To claim, however, that these banking failures caught everyone off guard is simply burying one's head in the historical sand. The blissful economic ignorance that marked the Reagan years masked early signs of the problem. Indeed, there were significant warning signs along the way. From 1985 to 1988, almost 500 banks had failed, with the number steadily increasing each year. Even big banks such as Citibank and Chase Manhattan were in trouble. Their problems mirrored those of the Savings and Loan Industry: deregulation has encouraged tremendous amounts of speculative lending. The problem was only exacerbated when the banks tried to cover their early losses by making even more speculative investments hoping for a quick and easy return. Again writing in retrospect, Greenspan said the banks were acting "like amateur gamblers trying to get square they'd bet even more by leading the whole industry into a binge of commercial real estate lending" (p. 117).

When the Savings and Loan Industry began to unravel, this ultimately had a chilling effect on lending practices at banks. Many chose to circle the wagons, and resist any type of new loans, and this created another economic challenge for an economy trying to pull itself out of recession. Significantly, Greenspan admitted in his autobiography, "Nothing we did at the Fed seemed to work. We'd begun easing interest rates well before the recession hit, but the economy had stopped responding. Even though we lowered the fed funds rate no fewer than twenty-three times" (p. 118). The parallels between the banks' reactions to the recession of 1990, and the economic collapse of 2008, are striking. And those who believe that the Fed holds the answers to solving all macroeconomic conundrums are clearly mistaken. People came to believe that Greenspan could save the world, but he now admits that the Fed was and is not up to the task.

Of course, he admitted precious little of this while he was actually Chair of the Fed or in the midst of the crises that unfolded during his tenure. More openness and honesty at the time might have gone a long way toward averting similar and more pronounced crises in the future. Instead, we received constant promises of liquidity and tropes of reassurance, both of which had the effect of convincing the public, and the markets, that nothing was fundamentally wrong and the nation could return to business as usual. The Savings and Loan debacle was not something that materialized overnight in 1989; it was something that had been brewing since at least the mid-1980s, but nobody chose to heed the warnings instead choosing to accentuate the positive in the hope of continuing profitable economic expansion ad infinitum. The Chair of the Fed at the time, while forthright in his autobiography about his concerns, did little to identify, or correct the issues that led to the debacle in the first place. He continued to maintain his unshaken belief in the virtues of the free market, despite growing corruption, greed, and massive economic crises.

President Bush, for his part, did little if anything to solve the problems, either. Indeed, he seemed to only continue the deregulatory excess of his predecessor, Ronald Reagan, and his infamous campaign pledge: "Read my lips: No new taxes!" only extended the Reagan Era tax breaks for big businesses and the wealthy. Given such ideological and political commitments, President Bush seemed totally baffled by the remarkably different results he endured during his one term in office when he compared them to the so-called successes of the Reagan Administration. He believed he had created the same political and economic conditions that Reagan had, so he expected that he would achieve the same results. He sought a scapegoat, and he found one in Alan Greenspan. There was a widespread belief in the Bush Administration that the Fed had created the Recession of 1990 by steadily increasing interest rates in the mid to late 1980s. What Greenspan was trying to do, of course, was engineer an elusive "soft landing" for the economy, but it forced several pointed public clashes between the President and the Chair of the Fed, episodes I will discuss in more depth in the following chapter. Still, turning Alan Greenspan into a scapegoat really diverted attention away from the real issues behind the economic crises of the Bush Administration, the culture of deregulation, greed, and self-interest that dominated the 1980s.

In the almost prescient 2003 film, *Head of State* (Rock, 2003), Mays Gilliam, played by Chris Rock, who also directed the film, is an alderman in a poor neighborhood in Washington D.C.'s 9th Ward. After one party's candidate for president Senator Sam Gaines and his running mate General Olson James died after their planes collided into each other over Virginia ten weeks before the general election, party leaders were discussing who should replace them. Realizing that they would most likely lose the election, they decided to recruit a presidential candidate who would set up a party victory in the following election. One party leader, Senator Bill Arnot, commented, "We need a candidate who will put on a good show." Another, Martin Geller, remarked, however, "It's not a circus, it's a presidential election. You cannot pick just some guy to run for president."

They settled on recruiting Gilliam to run as an unlikely candidate for president because he was recently featured in the news as a local "hero" after saving a woman and her cat from a home that was about to be demolished by explosives. The move was also a more cunning effort to rally and solidify the "minority vote" that party leaders decided that they could then use for the following election in 2008. Senator Arnot mused, "The smartest thing we can do is be the first party to nominate a minority for president. … He'll lose, of course, but the minorities will be happy and they will vote for us in 2008." Of course, Arnot had plans to be the presidential candidate in the following election.

Gilliam's campaign managers tried to mold and control his image initially to use him for their unscrupulous political purposes, but after a rough start to his campaign, Gilliam decided to simply be himself after a pep talk from his brother, Mitch, who tells him he needed to "speak [his] mind" and stand up for the "every day common folk, working people out there" before a major campaign speech in Chicago.

Gilliam decided to turn off the teleprompter, and go off script for that speech, and it was a turning point in his campaign. Gilliam began that speech: "They had a speech written for me about what the people need, but you guys are people; you know what you need: better schools, better jobs, less crime. How many of you, right now, work two jobs just to have enough money to be broke? That ain't right." He continued:

> Now we got these corporations, stealing all the money. They ain't stealing their money, they stealing our money. Your pension. You work for 35 years. You thought you wuz gonna leave your kids a "will," now you gonna leave them a "won't." You show up to get your pension; they give you a pen. They give you a damn pen. Now what the hell am I supposed to do with a pen?! I should just stab you in the neck with this pen, Mr. pension taker. Taking everybody's pension, and nobody going to jail. (Rock)

Feeding off growing enthusiasm from the audience, he concluded the speech:

> How many of you work in a city you can't afford to live in? That ain't right! How many of you work in a mall that you can't afford to shop in? That ain't right! How many of you clean up a hotel you ain't never gonna be able to stay in? That ain't right! And we got nurses that work in hospitals that they can't even afford to get sick in! It ain't right! It ain't right. It ain't right! It isn't right! That shit is wrong! It's dead wrong! I'm Mays Gilliam and I am running for President of the United States of America. (Rock, 2003)

We can learn a lot from comedians, especially ones that have a tinge of political satire embedded in their jokes and performances. As my colleague Kevin Howley succinctly put it in his book, *Drones: Media Discourse and the Public Imagination*: "Scholars have long observed satire's ability to articulate resistant sensibilities and practices" (2018, p. xxviii). One of the greatest political satirists in my estimation is Jonathan Swift. Among other works, he wrote the incisive *A Modest Proposal* in which he proposed consuming babies as a way to deal with the persistent problem of poverty in Ireland. In the Preface to his short satire, *The Battle of the Books*, Swift (2008) commented, "Satire is a sort of glass wherein beholders generally discover everyone's face but their own" (p. 104). Those in power seemed to be looking in all the wrong places to confront the real issues behind the economic crises of the time, and stood idly by as what Martin Mayer (1990) called *The Greatest-Ever Bank Robbery* unfolded on their watch. Indeed, he calls it, "[T]he worst public scandal in American history" (p. 1). While Alan Greenspan provided one distraction and scapegoat for President Bush, another was just over the edge of the horizon as he prepared the nation for war.

References

Beckhart, B. H. (1972). *Federal reserve system.* American Institute of Banking.

Beckner, S. K. (1996). *Back from the brink: The Greenspan years.* John Wiley & Sons.

Bernanke, B. S. (2013). *The federal reserve and the financial crisis.* Princeton University Press.

Calavita, K., Pontell, H. N., & Tillman, R. H. (1997). *Big money crime: Fraud and politics in the savings and loan crisis.* University of California Press.

Duke, Jr., P., & Seib, G (1989, February 7). U.S. taxpayers, thrifts to share cost of rescue. *Wall Street Journal*, A5.

Duke, Jr. P., & Smith, R. (1990, September 21). Fed allows J.P. Morgan to underwrite stocks. *Wall Street Journal*, p. C1+.

Farley, C. J. (1999, September 5). Seriously funny. *Time.* Retrieved August 26, 2014, from http://content.time.com/time/subscriber/article/0,33009,991949,00.html

Gallen, J. (Director). (2004). *Never scared.* Home Box Office.

Greenspan, A. (2000). Letter to Thomas Sharkey, Federal Home Loan Bank. 13 Feb. 1985. Qtd. In Martin, J. (2001). *Greenspan: The man behind money*, p. 191.

Greenspan, A. (2007). *The age of turbulence: Adventures in a new world.* Penguin.

Greider, W. (1987). *Secrets of the temple: How the federal reserve runs the country.* Simon and Schuster.

Hershey, Jr. R. D. (1989, August 10). Bush signs savings legislation: Remaking of industry starts fast. *New York Times*, pp. A1, D2.

Howley, K. (2018). *Drones: Media discourse and the popular imagination.* Peter Lang.

Labaton, S. (1990, September 14). Greenspan urges cautious moves to shore up the banking system. *New York Times*, p. A1+.

Martin, J. (2001). *Greenspan: The man behind money. Perseus.*

Mayer, M. (1990). *The greatest-ever bank robbery: The collapse of the savings and loan industry.* Scribner's.

Murray, A., & Wessel, D. (1990, May 23). Brady to seek new borrowing authority for S and L bailout, possibly tripling total. *Wall Street Journal*, p. A2.

Nash, N. C. (1989a, February 24). Federal reserve says it is ready with cash for savings and loans. *New York Times*, p. A1, D5.

Nash, N. C. (1989b, November 20). Greenspan's Lincoln Savings regret. *New York Times*, D1.

Pizzo, S., Fricker, M., & Muolo, P. (1989). *Inside job: The looting of America's savings and loans.* McGraw-Hill.

Rock, C. (Director). (2003). *Head of state.* DreamWorks SKG.

Strunk, N., & Case, F. (1988). *Where deregulation went wrong: A look at the causes behind the savings and loan failures in the 1980s.* United States League of Savings Institutions.

Swift, J. (2008). The battle of the books. In A. Ross & D. Wooley (Eds.), *A tale of the tub and other works* (pp. 104–125). Oxford University Press. (Original work published 1704).

White, L. J. (1991). *The S&L debacle: Public policy lessons for bank and thrift regulation.* Oxford University Press.

CHAPTER 10

Who You Fighting For? Desert Storm and the Recession of 1990

In 1935, retired United States Marine Corps Major General Smedley D. Butler published, *War Is a Racket.* After retiring from the Marines, Butler went on a nationwide tour giving a series of speeches and radio addresses that critiqued war profiteering, and the use of war to advance commercial interests, especially World War I. His speeches were so popular that he expanded his observations and arguments and published them in his book. The book is divided into five chapters: (1) War is a racket, (2) Who makes the profits? (3) Who pays the bills? (4) How to smash this racket! (5) To hell with war!

In the opening lines of his book, Butler (2016/1935) wrote, "War is a racket. It always has been. It is possibly the oldest, easily the most profitable, surely the most vicious. It is the only one international in scope. It is the only one in which the profits are reckoned in dollars and the losses in lives" (p. 1). He explained precisely what he means by racket: "A racket is best described, I believe, as something that is not what it seems to the majority of the people. Only a small 'inside' group knows what it is about. It is conducted for the benefit of the very few, at the expense of the very many. Out of war a few people make huge fortunes." Indeed, he estimated, "At least 21,000 new millionaires and billionaires were made in the United States during the World War" (p. 1). In the second chapter, Butler gave a detailed accounting of the profits earned by individual corporations that manufactured or provided material support for the war effort. There

G. D. Klinger et al., *Money Talks*,
https://doi.org/10.1007/978-3-031-00816-0_10

was literally no cap on the profit margins, so with inelastic demand and monopoly power over war materials, certain military-oriented corporations were able to essentially charge whatever they wanted. Importantly, he noted, that those who financed the war, bankers, have even greater latitude given the lack of government oversight: "If anyone had the cream of the profits it was the bankers" (p. 5).

While there was certainly money that was made from the Gulf War in 1990 both in its prosecution and aftermath, a fact that I must leave to other writers, the most remarkable things about the prosecution of this war, as it evolved from the defensively oriented Operation Desert Shield to the offensively oriented Operation Desert Storm, was the sheer spectacle of it. I was in graduate school at the University of Iowa at the time, and I remember watching television reporting on the war with shock, and with awe. Those who cared were glued to our television sets with dismay and disbelief. The images coming back from the offensive phase of the war seemed to be like a video game; they were surreal, and they were constant. Significantly, this was arguably the first television war, and it unfolded in real time. No longer did Americans have to wait for the nightly news, or the morning newspaper for updates. The newly evolving news cycle, filled with war images and stories, ran 24 hours a day, 7 days a week. As Andrew Hoskins (2004) observed in his book *Televising War*, "One of the most compelling features for audiences watching in 1991 was that this was the first war that appeared 'live'—unfolding on the screen in 'real time'" (p. 50). Sadly, the media only seemed too happy to oblige with eerily green night-vision images of artillery tracers at night, bold attention-grabbing sound effects and war-colored graphics, and talking heads such as CNN's appropriately named Wolf Blitzer who made a name for himself with his constant updates about the war. There was talk of "smart bombs," or precision-guided munitions, that were designed to limit so-called collateral damage or the loss of civilian lives and infrastructure. There were videos of bombing runs from the moment the bombs were released to the point of impact, and aptly named Patriot missiles shooting down clumsy Iraqi Scud missiles.

The military and the government tightly controlled both the script and the images from the war. As Communication professor Daniel C. Hallin (1994) noted, "The military controlled [journalists'] movements far more tightly than it had in Vietnam, giving them less access to soldiers in the field and making them more dependent on official briefers and experts who could comment on the official briefings" (p. 55). The public was only shown "successful" bombing runs, and military actions, and the independent press had its access significantly limited. Moreover, the Bush Administration purposefully withheld casualty counts on both sides of the conflict, and the short length of the war, lasting just over one month, prevented journalists from developing an independent and critical perspective on the war. President Bush, fully aware of what happens to war efforts that lose public support because of horrifying images and reporting of the war, such as what happened during the Vietnam War, sought to control the spin and distinguish the First Gulf War from that tremendously unpopular war. Indeed, he even made the distinction between the Gulf War and the Vietnam War a major talking point during his War Address announcing the commencement of hostilities in Kuwait and Iraq. As Jarol B. Manheim (1993), Professor of Political Science and Political Communication, noted, "The Bush administration came to the Gulf Crisis with its own lessons, experiences, and concerns. From Vietnam, the administration knew that it would not be possible to prosecute a war in the Gulf without the acquiescence, if not support, of the American people" (p. 165).

Manheim raises an important point: it is difficult for a nation to go to war and remain in the war without popular support. The Bush Administration not only carefully controlled images during the prosecution of the war, but also implicitly condoned the use of false images and information as a pretext for going to war. Indeed, one of the main pieces of evidence that the Bush Administration cited to justify the rush to war was the testimony of "Nayirah" who claimed in tearful testimony before a congressional caucus on October 10, 1990, that she was a volunteer in a Kuwaiti hospital and had witnessed Iraqi soldiers pulling newborns from incubators and leaving them on the floor to die. John R. MacArthur, the publisher of *Harper's Magazine*, claimed in an op-ed piece in the *New York Times* that Nayirah was actually the daughter of the Kuwaiti Ambassador to the United States and never worked in any capacity at the hospital in question. He contended that the whole story had been either totally fabricated or at least grossly exaggerated (MacArthur, 1992, p. A17). Kuwait, through its sponsored "Citizens for a Free Kuwait," actually hired Hill and Knowlton, the largest public relations firm in the world at the time, to manage Kuwait's public response to the invasion, and manipulate public opinion to support the war. Nayirah's allegedly false testimony before Congress was even known in advance and facilitated by

Rep. Tom Lantos of California, co-chair of the Congressional Human Rights Caucus ("Deception," 1992, p. A20). Tellingly, the Congressional Human Rights Foundation, which Lantos helped found, "rents space in Hill and Knowlton's Washington's headquarters at a reduced rate. The same Citizens for a Free Kuwait that produced the mysterious Nayirah also gave $50,000 to the foundation sometime after Iraq's invasion of Kuwait" (p. A20). Observers who were concerned about alleged Russian meddling in the 2016 election should look to the public relations efforts of Hill and Knowlton on behalf of Kuwait in the run up to the First Gulf War. With a total investment of $12 million, it was arguably the most significant foreign-funded attempt to manipulate American public opinion and much of that effort was based on blatant misinformation and misrepresentation, such as the congressional testimony of Nayirah (Goshko, 1992). John MacArthur, who first broke the story about the deception, concluded, "[T]he incubator story seriously distorted the American debate about whether to support the war" (p. A17). In fact, MacArthur noted that seven senators cited the story in speeches supporting the war, and that the war resolution narrowly passed in the Senate by six votes (p. A17). President Bush, for his part, publicly recounted the story at least ten times in his justification for going to war (Walton, 1995, p. 771).

One of the troubling consequences when one tries to control the images of war in an effort to publicize only its "successes" rather than its concurrent "failures" is that the institution of war itself becomes more palatable. As George Orwell reminded his readers in his short column responding to Vera Brittain's *Seed of Chaos*, attempts to sanitize war by setting up artificial rules regarding the conduct of the same only prolongs, even encourages war efforts in the future. It is only when we see how ugly and horrific war really is will there be the popular impetus required to end all wars once and for all. Or, in Orwell's (1944) words, "I can't feel that war is 'humanized' by being confined to the slaughter of the young and becomes 'barbarous' when the old get killed as well. … War is of its nature barbarous, it is better to admit that. If we see ourselves as the savages we are, some improvement is possible, or at least thinkable." As time moves forward, the ability to sanitize war efforts becomes more refined because "[a]s the art of managing conflict evolves so, too, does the art of managing the images of that conflict that are conveyed to the populations of the principals and, increasingly, to a larger world audience" (Manheim, p. 155).

In his jaw-dropping book, *The Fire This Time: U.S. War Crimes in the Gulf*, former U.S. Marine and Attorney General Ramsey Clark (1992) called the First Gulf War a "turkey shoot." He noted that there was a "near-constant roar of U.S. overflights [that] continued for 42 days at an average of one every 30 seconds," and that "[o]ver 80 million pounds of bombs were dropped on Iraqi military placements" (p. 40). Further, "U.S. generals ordered the use of fuel-air explosives (FAEs), napalm bombs, cluster bombs, and the GBU-28 'superbomb' in ways that are inconsistent with international law" (p. 44). The end result was "Iraq lost between 125,000 and 150,000 soldiers. The U.S. said it lost 148 in combat, and of those, 37 were caused by friendly fire" (p. 38). Countless Iraqi civilians lost their lives, as well. The number of lives lost in Iraq is difficult to estimate given the aforementioned steadfast refusal of government officials to gather or release casualty numbers in Iraq. This death and destruction, however, was not the main storyline of the First Gulf War, nor was it the dominant image. Instead, the American public, through the news media, got a precise, decisive, and sanitized war prosecuted with all due alacrity. It came complete with Desert Storm trading cards and a National Victory Celebration Parade in Washington D.C. on June 8, 1991, that cost United States taxpayers $12 million. The triumph of a carefully controlled narrative and image was complete, and the bread and circuses extended into a new decade.

Among other things, the First Gulf War also provided a convenient cover and distraction for a growing economic recession in the United States. It also became a convenient scapegoat for President Bush as the economy turned sour, although the economic downturn started well in advance of the hostilities in Iraq and Kuwait. Moreover, the U.S. Department of Defense estimated that the cost of the war to the United States was $61 billion, but that $54 billion of that was paid by other countries, so the overall financial impact of the war effort was negligible, at best (DOD, 1992, p. 634). U.S. weapons manufacturers, and war financiers, on the other hand, did remarkably well on somebody else's dime.

The third economic crisis is difficult to isolate from the crises described in the previous two chapters for they are intertwined with the larger problem of economic stagnation, but there were independent signs of a growing recessionary situation. In his outlook for the economy in 1988, Greenspan noted that there were "very few signs that we're about to trip over [into recession]" (Murray, 1988, p. 3). That guarded optimism was qualified by Greenspan's testimony before the Joint Economic Committee of Congress less than a month later in which he described the economic outlook for the nation as "satisfactory, but not without risks" (Kilborn, 1988, p. D11). Nevertheless, he held out hope that the possibility of positive economic growth was "relatively good." And such an outlook seemed to prompt the Fed, in what was called a "surprise step," to actually increase in the discount rate from 6.0% to 6.5% in August of that year, the highest level it had been since July 1986, a move that sent international markets tumbling (Sease & Winkler, 1988, p. 3). The increase was designed to check inflationary pressures and was consistent with Greenspan's aforementioned intellectual commitments for monetary policy. Again, however, only weeks after George Bush had been elected, Greenspan's rhetoric took a more pessimistic turn indicating that if the government did not act promptly to balance the budget, "the imbalances in the economy are such that the effects of the deficit will be increasingly felt and with some immediacy" and that failure to bring the deficit down "courts a dangerous corrosion of our economy" (Wessel, 1988, p. A2). Importantly, Greenspan was already shifting blame for the coming economic slowdown. It was not a more restrictive monetary policy that would cause the downturn, but the irresponsible fiscal policy pursued by the legislative and executive branches. In fact, in Greenspan's estimation, monetary policy was constrained by the government's fiscal policies. In this view, he had no choice but to raise rates because of these fiscal excesses.

At one point, growing concerns over the health of the U.S. economy forced a public clash between Greenspan and Bush. Greenspan remained committed to an interest rate policy that checked inflation; in his testimony before the House Banking Committee, for example, he indicated that inflationary pressures were "clearly too high and must be brought down" (Wessel, 1989, p. A2). President Bush, however, argued inversely the very next day that he did "not want to see us move so strongly against fear of inflation that we impede economic growth" (Stout, 1989, p. A2). Greenspan downplayed the clash, however, in testimony before the Joint Economic Committee of Congress seven days later when he characterized the difference between he and Bush as "negligible" (p. A2). Negligible, however, it was not.

The clashes between Bush and Greenspan began early and lasted for four years. Indeed, on the presidential campaign trail in 1988, Bush gave an early indication that he was prepared to pick a very public fight with Greenspan. He offered an early warning to Greenspan and the Fed: "I wouldn't want to see them … ratchet down, tighten down economic growth" (Beckner, 1996, p. 91). All told, "Greenspan and Bush would end up having one of the worst president-Fed chairman relationships ever" (Martin, 2001, p. 188). It got so bad that Bush had to seriously consider whether he was willing to reappoint Greenspan when his term expired. Reluctantly, and perhaps because he had no other viable alternatives, Bush renominated Greenspan during a recess of Congress. This temporary appointment allowed Greenspan to continue to serve until Congress returned and formally took up his nomination.

In a letter to President Bush on March 14, Republican Senators Trent Lott, Orrin Hatch, and Connie Mack urged the President to take a more confrontational approach with the Fed. They observed, "We do not deny that inflation has to be controlled. What we do deny is that it is presently out of control. ... If the Fed persists in tightening credit and raising rates we fear it will be sowing the seeds of a recession" (Beckner, p. 129). Greenspan was beginning to alienate even the most conservative voices in Washington D.C. in part because their own political fates rested on a growing and vibrant economy.

The public clashes between Bush and Greenspan aside, it was clear that the Fed was determined to pursue a policy of fighting inflation first. After a higher than expected rise in the consumer price index, and raising the discount rate to 7.0% in response, Greenspan testified before the Senate Budget Committee that "the risks are very substantially more in the direction of inflation than they are in terms of recession" (Murray, 1989a, p. A2).[1] Greenspan continued to justify his restrictive policy adjustments. In his semi-annual Humphrey-Hawkins testimony before Congress in February 1990, Greenspan claimed, "The current rate of inflation let alone an increase is not acceptable, and our policies are designed to reduce inflation in the coming years" (Beckner, p. 125).

By the summer of 1989, though, the converse situation was becoming slowly more obvious. In June, the Fed reversed course and began easing interest rates, initially refusing to comment on these moves. By late summer, Greenspan had told both the House and Senate Banking Committees that he was confident that the U.S. economy could achieve a "soft landing," (Nash, 1989, p. D2) a term with marked rhetorical significance for it simultaneously admitted the economy was headed down, but implied

[1] Indeed, Greenspan boldly announced that the Fed's long-term goal was to "eliminate inflation," and that the central bank should not even tolerate the 4–5% inflation of recent years (Murray, p. A2).

that it is nothing worse than a plane landing softly. In other words, Greenspan was again trying to paint a picture of financial stability amidst growing uncertainty; his rhetoric had changed in response to the growing perception of a crisis.

While publicly the Fed seemed comfortable with this soft landing language, and they even adopted it during meetings, some were more realistic behind closed doors. John LaWare, for example, claimed in the August 1989 FOMC meeting: "We talk about a soft landing, but this kind of landing looks more to me like being stuck in the mud" (Beckner, p. 139). There were significant differences of opinion on the Fed about the state of the economy, and appropriate Fed responses given the situation. Greenspan's view on the economy seemed to be overly optimistic.

Greenspan's public posturing seemed to be consistent with his private reflections. He was, some may argue, in denial about the state of the U.S. economy. In the August 21, 1990, FOMC meeting, Greenspan claimed, "I think there are several things we can stipulate with some degree of certainty: namely, that those who argue that we are already in a recession I think are reasonably certain to be wrong" (Beckner, p. 195). Ironically, of course, we know in retrospect that he made this statement in the midst of the recession. On the other hand, though, Greenspan hedged his bets, as he always did, and noted the sense of "economic/political turmoil," adding that the nation needed "some stable anchor in the economic system. ... It has to be the central bank. It's got to be we!" (Beckner, p. 195). At the end of the meeting, Greenspan called for a unanimous vote to demonstrate that stability and solidarity.

Martin observes, "Throughout the autumn of 1990, Greenspan refused to acknowledge that a recession had begun. ... Greenspan was willing to admit that the economy was in bad shape. He just wouldn't use the "R" word" (p. 195). It was as if he felt saying it was so, would make it so, and that belief is not too far off base. The Bush Administration was equally adamant about refusing to utter the word "recession," choosing instead, almost jokingly, to refer to it as the "big banana." In the December 18, 1990, FOMC meeting, Greenspan informed the committee that the then-current economic weakness was "without any parallel in the post-World War II period. ... [It was not a recession, but] a balance sheet suppression" (Beckner, p. 212).

Despite his optimism about avoiding a recession, Greenspan was preparing for the worst. The shift became apparent when Greenspan admitted before the House Banking Subcommittee on Domestic Monetary Policy,

"Recent developments suggest that the balance of risks may have shifted somewhat away from greater inflation ... [and that growing economic] softness conceivably could culminate and deepen, resulting in a substantial downturn of activity" (Murray, 1989b, p. A2). He urged, however, in darker tones than usual, that "the balance we are seeking is a delicate one. I cannot rule out a policy mistake as the trigger for a downturn" (A2). Seemingly cognizant of this rhetorical shift, the *Wall Street Journal* reported that the "Fed Chairman's comments were a far cry from his testimony at the beginning of the year" (A2).

The economic situation in the U.S. grew increasingly uncertain, however, as it moved toward a "technical" recession and it forced Greenspan, again, into a rhetoric of reassurance. One early symbol of growing uncertainty in the U.S. economy occurred on October 13, 1989, when the Dow Jones Industrial Average dropped 190 points, the largest drop since the crash in 1987. Greenspan privately told government officials both in the U.S. and abroad, in moves similar to those following the 1987 crash, that the Fed was prepared to make money available to avoid a financial crisis (Murray, 1989c, C1). This time, however, Greenspan made no public pronouncement of the same because he did not want, in the words of one government official, "to reinforce a sense of [market] crisis" (C1). In the *Wall Street Journal* of October 16, Greenspan suggested that he was surprised that his private sentiments were made public (C1); the next day, the market rallied some 88 points during the fourth largest trading day in its history. Thus, even in silence, the rhetoric of Alan Greenspan had a significant economic and political impact.

The following year, the reassurances of Greenspan grew stronger amid a growing public perception of recessionary times. On January 30, 1990, Greenspan testified before the Joint Economic Committee of Congress that "such imbalances and dislocations as we see in the economy today do not suggest anything more than a temporary hesitation in the continued expansion of the economy" and that he put "the probability of a recession the next six months at about 20 percent" (Wessel, 1990a, p. A2).[2] The Fed's semi-annual Monetary Policy Report before the House Subcommittee on Domestic Monetary Policy reaffirmed the following month that the

[2] Greenspan's testimony here marked the beginning of increased qualification of his statements regarding the health of the U.S. economy. For example, he qualified the fairly specific claim that the chance of recession for the economy was only 20% by claiming that he "wouldn't bet the ranch on such statistical figures" (Wessel, 1990a, p. A2).

chances of recession have been reduced and that the "point of weakness may have passed" (Wessel, 1990b, p. A2).[3]

In November of the same year, however, President Bush finally formally admitted that the U.S. economy was in a recession and he moved to link its occurrence with the tensions in the Gulf; it seems that everyone needs a scapegoat when the economy turns sour. Later that month, Greenspan declared that "a meaningful downturn in aggregate output" had occurred, but in his usual style, he tried to put the best face on this news by carefully avoiding the word "recession" and arguing, "The world out there, when you look at the hard data, is not in as bad [of] shape as it feels" (Murray, 1990, p. A2). In his annual report, Greenspan made what the *Wall Street Journal* called "carefully hedged comments." He testified, "It would be most unwise to rule out the possibility that the recession may become more serious than already is apparent. Nonetheless, the balance of forces does appear to suggest that this downturn could well prove shorter and shallower than most prior postwar recessions" and that signs were "very gradually emerging" that the recession would bottom out "in the very near future" (Murray, 1991, p. A2). On March 6 and March 13, Greenspan gave largely identical remarks before the House Ways and Means Committee and the Joint Economic Committee of Congress, respectively; in this testimony, he argued, "The scales appear to tip slightly in favor of suggesting that the current downturn might prove milder than most of the recessions in the past 40 years" and that "I think the turn [upwards] is going to occur in a reasonably short period of time" (Wessel, 1991a, p. A2). His discourse had, by now, taken a noted optimistic shift in looking for the light of recovery at the end of the recessionary tunnel.

When it became more apparent that this recession would be much deeper than other similar recessions, and after George Bush had coined the catchy and rhetorically powerful phrase "double dip" recession, a phrase which invoked pleasant thoughts of ice cream cones, Greenspan noted that the economy was "having significant difficultly in bouncing [upwards]" due to an "utterly unprecedented" credit crunch, but he held out hope for "a much improved long term economic outlook" (Bulkeley, 1991, p. A2). One month later, Greenspan admitted that the economy

[3] It seems now, however, there was a widening gap between the careful, reassuring picture Greenspan was attempting to create, and general perception among forecasters who suggested that his conclusion was "way premature," and that "the weakness hasn't passed, and the economy will grow weaker" (Wessel, 1990c, p. A2).

had entered "a pause," and that the recovery "clearly ha[d] faltered" (Wessel, 1991b, p. A16). The *Wall Street Journal* noted that his discourse had again taken a significant shift: "Mr. Greenspan, the nation's most powerful economist, painted a picture that was strikingly different from the one he provided in his last appearance on Capitol Hill in July" (A16).

On September 27, 1991, Greenspan was summoned to the White House. In public, Greenspan had focused on the positive aspects of what he believed to be a growing recovery, but he told President Bush that the economy was "moving into a 50-mile per hour headwind" (Beckner, p. 247). This was a phrase that he later repeated several times in public when it became clearer that the expected recovery was faltering.

Nevertheless, he still claimed amidst these comments that the "longer term outlook is actually improving" (A16). As the U.S. economy began to finally pull itself out of its second dip, Greenspan again hedged his bets in emphasizing that he was "cautiously optimistic," but that the new signs of economic growth "could just as easily peter out, as indeed the much more vigorous recovery of last spring petered out" (Wessel, 1992, p. A2). This time, the economy seemed to at least temporarily pull itself out of a technical recession and, once again, Greenspan had rhetorically negotiated his way through troubled economic waters with guarded optimism as the overarching message, but a message that consistently sent out mixed signals, at best.

As was the case with the previous two crises that we considered, there is the question about Fed complicity in causing the recession. Discussions in the FOMC before the onset of the technical recession seem to support this hypothesis. There was one FOMC meeting in 1989 where voting members seriously considered the prospects for zero inflation, and what would need to happen to achieve that goal. Most members admitted that such an ambitious move against inflation would stifle as least short-term economic growth. This seemed to be a price that Greenspan was willing to pay at the expense of a recession and George Bush's political future. At one point in the meeting, Greenspan contended, "[I]f we could come through this period even with a mild recession, or preferably none whatsoever, I think the credibility of this institution would be such by the fall of 1990 that we could probably write our own policy ticket" (Beckner, p. 157). While Greenspan marveled at the prospect, he was also concerned about the impact that such a belief, trading a recession for lower inflation, would have on the public. He advised members of the FOMC to not reveal the nature or content of their discussions on the issue.

Despite the differences of opinion and the potential political fallout on the issue, Greenspan adopted a tightening stance that in many ways enacted this hypothetical model. "In effect, Greenspan rolled the dice and hoped the economy would skirt recession so he could continue his battle against inflation" (Beckner, p. 193). The problem was, as was the case with the stock market collapse in 1987, things do not always go according to plan. Not only did the Gulf War provide a convenient scapegoat for President Bush, Greenspan blamed the recession on these hostilities, as well. "It is still a matter of considerable debate whether the sluggish economy would have gone into recession without [the Gulf War]. One thing is clear: economic data had already turned negative" (Beckner, p. 192). Greenspan's view on the subject was less than scientific: "my inclination is to presume that, were it not for the Gulf War, we would not have had a recession, but if you asked me to prove it I would not be able to do so" (Beckner, p. 214). Greenspan had hoped for a slowdown in economic growth aimed at combating future inflation; he most likely did not want to see a recession. That is perhaps why it took him so long to admit that the economy was in recession: he did not want to admit that he had been wrong.

Beckner argues, "Administration suspicions that the Fed was courting recession were not far wrong. ... Recently released FOMC transcripts reveal the Fed was consciously flirting with recession. It was a price some Fed officials thought was worth paying to kill inflation" (p. 69). Others, like Edward Kelley, another distinguished member of the Fed's Board of Governors, recognized that raising rates too quickly to fight future inflation would create a myriad of monetary and fiscal problems: exacerbating issues in the Savings and Loan industry, inviting recession, and worsening the budget deficit. His sentiments were almost prophetic, but Greenspan still held the line and continued to commit to higher rates, downplaying any signs of weakness in the economy.

In the end, President Bush blamed Alan Greenspan for losing his reelection bid in 1992. Indeed, in a 1998 interview, Bush claimed, "I think that if the interest rates had been lowered more dramatically that I would have been reelected president because the recovery that we were in would have been more visible. I reappointed [Greenspan], and he disappointed me" ("Bush pins the blame," 1998). Bush was not alone in his criticism: "There were those within the system who also questioned the way Greenspan had steered policy. The main charge: unpredictability" (Beckner p. 280). Some felt that a series of confusing, often-conflicting statements was undermining the credibility of the Fed. As it happened, though, the Fed was on the brink of perhaps its most pronounced credibility ever in the coming years. With a new administration, and a new set of economic circumstances, Greenspan grew in fame, and the Fed grew in power.

Desert Storm was little more than misdirection, a convenient scapegoat for those in political and economic power to blame their own poor forecasting and decisions on the cost of war. What is lost in this calculation, however, is the fact that the real cost of the war can never be reckoned with dollars and cents. As Major General Smedley Butler sadly concluded: "This bill renders a horrible accounting. Newly placed gravestone. Mangled bodies. Shattered minds. Broken hearts and homes. Economic instability. Depression and all its attendant miseries. Back-breaking taxation for generations and generations" (p. 1). As was the case with the Savings and Loan debacle, the confluence of economic crisis and the prosecution of war under President George H. W. Bush were just a preview of what was to come under another Bush presidency, when his son, George W. Bush, invaded Iraq in 2003 under the auspices of the Orwellian moniker "Operation Iraqi Freedom."

References

Beckner, S. K. (1996). *Back from the brink: The Greenspan years.* John Wiley & Sons.

Bulkeley, W. (1991, October 29). Greenspan, grim on economy, cites regulators, banks. *Wall Street Journal*, A2.

Bush pins the blame for '92 election loss on Alan Greenspan. (1998, August 25). *Wall Street Journal*, A16.

Butler, S. D. (2016). *War is a racket.* Skyhorse Publishing. (Original work published 1935).

Clark, R. (1992). *The fire this time: US war crimes in the Gulf.* Thunder's Mouth Press.

Deception on Capitol Hill. (1992, January 15). *New York Times*, A20.

Department of Defense. (1992). *Conduct of the Persian Gulf War: The final report to congress.* (Appendix P). United States Department of Defense.

Goshko, J. M. (1992, July 8). US ex-envoy indicted in Kuwaiti "fronts." *Washington Post.* Retrieved November 14, 2017, from https://www.washingtonpost.com/archive/politics/1992/07/08/us-ex-envoy-indicted-in-kuwaiti-fronts/b17e1a35-b902-4d71-91b4-1fe10dd5eaf7/.

Hallin, D. C. (1994). Images of Vietnam and the Persian Gulf. In S. Jeffords & L. Rabinovitz (Eds.), *Seeing through the media: The Persian Gulf War* (pp. 45–57). Rutgers University Press.

Hoskins, A. (2004). *Televising war: From Vietnam to Iraq*. Continuum.
Kilborn, P. T. (1988, March 16). Fed chairman finds economy is stronger. *New York Times*, D1.
MacArthur, J. R. (1992, January 6). Remember Nayirah, witness for Kuwait? *New York Times*, A17.
Manheim, J. B. (1993). The war of images: Strategic communication in the gulf conflict. In S. A. Renshon (Ed.), *The political psychology of the Gulf War: Leaders, publics and the process of conflict* (pp. 155–172). University of Pittsburgh Press.
Martin, J. (2001). *Greenspan: The man behind the money*. Perseus.
Murray, A. (1988, February 24). Greenspan confirms fed allowed interest rates to decline recently: but chairman is optimistic on economy, indicating more easing isn't likely. *Wall Street Journal*, 3.
Murray, A. (1989a, March 1). Fed chairman defends move to raise rates: Greenspan denies recession will be triggered, hints at further tightening. *Wall Street Journal*, A2.
Murray, A. (1989b, July 21). Greenspan predicts economy will slow, says there's risk of substantial downturn: Fed chief thinks recession unlikely; board poised for further rate cuts fed economic projections. *Wall Street Journal*, A2.
Murray, A. (1989c, October 16). Fed ready to inject big funds. *Wall Street Journal*, C1.
Murray, A. (1990, November 29). Greenspan says GNP likely to fall: Fed chief stops short of stating recession in 4th-period forecast. *Wall Street Journal*, A2.
Murray, A. (1991, February 21). Fed chief indicates agency isn't seeking lower rates Greenspan tells congress he sees signs recession will bottom out soon. *Wall Street Journal*, A2.
Nash, N. C. (1989, August 2). Greenspan says fed is continuing to ease credit. *New York Times*, D2.
Orwell, G. (1944, May 19). As I please. *Tribune*. Retrieved November 14, 2017, from https://orwell.ru/library/articles/As_I_Please/english/eaip_01.
Sease, D. H., & Winkler, M. (1988, August 10). Stocks, bonds plunge, dollar soars as fed lifts discount rate to 6.5%. *Wall Street Journal*, 3.
Stout, H. (1989, February 1). Greenspan defends fed's tightening, minimizes policy differences with Bush. *Wall Street Journal*, A2.
Walton, D. (1995). Appeal to pity: A case study of the argumentum ad misericordiam. *Argumentation, 9*(5), 769–784.
Wessel, D. (1988, November 17). Greenspan says federal deficit can't be outgrown, stresses cuts in spending over boosting revenues. *Wall Street Journal*, A2.
Wessel, D. (1989, January 25). Fed chief says inflation is "too high," warns of continued drop in jobless rate. *Wall Street Journal*, A2.
Wessel, D. (1990a, January 31). Greenspan sees a lower risk of recession: Current economic slowing is temporary, fed chief tells congressional unit. *Wall Street Journal*, A2.

Wessel, D. (1990b, February 21). Greenspan says economy might have hit nadir: Fed chief may welcome a slow economy in '90, to help cut inflation. *Wall Street Journal*, A2

Wessel, D. (1990c, February 22). Greenspan's optimism on US economy isn't widely shared among forecasters. *Wall Street Journal*, A2.

Wessel, D. (1991a, March 7). Greenspan sees recession's end relatively soon fed chief cites cheaper oil, ending of gulf conflict; but he adds a warning. *Wall Street Journal*, A2.

Wessel, D. (1991b, December 19). Recovery has faltered, Greenspan says, citing efforts to slash debts from '80s. *Wall Street Journal*, A16.

Wessel, D. (1992, February 20). Greenspan sees "stirrings" of recovery, comments suggest rate cut isn't likely. *Wall Street Journal*, A2.

CHAPTER 11

Telling Stories: Interrogating "Irrational Exuberance"

In the novel *A Tenured Professor*, Harvard economist John Kenneth Galbraith[1] (1990) tells the story of Montgomery Marvin, an aspiring young economist striving to obtain both tenure at Harvard and tremendous personal wealth. Trained at Harvard, Cambridge, and UC Berkeley, Professor Marvin developed a fairly unconventional measure of a company's financial health. Dubbed the "IRAT," or Index of Irrational Expectations, this econometric model "'identifies, isolates, measures and acts on irrational expectations,'" according to his colleague, Professor Grierson (1990, p. 9). By studying past instances of irrational thought and behavior, such as the manic speculation that ran rampant in the United States in the years leading up to the Great Depression, Marvin was able to isolate and analyze moments in history when "the intelligence of the individual had given way to the self-reinforcing delusions of the crowd" (p. 55). He realized that his model "applied not only to individuals. Institutions could also be lifted up to and forced down from euphoric heights" (p. 57). His first case study, appropriately, given what we know

[1] Ronald Reagan was no fan of Galbraith. In his 1975 speech to the Rotary Club in Oakland, Reagan commented: "John Kenneth Galbraith, who in my opinion is living proof that economics is an inexact science, has written a new book, Economics and the Public Purposes. In it he asserts that 'market arrangements in our economy have given us inadequate housing, terrible mass transportation, poor health care, and a host of other miseries.' And, for the first time to my knowledge, he gives socialism as the answer! But he deals in fairy tales" (p. 9).

G. D. Klinger et al., *Money Talks*,
https://doi.org/10.1007/978-3-031-00816-0_11

now, was Bank of America. In that case, Marvin sought to identify "how much of its present position and currently glowing prospect was based on reality, how much on the euphoria born of past success and unsupported hope" (p. 58). In order to develop an actual numerical measure for the IRAT as he applied it to specific companies, Marvin carefully studied "press comment, executive speeches, interviews in the San Francisco financial community, company advertising and some discreet conversations with middle and upper management" (p. 58).

The IRAT was a unique model because its predictive power was built upon an assumption of irrationality in the marketplace rather than the traditional rationality assumption embedded in the vast majority of microeconomic and macroeconomic models, a presupposition that we challenged in the introduction. Indeed, as Professor Grierson observed, "Other models, other perceptions of the future, assume rational behavior, rational responses, rational expectations" (p. 9). Marvin used his model to identify companies that were built on irrational hype, rather than solid economic fundamentals, and sold them short in the stock market resulting in significant profits when the hype was revealed, and the stock price spiraled downward.

Marvin's second case study was a collection of banks and savings and loan associations in Texas. He recognized that the financial position of many of these institutions, as was the case with Bank of America, was built upon hype, past successes, and unwarranted faith. Specifically, it was built off the belief that one "must have faith in Texas, faith in America, faith in the free enterprise system and faith in oil" (p. 66). Moreover, the FDIC and FSLIC insurance programs that sought to assure citizens and customers that their deposits were safe in these banking and savings and loan institutions further buttressed this unwarranted faith. In short, these insurance programs both assured depositors, but simultaneously encouraged risky lending practices because if these investments failed, the government would step in with relief funding to bailout any financially distressed banking institutions. Writing in 1990, and with a sage sense of foreshadowing, Galbraith identified an inherent problem with the deregulatory schemas of the 1980s; they essentially created institutions that were "too big to fail." Marvin essentially realized the same unsettling state of affairs in the banking and savings and loan industries that he was studying in Texas, and the insurance programs designed to assuage depositor anxiety while emboldening bad behavior by these institutions' money managers, namely, "the certainty that no really large financial institutions would be allowed to fail" (p. 66). The free market was and continues to be embraced only when there are profits to be made, and results trend in a positive direction. When things turn sour, and profits turn to losses, this unmitigated faith in the free market is quickly jettisoned by even the most ardent supporters of laissez-faire capitalism. In short, the banking insurance programs ensured "business could expand, risks could be taken, without the threat or thought of a devastating end. Free enterprise but with the ultimate and benign support of socialism" (p. 66).

Importantly, Marvin recognized that the "dementia that they measured could be individual … institutional … collective … [or] a further possibility, as here in Texas: it could be compelled. There was no other choice but to conform, march in lock step to the inevitable collapse" (p. 68). Originally, Marvin used his model only to identify irrational hype in individual corporations, but he came to realize that it had much broader implications. By the middle of the 1980s, Marvin observed, "Irrationality was becoming general; euphoria was becoming endemic and universal" (p. 83). This tendency was nowhere else more evident than in the unrelenting march upward of the stock market during the 1980s. The rise of program trading, portfolio insurance, index trading, and option trading only exacerbated this tendency (p. 84). The euphoric bubble that this trend engendered was burst on October 19, 1987, during what came to be known as "Black Monday." Of course, positive spins were immediately placed on this catastrophic downturn, as continues to be the case with any significant market downturn, it was nothing more than a healthy "correction." In this case, it was "'[a] major correction,' said Marvin, falling easily into the approved reference" (p. 90). Of course, Marvin saw this coming given the accuracy of his IRAT model, and he bet heavily on the downturn, making perhaps his most significant market gains to date. Trying to hide the fact that he was making enormous sums of money while others were having their life savings erased, Professor Marvin listened empathically to an unnamed Harvard Alumnus who commented on the market crash: "'It was bad. I hope someone in Washington comes out tomorrow—should be Reagan himself—with a reassuring statement. Stress that the economy is fundamentally sound'" (p. 93). We know now that this responsibility fell to Alan Greenspan, as it did every time there was an economic crisis during his tenure as Chair of the Federal Reserve. Galbraith observes, "At all cost the sanctity of the securities market had to be protected. … One cannot harbor doubts as to the essential virtue of the greatest of free enterprise institutions" (p. 95). As such, the rhetorical and monetary responses of figures like Alan Greenspan and Ben Bernanke are entirely predictable. They sought to prop up the market, and the institutions that dominate the market during times of economic crisis. They were essentially the voice of capital. The mechanisms of the market were never to blame. Indeed, in the "ensuing months [after Black Monday] diverse commissions were impaneled to identify a deeper, more persuasive cause. It was decided that the casino adjuncts of the market—program trading, index trading, option trading, and portfolio insurance ... were to blame" (p. 96).

Despite the impeccable accuracy of his IRAT model, Marvin's goal was not simply to get rich, but to use his new wealth for what he perceived to be positive social change in society. In explaining his vision to his Harvard colleague Professor McKrimmon, Professor Marvin mused, "I'm going to be an economist, but I want to make my small contribution to the liberal agenda. Peace, a better break for the poor and the inner cities, greater equality in income distribution, government assuming its proper responsibilities" (p. 38). McKrimmon advised that such a goal was "most unwise" because "[y]ou simply will not get tenure" (p. 38). The tenure system, according to McKrimmon, was originally designed to "protect radical professors," but now it works to screen such professors out (p. 38).

True to his word, Marvin invested in initiatives like the EXEGES program, a program supported by his partner, Marjorie Bradford, aimed at increasing the ranks of women executives at major corporations. He also relieved Harvard of its investments in South Africa because of their direct and indirect support of Apartheid. Marvin also funded peace professorships and programs at U.S. Military Academies, and took controlling interests in major defense contractors requiring them to begin to pursue peace initiatives, and defund the development of programs like the Strategic Defense Initiative, or "Star Wars" program. Finally, he created a program of PRCs, or Political Rectitude Committees as a counter-balance to the increasing influence of largely unregulated influence of Political Action Committees in American politics.

Because of the remarkable success of the IRAT, his massive accumulated wealth, and his subsequent political and economic interventions, Professor Marvin was investigated by the SEC, the FBI, and the OMB, he was called before a Congressional committee, and he even drew some criticism from groups at Harvard. The reasons for this increased scrutiny and disdain were varied, but they seemed to coalesce around three major threads: betting on market failures was inherently un-American, political and economic activism in defense industries especially was unpatriotic and dangerous, and, finally, anyone who makes such enormous sums of money in so little time must be doing something unethical. During their first visit to Professor Marvin, agents from the SEC commented, "'[T]here's something odd about your being so much on the negative side. Americans are meant to be optimistic. This country is built on optimism'" (p. 137). Marvin's interrogation by the House Banking, Finance, and Urban Affairs Committee seemed to echo this concern. Indeed, one committee member asked, "'[D]on't your operations imply a serious lack of faith in the American free enterprise system?'" (p. 159), and another "asked Marvin if his exploitation of irrationality was not out of step with the system" (p. 161). Because of the limits he was trying to place on the defense industry, the Assistant Deputy Under Secretary of the Army remarked, "'This company by its arrogance is putting the very essentials of our nation's defenses at risk'" (p. 179). This was deemed unpatriotic because "[t]he American commitment to a strong defense is no casual thing; it is permanent and enduring" (p. 181). Finally, there was a widespread belief that penetrated even the walls of Harvard that "no one can get very rich in a very short time without crossing the ill-guarded border into chicane or outright crookedness" (p. 133).

In previous chapters, I demonstrated that the vast majority of Greenspan's power stemmed from his image and his rhetoric. Indeed, reflecting upon the monetary power of the Fed in the years leading up to the Recession of 1990, Greenspan admitted in his autobiography that the actual monetary intervention of the Central Bank in the economy had little, if any, practical effect. While attentive to the power of his words earlier in his tenure, Greenspan seemed to come to believe that he could move markets, engineer soft landings, burst bubbles, and foment recoveries simply through his rhetorical power. Perhaps nowhere else is this self-deluded belief in the power of his rhetoric evident than in his use of the phrase "irrational exuberance" as an attempt to stem the speculative bubble that had developed in the marketplace. Perhaps concerned that the Fed's proactive policy initiatives had failed to engineer a soft landing instead of a full-blown recession in 1990, Greenspan turned more vigorously to a proactive rhetorical program.

After the "irrational exuberance" comment, "Greenspan the mortal was fast becoming Greenspan the myth—a man who could literally move markets" (Martin, 2001, p. 216). Greenspan came to see himself as someone who was larger than life, and the media only reinforced this view. While he had negotiated his way into the limelight, the media was complicit in placing Greenspan in a position that no other Fed president before him had enjoyed. He became the defining voice for nearly every economic issue, and given the new centrality of the economic paradigm in everyday life, he became the central figure of contemporary popular culture.

As I noted above, while the only formal tool available to the Fed to impact the economy is monetary policy, the Fed generally, and Greenspan specifically, developed a novel new dimension of their power: rhetoric. And this new power was one that Greenspan used more boldly later in his tenure. Besides policy adjustments, "[a]bout the only other tool the Fed has is talk. Many of Greenspan's public statements were seen as jawboning, an effort to talk the stock market down into more comfortable territory" (Martin, p. 232). As I noted earlier, the Recession of 1990 was a test case, an attempt to check back speculative excess to ensure more sustainable economic expansion. In that case, the Fed relied more on its traditional tools of manipulating the economy: managing monetary policy through interest rate adjustments. This effort failed as the economy tripped over into a fairly pronounced recession. And the attempt to revive the economy from its recession through its traditional monetary tools was equally deemed a failure by Greenspan. The problem was that monetary tools provided little power to effect significant policy change with any alacrity:

> The Fed has limited influence on inflation because the problem can come from many sources, both domestic and international. ... The Fed can tweak overnight interest rates, and fine-tune the language in its press releases, but neither will have much influence on real growth and inflation. The transmission belt between monetary policy and real growth can be long and complex, and the transmission belt between monetary policy and inflation is even less direct and more complex. (Santow, 2009, p. 227)

Greenspan apparently came to believe that more was needed from the Fed than these traditional policy tools if it were to succeed at engineering a soft landing or smooth recovery in the future.

That future was not too far off. President Bush lost his reelection bid in 1992, and a Democrat was elected president for the first time in 12 years. Many observers believed that the single issue that cost Bush the election was the sputtering economy. Indeed, even those on the Clinton election campaign recognized this important single issue in emphasizing its bid for the presidency by articulating its simple one-line theme for the campaign: "It's the economy, stupid."

Despite their obvious political and ideological differences, Greenspan seemed to value his relationship with Clinton. In his biography, he reserved his most outspoken praise for President Clinton. He was particularly enamored by Clinton's grasp of economic policy. While he shared intellectual commitments with Reagan about the merits of a free market, he felt that only Clinton truly grasped how fiscal and monetary policy must work in unison. Monetary policy, in his estimation, worked best when a nation's fiscal economic house was in order. So, while he shared basic free market sentiments with Reagan, he loathed the fact that Reagan built so much of his economic expansion upon significant and growing budget deficits. Clinton demonstrated more fiscal responsibility than either of his predecessors and turned the massive budget deficits of the Reagan-Bush years into budget surpluses.

Greenspan first met President-elect Clinton in December of 1992, just weeks after the presidential election. Clinton had not even moved to Washington D.C. yet, so Greenspan was summoned to the Governor's mansion in Little Rock, Arkansas. Clinton clearly had his priorities straight and recognized the power that Greenspan held over the economy. Given that President Bush had blamed his loss squarely on Greenspan, Clinton wanted to make friends with the Chair of the Fed as soon as he could. Greenspan left the meeting with the following impressions: here was a president who was "fully engaged," who "asked a lot of smart questions," and was a "fellow information hound" (Greenspan, 2007, p. 144). In assessing the President overall, Greenspan had this to say: "I walked away impressed, yet not entirely sure what I thought. Clearly, for sheer intelligence, Bill Clinton was on par with Richard Nixon, who, despite his obvious flaws, was the smartest president I'd met to that point" (p. 144). He continued, "[E]ither Clinton shared many of my views on the way the economic system was evolving and on what should be done, or he was the cleverest chameleon I'd ever encountered" (p. 144).

A difficult fiscal road confronted Clinton. While the economy had derailed the Bush presidency, that same economy threatened to sour his first years as president. Under the Reagan-Bush years, the federal deficit had ballooned to over $3 trillion. Such a dire fiscal situation certainly constrains policy initiatives. Greenspan concurred about the troubling fiscal legacy of the Reagan-Bush years: "Though I hadn't put it in so many words, the hard truth was that Reagan borrowed from Clinton, and

Clinton was having to pay it back" (p. 147). The same dynamic unfolded during the George W. Bush presidency. Bush the younger left Obama with a financial catastrophe, and the early years of Obama's presidency were dominated by his efforts to right the ship.

Clinton worked mightily during his first two years in office to set the United States' fiscal house in order. He crafted fiscally responsible budgets, and both the economy and the markets responded favorably. The real GDP had grown at an 8.5% pace since the end of the recession, and had settled on a robust annual rate of 5.5%. While Greenspan seemed pleased with the economic turnaround, economic growth raised the specter of Greenspan's white whale: inflation. While the actual evidence of inflation at the time was scant, Greenspan always endeavored to move against inflation before it reared its ugly head. Consistent with Greenspan's beliefs about acting early to combat inflation, the decision to begin raising rates was a proactive move to stop future inflation. Indeed, on the surface at least, inflation seemed dormant. The Consumer Price Index had only risen 2.6% in 1993. Greenspan commented on the move to proactively act against inflation despite the lack of evidence of the same in his biography. The move, he admitted, was a "more radical approach: moving gently and preemptively before inflation even appeared" (p. 154). Importantly, he continued, "It was a matter of psychology" (p. 154). The last point is significant given the aforementioned connections between rhetoric and social psychology. Greenspan was steadily becoming more aware of his rhetorical power, and the rhetorical implications of his monetary policies. He was more attentive to his discourse, especially that which accompanied policy changes.

Consistent with the above, and despite actual evidence of inflation, Greenspan decided it was time to put on the brakes, and begin steadily increasing interest rates beginning in 1994. It was his second attempt at engineering a soft landing, and he hoped to have more success this time. On January 21, 1994, Greenspan informed Clinton and his economic advisers that he intended to raise interest rates. "Clinton was furious and viewed the move as a betrayal. It seemed as though Greenspan was going back on his word" (Martin, p. 204). In early meetings, Clinton and Greenspan seemed to have reached a mutual agreement: if Clinton would get serious about deficit reduction, Greenspan would have more flexibility in pursuing a looser monetary policy. In Clinton's estimation, he had kept his end of the bargain, but Greenspan seemed to renege on this agreement.

Beginning the following month, over the course of a year, the Fed tightened monetary policy a total of seven times. Importantly, this was the first time that the Fed announced a policy change, instead of leaving it to the Fed watchers to decipher the decision based on the Fed's action in the market. Cognizant of this change and the impact it might have on financial markets, Greenspan began dropping hints that this change in policy was coming. In his autobiography, he reflected, "I worried that the news would rattle the markets. So, with the FOMC's consent, I strongly hinted in advance that a policy shift was imminent" (Greenspan, p. 154). Despite the early warnings, and a new rhetorical evolution in announcing monetary policy, the markets did not like the decision to raise rates. The day of the announcement, the Dow lost nearly 100 points, or 2.5%. The losses continued to spread through the end of March with the Dow losing a total of 400 points over a two-month period. Publicly, Fed officials downplayed the decline in stock and bond prices as a "speculative correction," but privately they were worried. The concern about a repeat of 1990 hung over their deliberations.

Greenspan lamented the fact that the markets did not react to his new rhetorical initiative: warning the markets in advance before actually making a policy change. He commented, "The rest of the world … seemed to turn a deaf ear. The markets did nothing to discount a rate hike" (p. 154). He subsequently became more aggressive in his rhetorical interventions later in his tenure. Despite being disappointed with the markets' lack of reaction to his new rhetorical initiative, Greenspan seemed fairly pleased with the end result of both his rhetorical and monetary interventions. In 1995, he declared that the economy had achieved a soft landing, and by 1996, economic activity began to pick back up again. "In hindsight," Greenspan reflected, "the soft landing of 1995 was one of the Fed's proudest accomplishments during my tenure" (p. 156).

Greenspan was reappointed to a third term in June 1996, but it was a rough ride. Tom Harkin threatened to filibuster the nomination, and succeeded in having it delayed for several months. He contended that Greenspan's "blind pursuit of inflation control … [was] cold to the needs of families" (Beckner, 1996, p. 417). Harry Reid claimed that a "cloud of suspicion" hung over the Fed because of "mismanagement" of the Fed's budget. They pointed to a recent Government Accounting Office audit of the Fed that revealed that its operating expenses had risen 50% over a six-year period, and that the Fed had built up a $3.7 billion "slush fund" (pp. 417–418). The slush fund, and the expansion of the Fed's economic power and purpose, is an important issue that we will revisit in the next chapter.

With the pickup of the economic expansion in 1996, there was a concurrent speculative event unfolding in the markets. The year 1995 marked the first year of the infamous "dot com" bubble in the markets. While many factors flowed together in a confluence to create the dot com bubble, the triggering event was arguably the initial public offering of Netscape. In one day, the stock nearly tripled in value and set the precedent for other internet startups. The dot com boom helped fuel an enormous run up in the stock markets with the Dow Jones Industrial Average up more than 30% in 1995, and the Nasdaq up more than 40% the same year. While Greenspan claimed that the Fed paid little attention to the stock markets, this significant uptick had caught their eye. At an FOMC meeting in December 1995, Greenspan admitted, "[C]lueless we were about the growing strength of the stock market" (p. 166). He continued, "I've been looking at the business cycle since the late 1940s. There has been nothing like this" (p. 167). Subsequently, he concluded, "time-honored rules of thumb might not apply" (p. 167). While awed by the strength of the economy, and the incredible run up in stock prices, Greenspan privately worried at the time: "The real danger is that we are at the edge of a bond and stock bubble" (p. 166).

The question was: what, if anything should the Fed say, or do about this? If Greenspan was serious that the Fed can and should pay little attention to the markets, perhaps it should just ignore the massive run up in stock prices, and allow the "self-correcting" aspect of all markets run its course. Indeed, this seemed the most consistent policy for a Fed chair who championed the free market. The run up in stock prices presented Greenspan with an obvious dilemma: allow the free market to run its course or intervene in order to "pop" what he perceived to be a "bubble." Greenspan thought long and hard about how to resolve this dilemma. He finally concluded, "I still didn't agree that raising the issue [of a market bubble] was necessarily a bad idea. The growing importance of the stock market was impossible to deny. How could you talk about the economy without mentioning the eight-hundred-pound gorilla?" (p. 175) (Fig. 11.1).

Greenspan first spoke of "irrational exuberance" on December 5, 1996, at an American Enterprise Institute's reception held in his honor. He said that he first arrived at the concept in the bathtub (p. 176). "It was a mere two words, buried in an avalanche of highly technical and otherwise

Fig. 11.1 President Bill Clinton listens to the Fed Chair's remarks on U.S.-China trade policy. Clinton added, "We all know that when Alan Greenspan talks, the world listens." (REUTERS/Alamy Stock Photo)

befuddling words. But it served to capture people's imagination. For better or worse, those two words were to become for a time Greenspan's catchphrase, his tag line, and his slogan" (Martin, p. 214). The phrase was excerpted from a speech that was 18 pages long, entitled "The Challenge of Central Banking in a Democratic Society." Greenspan admitted, "I carefully hedged what I had to say in my usual Fedspeak" (p. 176). It is important to note that Greenspan did not say directly that the stock markets were irrationally exuberant, but instead couched the phrase in a rhetorical question. Specifically, he mused, "How do we know when irrational exuberance has unduly escalated asset values …?" (Norris, 1996, p. 1). Nevertheless, news outlets quickly stripped the phrase "irrational exuberance" from its original context, and used it to promulgate the view that Greenspan believed the market to be wildly overvalued.

In response to his comments, stocks in Japan fell 3%, and they dropped 4% in Germany and Great Britain. While stocks in the U.S. initially plunged as much as 145 points, the Dow ended the day closing down only about 1% (Norris, p. 1). Still, though, the stock market largely shrugged off his infamous comments as the U.S. stock markets ended the year up well over 20%. Despite the short-term reaction, Greenspan's bold rhetorical experiment proved to be a failure.

Greenspan admitted the move to address perceived speculation in the stock market was new. "Directly addressing the stock market is a highly unusual move for the Chair of the Fed. ... Prior to Greenspan's 1996 speech, in fact, Fed chairmen have publicly commented on the stock market per se on only two occasions. ... Greenspan's comments were virtually without precedent" (Martin, pp. 215–216). Greenspan noted, "The Fed has no explicit mandate under the law to try and contain a stock-market bubble" (p. 178). But try to contain it he did, moving first rhetorically, then monetarily, in an effort to stem what he perceived to be the unsustainable growth of the stock market. In early 1997, the stock market dipped about 7% over a two-month period in response to Greenspan's rhetorical and monetary initiatives, but the market more than made it up by the end of the year. Greenspan concluded, "[Y]ou can't tell when a market is overvalued, and you can't fight market forces" (p. 179). Subsequently, "[The Fed] did not raise rates any further, and we never tried to rein in stock prices again" (p. 179). Despite his claims to the contrary, though, Greenspan continued to expand his rhetorical power in the years to come: "Although all Fed chairmen have at one time or another taken advantage of their special exalted status, the one who seemed to perfect this role was Alan Greenspan. He was asked to pontificate on a wide variety of subjects, many of which had nothing to do with monetary policy" (Santow, p. 6).

Greenspan's phrase, "irrational exuberance," is significant for several reasons. First, like "Reaganomics" years earlier, it functioned as an ideological, political, and economic amalgam that wielded tremendous rhetorical power. Second, it was marked a virtually unprecedented expansion of the power of the Fed, taking on an issue, valuations in the stock market, that was clearly outside its purview. Certainly, stock market levels have at least an indirect relationship with economic policy, but that could be said about almost anything. Indeed, foreign policy, for example, also has an indirect impact on monetary policy; does this authorize the Chair of the Fed to publicly comment on issues of foreign policy, as well? When cast in this way, the public may be less comfortable with such an expansion of the Fed's power and influence. Nevertheless, Greenspan chose to push into new frontiers, both substantively and rhetorically. Substantively, he chose to address an issue that even he admitted was outside of the Fed's congressional mandate. Rhetorically, he coupled traditional monetary tools with novel public commentary, a marked expansion of the power of the Fed.

The third reason why the phrase "irrational exuberance" is significant is because of the meaning attached to these words, and this deserves more detailed attention. As we learned in the introduction, the concept of "rationality" is a rhetorical construct. What is deemed "rational" is simply an idea that reveals particular ideological, psychological, and political commitments. Historically, "rationality" has often been used as a club to beat those deemed "irrational" into submission. Rationality was the line of demarcation that kept women from the public sphere, safely locked away in the private sphere deprived of basic human rights for almost the entirety of Western Civilization. Rationality was the intellectual substructure for shameful institution of slavery, and countless colonial conquests. Rationality was the torch that burned "irrational" women at the stake based on the unsupported belief that they were witches. Rationality was the wedge that forced Native Americans from their homes and traditional hunting grounds, and legitimized nothing less than an American genocide. In my home state, Indiana passed what is widely regarded as the first eugenics legislation in the world in 1907. There is a historical marker by the state house in Indianapolis that recounts our complicity in a broader eugenics project. As part of that initiative, citizens who were deemed "idiots" or "imbeciles" were forcibly sterilized to prevent them from producing offspring and potentially tainting the public genetic pool. The law was revised in 1927 to meet constitutional muster and was not repealed until 1974. In all, over 2300 people deemed "mentally defective" were involuntarily sterilized under this program.

In his seminal book, *Whose Justice? Which Rationality?*, philosopher Alasdair MacIntyre (1988) problematizes a singular, shared view of rationality. He reflected:

> The perspective of a tradition [e.g., "rationality"] originally rooted in contingent circumstance, arising out of problems, perplexities, and disagreements in some particular social order, articulated in the terms of the particularities of the language and culture of that order, does not permit any generalized confidence about the potential hospitality of other languages and cultures to the articulated statement of, let alone allegiance to, that particular tradition. (p. 327)

In other words, concepts like rationality are anything but neutral and universal, but are instead contingent upon particular circumstances, ideological preferences, and historical actors. Despite this, Greenspan positioned himself the neutral arbitrator of what was a "rational" market, and what was "irrational." Not only was public commentary on stock market valuations beyond his professional responsibilities and expertise, but he also seemed to be comfortable with his self-anointed new role. Indeed, a "modern version of the prophets who spoke in riddles, Greenspan likes to pose questions rather than make pronouncements. In the public exegesis of his [irrational exuberance] remarks, it is often forgotten that, when it comes to such questions, even he does not know the answers" (Shiller, 2000, p. 14). Nevertheless, Greenspan continued to portray himself as the person with all the answers, and the only public official who could and should speak authoritatively about economic policy. This seems to be a common characteristic of Fed chairs. Indeed, economist Leonard J. Santow observed:

> During these Congressional appearances, chairmen were often asked questions on subjects for which they had little or no personal responsibility. It was as if they were viewed as the wise men who would help guide Congress in its legislative tasks. Of course, some of the chairmen played their role to the hilt. ... When it came to areas outside their bailiwick, they were preaching to the choir and tried to impress Congress with their knowledge and independence. Consciously or not, they tried to come off as wise men, above and beyond any fray. The image they tried to portray was that they could walk on water. (p. 5)

The important thing for Greenspan seemed to be a structural consolidation of economic and moral authority to make the markets continue to hang on his every word. His remarks on "irrational exuberance," however, represented another deeply ironic inconsistency for someone who was ostensibly committed to the principles of the free market. To ask, rhetorically, or otherwise, if the market suffered from "irrational exuberance" was nothing less than an unwarranted intervention in the marketplace. To a free market disciple, the market itself should be the sole determinant of "rationality," not actors who may believe that values are too high. As was the case when Greenspan modestly increased the wine budget of the Fed, the message was clear: there would be a party, but it would not be allowed to get out of hand. This implied, of course, that despite his ideological commitments to the free market, Greenspan did not have full confidence in the so-called self-correcting mechanisms of the market. As stock market valuations indicated, many investors did not agree with Greenspan's definition of "rationality," nor did the market itself. As Yale economist Robert J. Shiller wrote in his book *Irrational Exuberance*:

> The trouble with such exercises of moral authority is that, although views that the market is either very overpriced or very underpriced may become commonplace among the experts, they are never universally held. The leaders who make such statements find themselves doing so based on personal opinion: an intuitive judgment that is so hard to prove that they probably feel that it takes an act of courage to make such a statement in the first place. (p. 225)

Like "rationality," the word "exuberance" is also normatively loaded. *Merriam-Webster* (2018) defines "exuberant" as "joyously unrestrained," and "extreme and excessive in degree, size, or extent." It has negative pejorative implications. It suggests a situation that is "abnormal," one fueled by "hysteria" rather than fundamentals. Clearly, this is the way that Greenspan intended to use the word. And when he coupled it with the word "irrational," the overall meaning was unmistakable: stock market valuations lacked what he perceived to be a rational basis. While such a public rhetorical intervention in the market is troubling in and of itself, it also set a precarious precedent for both Greenspan and future Fed chairs. When Greenspan positioned himself as the most important voice in determining market rationality, it invited continuing public commentary on issues that may, directly or indirectly, affect monetary policy. Further, it placed a tremendous burden on future Fed chairs because the market and the public, not to mention the media, have become dependent upon the blessing, or criticism of the Fed chair. If future chairs do not comment on market valuations as Greenspan just had, then the market would have no grounding rhetorical and moral compass. What would occur when the oracle, the conductor, the maestro of the market retired? When that happened in 2006, Greenspan left big shoes to fill, a Fed that was now more powerful than ever before, and the chairs that followed him did not seem eager to embrace the same public persona, or scope of responsibility that Greenspan has cultivated for himself. The market told us precisely what it thought about this situation shortly after Greenspan's retirement. Ben Bernanke, the next Chair of the Fed, inherited a crisis in the making on the heels of Greenspan's exit from the stage, and he was uncomfortably thrust into the limelight in a role that he never seemed to fully comprehend, or enjoy.

In a clear swipe at Reaganomics in his book, *A Tenured Professor*, John Kenneth Galbraith commented on "President Ronald Reagan— [a growing] presence in the community ... the budget priorities of David Stockman, the monetary magic of Professor Milton Friedman, [and] the now compelling doctrine that the rich were not working because they had too little money, and the poor because they had too much" (p. 75). In Galbraith's (1990) view, this was an economic theory, symbolically portrayed in econometric models like the Laffer Curve, that was "engagingly unsupported by evidence" (p. 76). As we saw above, catchphrases like "irrational exuberance" function the same way in our public discourse insofar as they are based more on opinion, intuition, and ideology than incontrovertible evidence. In his previously cited book, *The Great Crash*, Galbraith (1955) commented, "A bubble can be easily punctured. But to incise it with a needle so that it subsides gradually is a task of no delicacy" (p. 30).

Just as Professor Marvin did in his quixotic quest to find "irrationality" in the marketplace in order to turn a profit, Alan Greenspan positioned himself as the one true voice on market rationality in an attempt to "burst the bubble" by "jawboning" stock market valuations that he perceived to be excessive, or "irrational." As such, he exponentially expanded the power, scope, and reach of the Fed; he set a precedent for rhetorical interventions in the marketplace going forward; and he put future chairs of the Fed in a disquieting position that encouraged them to publicly comment on areas both within and outside of the Fed's traditional domain.

References

Beckner, S. K. (1996). *Back from the brink: The Greenspan years.* John Wiley & Sons.

"Exuberant." Merriam-Webster Dictionary. Accessed 15 June 2018.

Galbraith, J. K. (1955). *The great crash: 1929.* Houghton Mifflin.

Galbraith, J. K. (1990). *A tenured professor.* Houghton Mifflin.

Greenspan, A. (2007). *The age of turbulence: Adventures in a new world.* Penguin.

MacIntyre, A. (1988). *Whose justice? Which rationality?* University of Notre Dame Press.

Martin, J. (2001). *Greenspan: The man behind money. Perseus.*

Norris, F. (1996, December 7). Greenspan asks a question and global markets wobble. *New York Times*, 1.

Santow, L. (2009). *Do they walk on water? Federal reserve chairmen and the fed.* Praeger.

Shiller, R. (2000). *Irrational exuberance.* Princeton University Press.

CHAPTER 12

The Disappointed: The "Great Recession" of 2008

In a Season 13 episode of *South Park* entitled "Margaritaville" (Parker, 2009), residents of South Park seem at their wits' end about what to do about a deep economic downturn that had enveloped their community. This particular episode won the 2009 Emmy Award for the Outstanding Animated Program (Programming Less Than One Hour). In the episode, Stan Marsh asked his parents, "Mom, Dad, how come there's suddenly no money?" Randy, Stan's father, replied:

> I will tell you what happened son. You see, there is a bunch of idiots out there who weren't happy with what they had. They wanted a bigger house and materialistic things that they didn't even need. People with no money who got loans to buy frivolous things that they had no business buying. These assholes just blindly started buying any stupid thing that looked appealing because they thought money was endless. (Parker)

His voice drowned out by his new Margaritaville blender, Randy continued: "and these idiots couldn't see that by doing all of this frivolous spending, they were mocking the economy, and they made the economy angry. We're all feeling the economy's vengeance because of materialistic heathens who did stupid things with their money. Do you understand, son?"

Randy Marsh's personification of the economy is only a simple satirical step removed from our own economic experiences. In invoking religious

G. D. Klinger et al., *Money Talks*,
https://doi.org/10.1007/978-3-031-00816-0_12

overtones to understand this personified economy, Randy commented, "Yea, it is an angry and unforgiving economy," and later reconfigured the oft-quoted *Psalm 23* to pacify the angry economy: "The economy is our shepherd; we shall not want" (Parker).

Stan's friend, Kyle Broflovski, however, called both the personification of the economy and the quasi-religious devotion it into question: "The economy is not a supernatural, all-knowing entity. The economy is just an idea, made up by people thousands of years ago." He insightfully recognized, "Faith is what makes an economy exist. Without faith, its only plastic cards and paper money" (Parker).

The "Great Recession" of 2008 was arguably the most significant economic crisis that confronted the United States since the Great Depression. The stock market lost over half of its value, with the Dow Jones Industrial Average peaking at 14,164 on October 9, 2007, and dropping to a low of 6443 on March 6, 2009. The crisis in the housing market was equally if not more significant. Nobel Prize-winning economist Paul Krugman (2009) estimated that the housing bubble wiped out "about $8 trillion of wealth. Of that, around $7 trillion will have been losses to homeowners" (p. 169). Including the collapse in the stock market, Princeton economist and former Vice-Chair of the Fed Alan Blinder opined, "In total, the wealth of U.S. households fell by something on the order of $18 trillion" (Blinder, 2013, p. 354).

To view the Crash of 2008 as an isolated event that happened in and around 2008, or to view it as a uniquely American phenomenon is to see it falsely. It has much deeper historical, structural, and international roots. While the economic and market collapses of 2008 came suddenly, they did not arrive without warning. In the years leading up to 2008, there were significant and undeniable signs that a collapse of this magnitude was forthcoming, and many of the policy responses had already been played out in similar crises both within the United States and around the globe.

Specifically, there were a series of international fiscal and monetary crises that rattled the economic boom underway in the United States in the 1990s. The first was Mexico who appealed for international help claiming that it was on the brink of financial collapse. Both the IMF and the U.S. Federal Government quickly came to its aid. The aid package, totaling $50 billion in short-term loans, helped stem the tide in the devaluation of the Peso, and a broader crisis was averted. Interestingly, Mexico actually only used a portion of the credit it was extended, so the mere promise of aid was the mechanism that created reassurance much as the promise of liquidity was a rhetorical tool that the Fed had used to stave off domestic economic crises.

In 1997, similar financial crises hit several countries in Asia, starting in Thailand and Malaysia, and spreading to Hong Kong, the Philippines, Singapore, and Indonesia. One of the biggest economies in the region, South Korea, was at risk, as well. It seems that the South Korean government had used its economic reserves to prop up commercial banks to cover bad loans (Greenspan, 2007, p. 189). The growing crisis in these countries led to the development of the phrase, "The Asian Contagion." The concern was that the economic contagion would spread to other economies outside of the region like an infectious disease. Paul Krugman (2009) was one writer who presciently recognized the potential danger: "Where some saw the crisis as a specifically Asian phenomenon, I saw it as a troubling omen for all of us, a warning that the problems of depression economics have not disappeared in the modern world" (p. 4). Like many others, he mobilized the disease metaphor in describing the phenomenon: "At the time [following the financial crises in Asia in the 1990's], I thought of it this way: it was as if bacteria that used to cause deadly plagues, but had long been considered conquered by modern medicine, had reemerged in a form resistant to all the standard antibiotics" (Krugman, 2009, p. 5). It was not so much that the "disease" would spread, but the economic crises in Asia illustrated the fact that modern economic policy was ill equipped to deal with significant downturns in economic activity.

On October 27, 1997, the Dow plunged 554 points mostly based on concerns that the Asian economic crisis would spread. It was the largest drop in ten years. The next day, Greenspan testified before Congress. As he read his prepared statement, "an aide handed him notes on the state of the Dow. Greenspan wanted to make sure that nothing he said roiled the skittish markets" (Martin, 2001, p. xv). In this case, it seems that rhetoric was the tool that worked: "Merely uttering soothing words was enough to temporarily stabilize the markets" (Martin, p. xv).

While significant, the amount devoted to containing the economic crisis in Mexico paled in comparison the aid commitment required to bail out the Asian economies. The concern, of course, was that if the United States and the International Monetary Fund came to the rescue of these economies, they were essentially intervening in the operation of the free market. By not allowing market forces to collapse these economies, it sent a powerful symbolic message to both companies and countries that had engaged in similar risky fiscal, monetary, and investment policies. Taking such speculative risks was acceptable because the governmental and international agencies would step in to prevent the downside consequences of these irresponsible policies. In short, if you were an economy that was "too big to fail," given the consequences it would have for the world economy, governments and international agencies would intervene to prevent such a monumental collapse. "This was a version of what the insurance industry calls the 'moral hazard' of protecting individuals from risk. The bigger the safety net, the theory goes, the greater the recklessness with which people, businesses, and governments will tend to behave" (Greenspan, 2007, p. 189). This rhetorical and economic posturing, of course, was simply a dress rehearsal for the inevitable economic collapse of 2008.

A third international economic crisis emerged less than a year later in 1998. In August of that year, Russia defaulted on its debt. By 1998, almost half of the world's economies were in recession. Privately, "Greenspan confided to colleagues that he had never seen anything quite so extreme during his half century of observing the economy" (Martin, p. xvii). For years, speculative investors poured billions of dollars into the Russian economy as it continued its transition to capitalism. Much of the speculation was fueled on the belief that there was no downside to the investments insofar as the international community would never allow the Russian economy to fail. "Many operated on the assumption that the West would always bail out the fallen superpower—if for no other reason, the saying went, than that Russia was 'too nuclear to fail'" (Greenspan, 2007, p. 191). Unlike the crisis in Mexico and Asia, however, the initial IMF aid package committed to Russia was withdrawn, and the scope of the Russian default grew in magnitude. While it had a significant impact on the markets, the markets and world economy quickly recovered. Here was a case where economic authorities picked and chose which economies to bail out, and which they would allow to fail, an uneven policy that foreshadowed similar inconsistencies in the Federal Government's response to the Crash of 2008.

Greenspan took significant steps to ease the impact the Asian Contagion and the Russian default would have on the U.S. economy. Greenspan and the Fed decided to begin cutting interest rates. On September 29, 1998, the Fed lowered the Federal Funds rate a quarter point. On October 15, Greenspan cut the rates again in between meetings of the Fed. In reaction to that move, announced in the final hour of trading on Wall Street, the Dow rallied over 300 points. Martin (2001) concluded that the two-tiered approach of Greenspan: monetary policy adjustments, and reassuring rhetoric, had blunted the impact these international crises had on the U.S. economy: "The threat of financial disaster—pressing just weeks before—had been contained through a combination of soothing words and savvy interest-rate policy" (p. xvii).

Domestically, the United States economy got its first early taste of the impact of reckless and speculative investments with the collapse of one of the nation's largest hedge funds, Long-Term Capital Management. The firm "specialized in risky, lucrative arbitrage deals" and "carried some $1.25 trillion in financial derivatives" (Greenspan, 2007, p. 193). Concerned that the sheer size of the potential failure would send massive shock waves through the U.S. economy, the New York Fed chose to intervene rather than allow the company to fail. This was the first run at the "too big to fail" trope that became an all too familiar theme during the Collapse of 2008, and the subsequent bailouts of these companies, such as AIG, General Motors, and Chrysler that were deemed "too big to fail." The *New York Times* decried, "Seeing a Fund as Too Big to Fail, New York Fed Assists in Bailout" (Morgenson, 1998). In that article, Pulitzer Prize-winning journalist Gretchen Morgenson noted, "The Federal Reserve Bank of New York has helped organize the rescue of a large and prominent speculative fund, indicating that regulators recognize that the failure of such a fund would damage already fragile world markets" (Morgenson, 1998).

The *New York Times* saw the parallels between this case, and the federal bailouts of 2008. On December 26, 2008, George Mason Professor of Economics Tyler Cowen (2008) recognized, "The financial crisis is a result of many bad decisions, but one of them hasn't received enough attention: the 1998 bailout of the Long-Term Capital Management hedge fund. If regulators had been less concerned with protecting the fund's creditors, our current problems might not be quite so bad." He continued, "But 1998 should have been the time to send a credible warning that bad loans to overleveraged institutions would mean losses, and that neither the Fed nor the Treasury would make these losses good" (Cowen, 2008).

While the failure of Long-Term Asset Management was significant, there were no substantive policy adjustments to prevent similar situations from recurring in the future. Indeed, it was right around this time that Congress passed the Financial Services Modernization Act that formalized the aforementioned repeal of the Glass-Steagall Act that had created a wall between the banking, investment, and insurance industries. So the government was actually moving in the opposite direction by pushing even harder in the areas of deregulation and the loosening of restrictions. The end result of these deregulatory moves was increased consolidation within the banking and investment industries. As Henry Kaufman (2008) noted, this was a trend that would continue: "Financial concentration will gain even greater momentum and influence. This is the most profound long-term consequence of the current credit crisis" (p. A11). More specifically, he observed:

> Leading independent investment banks already have been taken over by large financial conglomerates that are controlled by commercial banking entities, as have giant deposit institutions. Within the next year, many smaller and medium-sized financial institutions also will lose their independent identities. Today more than half of all nonfinancial debt (debt held by households, nonfinancial companies and government) is held by the 15 institutions. (p. A11)

There are two direct consequences of this consolidation: less economic democracy, and increased vulnerability of all markets. Indeed, Kaufman (2008) warned, "In the years ahead, the influence of these financial conglomerates will be overwhelming—and they will limit any moves toward greater economic democracy" (p. A11). Further, "because there will be fewer market participants of importance, the price volatility of financial assets likely will remain high. Through their global reach, these firms will transmit financial contagion even more quickly than it spread in the current credit crisis" (p. A11).

Despite its sheer size, the collapse of Long-Term Asset Management was treated as an anomaly, a blip on the monetary radar of an economy and market that was growing at an unprecedented pace. Since this early crisis was largely ignored, the unequivocal message was clear: it's safe to return to business as usual. As such, the following years were marked by increased deregulation, loosened restrictions, and accelerated consolidation all of which combined to create a tremendously powerful economic monopoly, and an incredibly vulnerable marketplace.

This situation in a large part was fueled by the aforementioned dot com boom. Concerned once again about an overheated economy and its implications for potential future inflation, the Fed began raising rates again from July 1999 to June 2000. In Greenspan's words, "We were hoping we might achieve another soft landing" given the alleged success it had with the same in 1995 (2007, p. 207). The economy this time, however, was in for a rougher ride. Right around the same time, George W. Bush had won the election of 2000. Greenspan advised President-elect Bush at the time that there were real short-term dangers in the economy. The markets turned decidedly downward as a result of three factors: the dot com bubble burst, there was a spike in oil prices, and the threat of recession was very real. Still, Bill Clinton had left Bush on solid fiscal footing: the projected budget surplus for 2001 was $270 billion.

Perhaps emboldened by this sense of fiscal security, President Bush and Congressional Republicans pushed through a $1.35 trillion tax cut, the largest since the Reagan era tax cuts. Like the Reagan cuts, they seemed to favor big business and the wealthiest Americans. Before the tax cuts took effect, and the much-ballyhooed tax rebate checks hit the mail, the projected budget surplus vanished, partly a result of the projected rosy returns on investments predicated upon continued explosive market growth.

2001 was an economic turning point for so many different reasons. The economic impact of the attacks of September 11 cannot be underestimated, but the economy was already beginning to unravel before that unforgettable day. In December 2001, amid a headline-grabbing scandal, Enron declared bankruptcy, and it seemed to only be the tip of the iceberg. "[I]t touched off a wave of accounting scandals and bankruptcies exposing the infectious greed and malfeasance that had been the dark side of the great economic boom" (Greenspan, 2007, p. 226).

Around the same time, dissatisfied with diminishing returns in the stock market, speculators turned to a new market to drive up prices and reap outrageous profits: the real estate market. Speculators who had enjoyed years of easy money with little risk with the dot com boom saw the opportunity to grow another bubble, and manipulate another market. "*The Economist*, which tracks home prices in twenty countries, has estimated that between 2000 and 2005 the market value of residential property in developed nations rose from $40 trillion to more than $70 trillion" (Greenspan, 2007, p. 231). Coupled with the outrageous profits reaped during the dot com boom, the real estate bubble created a troubling fact: "The post-9/11 recovery had a dark side, however. It was marred by a disturbing shift in the concentration of income" (p. 232). As I noted at the outset of the project, one of the inevitable consequences of a blind faith in the free market is that capitalism, left unchecked, tends to widen the rich-poor gap, a fact that was empirically verified by the unsettling acceleration of the same that occurred under the Reagan Administration. By the time we reached the George W. Bush Presidency some 20 years later, even conservative writers such as Alan Greenspan were concerned with what they saw, but they did not act on these concerns: "Greenspan warned about irrational exuberance but he didn't do anything about it. And in fact, the Fed chairman holds what I believe is a unique record among central bankers: he presided over not one but two enormous asset bubbles, first in stocks, then in housing" (Krugman, 2009, p. 144). Indeed, Greenspan's response to the recession of 1990, aggressively lowering interest rates to jumpstart the economy, was intimately connected to the Great Recession of 2008. "Cynics said that Greenspan has succeeded only by replacing the stock market bubble with a housing bubble—and they were right" (Krugman, 2009, p. 152). It was a simple illustration of kicking the underlying structural economic problem down the road.

Unfazed by this, the Bush Administration undertook an economic campaign of continued tax cuts and carefree government spending. Greenspan (2007) later lamented, "'Deficits don't matter,' to my chagrin, became part of Republicans' rhetoric. It was a struggle for me to accept that this had become the dominant ethos of economic policy of the Republican Party. … My sensibilities as a libertarian Republican were offended" (pp. 237–238). He continued, "The Republicans in Congress lost their way. They swapped principle for power. They ended up with neither. They deserved to lose" (p. 244). Other Republican critics were more pointed in their criticism of President Bush. Bruce Bartlett (2006), for example, claimed in his book *Imposter* that George W. Bush had bankrupted America, and advanced economic, trade, tax, and budget policies that were among the worst of any president on record. In their book, *Lost Decades*, Chinn and Frieden (2011) contend that the 2008 crisis was created by irresponsible fiscal and monetary policies. On the fiscal side, they laid the blame on George W. Bush's feet. President Bush, after all, turned a $236 billion budget surplus in 2000 into $650 billion budget deficit by 2004. On the monetary side, they placed blame on the Fed who kept interest rates too low for too long, something that created massive spending, much of it debt financed, by corporations and consumers alike.

As I note above, the housing bubble played a significant part in the Crash of 2008. Like many others, I lived in the midst of the housing crisis. When I purchased my first home in 2003, I financed the purchase of the house with Countrywide Financial. In 2004, it was the largest mortgage company in the nation, and it originated nearly $500 billion in mortgages the following year (McLean & Nocera, 2010, p. 144). In many ways, it was the symbol of overextension, profiteering, and unwarranted risk taking in the mortgage business. Because of its suspect business practices on a variety of fronts, several states and a group of investors sued Countrywide starting in 2008. Inexplicably, in the midst of this unfolding crisis, Bank of America announced it was acquiring Countrywide in January 2008, a deal that was finalized in July of that year. It was arguably one of the worst business acquisitions in history, and Bank of America continues to pay for the fallout, both in terms of its core business and in terms of its reputation. I remember getting my first new mortgage statement from Bank of America, but did not think much of it at the time. But as news of Countrywide's abuses continued to grow in significance, I began to realize that something was amiss, and it was not just limited to Bank of America's acquisition of Countrywide, it was something that was industry wide. It prompted me to investigate further.

The roots of the problem in the mortgage industry can be traced back to the Savings and Loan debacle in the late 1980s, and before. Since the Savings and Loan industry's primary business at the time was to originate new mortgages, the industry's exit from the marketplace left a hole in the mortgage business, and other companies swooped in to fill the gap. Two of those companies, Fannie Mae and Freddie Mac, were peculiar institutions, and their growth in the mortgage industry had started years earlier. They were quasi-private, quasi-government entities. They functioned largely as private corporations but were essentially insured by the Federal Government. This dynamic created an inherent moral hazard and encouraged them to take on increasingly risky mortgages given the fact that the government implicitly agreed to cover any losses that they would incur. The shift was significant: "S&Ls, which held almost 75 percent of the nation's home mortgages in 1975, held only about 35 percent six years later" (Mayer, 1990, p. 51). Moreover, "In 1981, Fannie Mae held $62 billion of home mortgages—more than the ten largest S&Ls put together—and if you valued those mortgages at the price they would bring on the market, Fannie Mae was insolvent by no less than $10.8 billion" [endnote omitted](Mayer, 1990, p. 51). In other words, the insolvency at Fannie Mae was evident over 30 years prior to the Crash of 2008, but government officials turned a blind eye to the situation based on the mistaken belief that home prices would never decline. The trend continued into the mid to late 1980s: "Paradoxically, during the Reagan Administration—with all its emphasis on reducing the federal government's role in American life—the government's role and influence in the residual mortgage market has, in fact, been substantially expanded" (Strunk & Case, 1988, p. 53). In fact, "of the one-to-four-family mortgage loans outstanding, federal credit agencies accounted for 38.6% of the total at year-end 1986, compared with only 28.5% at year-end 1980" (Strunk & Case, 1988, p. 53).

Other companies, such as Countrywide, wanted in on the action, and behaved as if they had the same implicit assurances that Fannie Mae and Freddie Mac received: that the Federal Government would cover any of their losses. Mortgage originations grew exponentially, and they assumed ever-increasing risk:

> This, then, was the situation in May 2006: risk was building up everywhere in the system; the housing bubble was reaching its frenzied finale; Wall Street firms were madly churning out CDO's [Collateralized Debt Obligations]; subprime originators were making loans to anyone with a pulse; everything was interconnected in ways that were dangerous for the financial system; and the regulatory apparatus, charged with protecting the safety and soundness of the banking system, was in complete denial. (McLean & Nocera, 2010, p. 245)

Importantly, McLean and Nocera continued:

> The banks' dirty little secret was now out in the open. It wasn't just Fannie and Freddie that had been creating moral hazard all these years. So had the nation's big banks. They had taken on terrible risks, built up immense leverage, and created such tight interconnectedness with their derivatives books that the failure of any one of them could bring down all the others. When things got bad, they assumed they had an "implicit government guarantee," just like Fannie and Freddie. (pp. 347–348)

The problems in the mortgage industry spread to investment banks and other financial institutions through a mechanism known as the Collateralized Debt Obligation (CDO). In effect, this allowed mortgage companies to bundle together mortgages and sell them in the marketplace as a security, a practice instituted by Freddie Mac years earlier. The underlying collateral was the mortgage on the relevant homes. The problem was that the underlying collateral was losing value with increasingly alacrity as foreclosures skyrocketed, and home prices subsequently dropped precipitously. Several investment banks were left holding CDOs that suffered monumental losses with no end in sight. Bear Stearns was one such investment bank that was overleveraged in this market. Despite being outside of its safety net, the Federal Government intervened, and helped facilitate the sale of Bear Stearns to none other than JP Morgan Chase for pennies on the dollar. When Lehman Brothers suffered the same fate later that year, though, the Federal Government chose not to intervene, one of the most significant triggering events of the economic crisis. The inconsistency in handling these cases echoed back to the decision to bail out Mexico, and distressed countries in Asia, but allow Russia to default in the late 1990s. Alan Blinder (2013) commented on the disparate treatment of these two investment banks:

> In March, the Federal Reserve, supported by the Treasury, kicked in almost $30 billion to facilitate the shotgun marriage of Bear to JP Morgan, presumably because a disorderly failure of Bear *might have* devastated the financial system. But in September, the Federal Reserve, again with the full support of the Treasury, refused to provide any money at all to facilitate a sale of Lehman—even though Lehman's failure *did* devastate the financial system. Go figure. (p. 100)

A week after Lehman Brothers was allowed to slip into bankruptcy, the five major investment banks in the United States no longer existed. Indeed, "Bear Stearns and Merrill Lynch had been absorbed into actual banks. Lehman was in the early stages of bankruptcy proceedings. Morgan Stanley and Goldman Sachs had become banks in name only" (Blinder, 2013, p. 154). The ripples spread to the thrift and banking industry, as well. Shortly thereafter, Washington Mutual, the largest Savings and Loan at the time, became the largest bank failure in U.S. history. As was the case with Bear Stearns, JP Morgan Chase acquired its banking operations at fire sale prices, and the rest of the company filed for bankruptcy. Wachovia, the nation's fourth largest bank holding company at the time suffered a similar fate, and fell into the waiting arms of Wells Fargo in another government forced sale.

Any attempt to pinpoint the "cause" of the Crash of 2008, or to lay blame on a single individual, group, or company, would be an exercise in futility. The opinions vary as much as they did in trying to unravel the mysteries of the Great Depression. While there are certainly some contributing factors, many that I have outlined above, what is far more interesting to me as a communication scholar are the rhetorical responses that emerged as a result of the Crash.

As a threshold matter, the attempt to frame the crisis as the "Great Recession" is rhetorically significant. Indeed, pundits quickly leapt to this moniker in an effort to assiduously avoid talk of another economic "depression." A recession indicated a normal downturn, and the adjective "great" at least admitted that it was worse than past recessions. As noted earlier, the same rhetorical manipulation occurred during the recession of 1990 when the Bush Administration invoked the phrase "double dip" recession to characterize a recession that was worse than what they had anticipated. Judge Richard Posner (2009) astutely observed, "The word [depression] itself is taboo is respectable circles, reflecting a kind of magical thinking; if we don't call the economic crisis a 'depression,' it can't be one" (p. ix). Ironically, President Herbert Hoover infamously applied the word "depression" to the economic conditions of the 1920s and 1930s as "part of his psychological campaign to keep up confidence. He believed 'depression' has a less ominous ring to it than the more common previously used words 'panic' and 'crisis'" (McElvaine, 1984, p. 72).

The tropes that played out in the earlier crises were repeated during the economic and market collapses of 2008. The insolvency of Fannie Mae and Freddie Mac was only a small piece of the puzzle. The tropes of "too big to fail" and the need for government "bailouts" emerged in the days and weeks that followed. The time-tested tropes of increased liquidity, reassurances of stability, and the call for more regulation and oversight were trotted out again in an attempt to restore confidence in the financial markets. In a highly symbolic act, on September 18, 2008, the Securities and Exchange Commission announced that it was banning the practice of short selling of 799 financial institutions in an effort to "protect the integrity and quality of the securities market and restore investor confidence" (U.S. Securities and Exchange Commission, 2008). This move, of course, hearkens back to the way government officials deemed the short selling by Professor Marvin "unpatriotic" in John Kenneth Galbraith's (1990), *A Tenured Professor*. Apparently, the free market is only embraced when the markets are moving in an upward direction. One suspects that there will never be a ban on securities when prices are moving decidedly higher (Fig. 12.1).

Writing in the midst of the crisis, Posner (2009) commented, "[The Government's response] to the crash has moved through four phases, with a fifth that at this writing is wending its way through Congress. The first

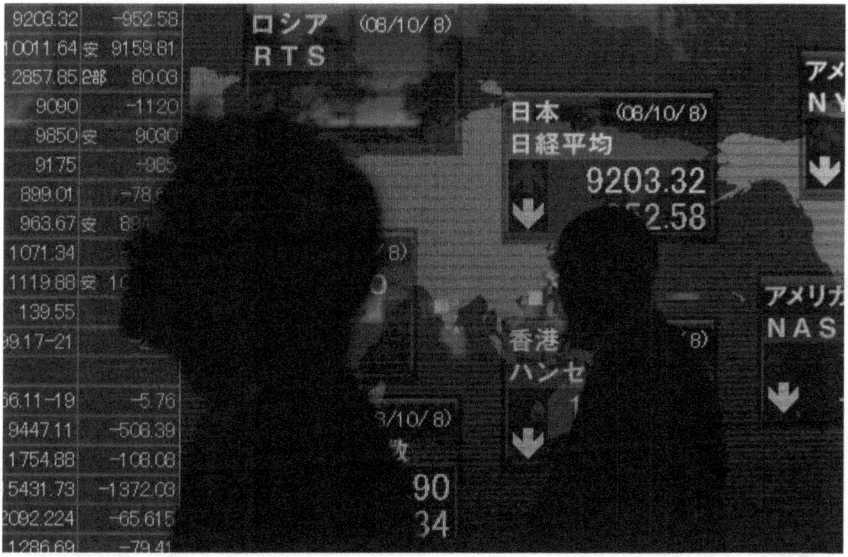

Fig. 12.1 On October 8, 2008, Japan's Nikkei Index plunges 9.4% in the largest single-day drop since 1987 Stock Market crash, stoking fears of global recession. (REUTERS/Alamy Stock Photo)

three phases are collectively the 'bailout'; the fourth (running simultaneously with the bailout) I'll call 'easy money'; and the fifth will, when executed, be the 'stimulus.'" (p. 148). The bailout took many different forms. The most significant initial move was the decision by the Fed to loan Bear Stearns $13 billion to help it deal with its liquidity crunch. The Fed has to use JP Morgan Chase as an intermediary because it did not have the legal authority to loan money to Bear Sterns directly insofar as it was not a conventional bank, and outside the purview of the Fed. Alan Blinder (2013) noted, "That decision was both stunning and monumental. It constituted crossing the Rubicon" (p. 105). "To justify its unprecedented action, the Federal Reserve invoked a little-known clause of the Federal Reserve Act, Section 13(3)" (Blinder, 2013, p. 105). This allowed the Fed to make loans to "any individual, partnership, or corporation" in "unusual and exigent circumstances." It was an "obscure power that had not been used since 1936" (Blinder, 2013, p. 105). It set the precedent for additional unconventional government intervention in the marketplace.

American International Group (AIG) had to accept an $85 billion loan, authorized by the Federal Reserve Bank's Board of Governors, from the Federal Reserve Bank of New York to keep them out of bankruptcy. This loan is significant because it was the first time in history that the Fed loaned money to a company that was not a bank. In addition to the Fed loan, the FBI launched an investigation for fraud (they did the same with Fannie Mae, Freddie Mac, and Lehman Brothers). In exchange for the loan, extended at 11.5% interest, the government assumed 79.9% of the company. Despite some shareholder resistance, this move essentially nationalized AIG. Importantly, this was the largest government bailout of a private company in U.S. history.

The government also effectively nationalized Fannie Mae and Freddie Mac, and by "August 2012, the government had spent about $140 billion, net, to keep Fannie and Freddie alive and functioning" (Blinder, 2013, p. 119). The unprecedented bailouts for General Motors and Chrysler were not far behind at a price tag of over $80 billion, again nationalizing private companies, and further deepening the moral hazard that the government was creating for companies that the government deemed "too big to fail." Blinder (2013) concluded, "By the time the post-Lehman panic subsided, the wreckage was everywhere. Bear Stearns, Merrill Lynch, Goldman Sachs, Morgan Stanley, Citigroup, Bank of America, Wachovia, Washington Mutual, Fannie Mae, Freddie Mac, and others had all been rescued, in one way or another, by the federal government" (p. 165).

The next phase of the government intervention in the marketplace was its so-called stimulus efforts. CNN estimated that the total price tag for the Federal stimulus program was $2.8 trillion (Isidore, 2010). The initial costs were a $700 billion bailout plan, called the Troubled Asset Relief Program (TARP) that allowed the Secretary of the Treasury, Hank Paulson, formerly of Goldman Sachs, to relieve financial institutions of toxic "assets," and a $787 billion stimulus program that was directed toward job creation, and investments in infrastructure, education, health, and renewable energy. President Bush signed the former into law in October 2008, under the auspices of the Emergency Economic Stabilization Act of 2008, and President Obama signed the latter into law in February 2009 under the moniker the American Recovery and Reinvestment Act of 2009.

The Fed, in concert with the fiscal efforts, engaged in three waves of what later came to be known as "Quantitative Easing" (QE). Quantitative

Easing began in November 2008 "when the Fed announced it would purchase $600 billion of loans and securities from Fannie Mae, Freddie Mac, and the Federal Home Loan Banks and created the TALF to buy $180 billion of consumer loans" (Eichengreen, 2015, pp. 304–305). There were two waves of quantitative easing, and arguably a third, dubbed "Operation Twist." "This, now, was a significant departure from prior policy. For the first time, the Fed made an open-ended commitment to keep interest rates low and continue its security purchases until the economy healed" (Eichengreen, 2015, p. 309). This unconventional policy ended in October 2014. All told, the Fed accumulated a staggering $4.5 billion in assets during its quantitative easing efforts (Wolfers, 2014).

This massive fiscal and monetary intervention by the Federal Government and the Federal Reserve in the marketplace was simply unprecedented in the history of the United States, both in terms of its size and scope. Individuals felt that the government was bending over backward to assist banks and businesses that had created the crisis in the first place because of their unsound, risky, and speculative practices. Further, little to nothing was being done to assist individuals who had suffered tremendously because of the crisis, and, to add insult to injury, it seemed that the risk and cost of these bad investments by greedy banks and businesses were once again being passed along to taxpayers. Finally, many felt that officials from both the government and Fed seemed to be intervening in the marketplace in unconventional ways, something that only deepened the moral hazard and incentivizing similar bad behavior in the future.

Importantly, Alan Blinder (2013) contended, "When you are promulgating policies that both feel wrong and are unfair by any objective standard, the communication burden is heavy and doing it well is critical. Explanations by the people in power should have been offered dozens, if not hundreds, of times. Instead, the job was shirked" (p. 257). He concluded, "[E]fforts to *explain* the bank bailout to the public were both *minimal* (give them a D for effort) and highly *ineffective* (give them an F for results)" (Blinder, 2013, pp. 356–357).

On April 21, 2009, Treasury Secretary Geithner claimed in remarks before a congressional oversight panel that large financial institutions can and do pose risks to the entire financial system, so allowing them to fail would create an untenable economic impact. Consequently, in his view, the Treasury's bailout was justified. This was simply a repeat performance of the "too big to fail" trope that had been fully rehearsed years earlier. Ben Bernanke went on *60 Minutes* in 2009, the first time the Chair of the

Fed had done so. In that interview, he went to great lengths to justify the bailout on "Wall Street" while neglecting more direct assistance to "Main Street." His argument was that when the government helps Wall Street, we indirectly help Main Street. This, of course, is just a simple re-articulation of the central principle of Reaganomics: that tax breaks and subsidies that help big business and the rich will "trickle down" to those in lower economic classes, a policy that had been repudiated by compelling empirical evidence.

Bernanke's post hoc justification did little to relieve him of the responsibility he held as the crisis unfolded. His earlier comments indicated that he was either ignorant of the coming crisis or intentionally misleading the public. For example, "[i]n late 2005, Bernanke said that home prices, rather than being in bubble territory, 'reflect strong economic fundamentals.' In 2006, he said that he expected the housing market to 'cool but not to change very sharply'" (McLean & Nocera, 2010, pp. 249–250). Indeed, invoking memories of Greenspan's infamous "soft landing" phrase, Bernanke claimed that "this cooling was 'orderly and moderate' and that the market appeared to be heading for a 'safe landing'" (Posner, 2009, p. 253). Further, "[a]s late as 2007, he said, '[W]e believe the effect of the troubles in the subprime sector on the broader housing market will be limited, and we do not expect significant spillovers from the subprime market to the rest of the economy or the financial system'" (McLean & Nocera, 2010, p. 250).

Like Greenspan before him, Bernanke was a free market disciple, and believed that the market, left untended and unregulated, would eventually correct itself. Economist Leonard J. Santow (2009) observed, "Both Greenspan and Bernanke share the blame for concentrating too much on interest rates with not enough emphasis placed on the regulatory portion of monetary policy" (p. 198). Still, it is hard not to feel sorry for Bernanke. He inherited an economic crisis in the making of mammoth proportions. In many ways, to tweak a lined cited earlier from Greenspan himself, Greenspan borrowed from Bernanke, and Bernanke had to pay it back. That being said, though, Santow (2009) recognized:

> It is important to note that while the Fed is a bank regulator, it is also a regulator of the government securities dealers and the government securities market. Bear Stearns happened to be one of the dealers in government securities, and the Federal Reserve dealt with them on an ongoing basis and therefore had to be aware of the problems, especially when looking at their

financials. This is another regulatory black eye for the Fed, and this one is primarily on Bernanke's watch. (p. 198)

While there were significant calls to reform and regulate entire industries, at least initially, as the crisis abated, and the market began to regain a portion of what it had lost, very little was done to change companies and industries to prevent a similar collapse in the future. It was, as it had been in the past, back to business as usual. Indeed, several Republican presidential candidates in the 2008 primary debates claimed that the long-term solution for the economy is simply to rearticulate many of the economic and political principles of the Reagan Era. Such a call was ironic, indeed, given that many of the problems that arose during the Collapse of 2008 were the direct result of Reagan Era policies: biased tax cuts, massive government spending, unsustainable budget deficits, and industry wide deregulation.

Alan Greenspan was no longer chair of the Fed when the Collapse of 2008 hit. Perhaps attentive to the warning signs of the coming crisis, Greenspan stepped off the stage in 2006. But he was demonized by major media outlets as one of the main architects of the crisis. Anderson Cooper identified him as one of the "10 Most Wanted Culprits of the Collapse" on CNN. And in the days after the collapse, David Blake claimed in the *Financial Times* that "Greenspan's sins return to haunt us," in an article entitled the same (Blake, 2008). How far and how quickly his star had fallen. In 2002, Greenspan was lauded as "The Man Who Saved the World." Now he was a "Culprit of the Collapse."

Both the media and the markets did a Herculean job of trying to get his replacement, Ben Bernanke, to fill the role that Greenspan had played in his 20 years on the Fed. Despite being named "Person of the Year" in 2009 by *Time* magazine, and making an unprecedented appearance on *60 Minutes* to sell the government bailouts of these failing banks and corporations, Bernanke has stayed mostly out of the limelight that his predecessor seemed to embrace. Perhaps the tide is turning, and people are finally beginning to move economics out of the central place it assumed in popular culture for just over 40 years. The contrition of Goldman Sachs, who issued a public apology for its mismanagement and malfeasance, was a positive sign, but did not heal the economic carnage created by the firm nor did it promise that substantive structural changes would occur (Zaki & Gomstyn, 2009). The $500 million it pledged to help small businesses is little more than a public relations gimmick designed to enhance its credibility and maintain the status quo, and the amount pales in comparison to the losses it helped to create. The formation of the group "Patriotic Millionaires for Fiscal Strength" was another positive sign insofar as the group recognized that many of the tax cuts created under the George W. Bush presidency were biased toward the rich. That group, a varied collection of millionaires, urged President Obama to let the Bush tax cuts on incomes over $1 million to expire at the end of the year in 2010. Regretfully, though, in a nod toward big business, Obama chose to extend the Bush Era tax cuts. Even if one applauds the surface magnanimity of this group, it does little to address the structural problems of an inherently inequitable economic system.

Greenspan and Bernanke's attempt to talk to and reason with a personified economy met with about the same success as policy makers at the Treasury Department in *South Park*. In the "Margaritaville" episode, their secretive method for pacifying an angry economy, and assist a failing insurance company that was presumably "too big to fail," was to chop off the head of a chicken and let it run around on a wheel of fortune that outlined various policy options. Wherever the chicken landed was the option that the government would pursue. In this case, the chicken collapsed on a "bailout." Once again, satire is not far removed from our own economic experiences. Indeed, our policy makers from both the government and the Fed decided that "jawboning" the market did not and could not work, and that a "bailout" was the only way to deal with the economic downturn of 2008, effectively covering massive losses by corporations and banks and leaving taxpayers to pick up the total tab of the initiative.

Fortunately, in a nod to consumers after the staggering and unprecedented corporate welfare programs enacted in response to the Crash of 2008, Congress finally passed legislation with an eye toward protecting individuals from similar economic catastrophes in the future. The Dodd-FrankWall Street Reform and Consumer Protection Act was signed into law on my birthday, July 21, in 2010. Before signing the legislation into law, President Obama hopefully remarked, "Because of this new law, the American people will never again be asked to foot the bill for Wall Street's mistakes. There will be no more taxpayer-funded bailouts. Period" (Cooper, 2010). If this sounds vaguely familiar, it should. President George H. W. Bush used strikingly similar language in 1989 when the government used taxpayer money to bail out the Savings and Loan Industry. Apparently, unlike what the song says, we will be fooled again. Further, this legislation did nothing to address the "too big to fail" conundrum; instead, the problem only grew worse. Indeed, "the six biggest banks—JP Morgan, Goldman Sachs, Bank of America, Citigroup, Wells Fargo, and Morgan Stanley—were allowed to grow 37 percent larger by the end of 2013 than in 2008–09, at the height of the crisis" (Eichengreen, 2015, p. 323). While the interventions of the Federal Government and the Federal Reserve in the marketplace may have staved off a deeper financial crisis, they did next to nothing to address the structural issues that led to the crisis in the first place. Finally, of course, the confidence President Obama's remarks inspired was fairly short lived given that President Donald Trump vowed to "do a big number on Dodd-Frank" (Thrush, 2017). As we will see in the next chapter, this is merely one of the many steps that President Trump took in precisely the wrong direction.

References

Bartlett, B. (2006). *Imposter*. Doubleday.

Blake, D. (2008, September 18). Greenspan's sins return to haunt us. *Financial Times*.

Blinder, A. S. (2013). *After the music stopped: The financial crisis, the response, and the work ahead*. Penguin.

Chinn, M. D., & Frieden, J. A. (2011). *Lost decades: The making of America's debt crisis and the long recovery*. W.W. Norton.

Cooper, H. (2010, July 21). Obama signs overhaul of financial system. *New York Times*. Retrieved June 27, 2018, from https://www.nytimes.com/2010/07/22/business/22regulate.html?dbk

Cowen, T. (2008, December 26). Bailout of long-term capital: A bad precedent? *New York Times*. Retrieved August 12, 2012, from http://www.nytimes.com/2008/12/28/business/economy/28view.html

Eichengreen, B. (2015). *Hall of mirrors: The Great Depression, the Great Recession, and the uses—And misuses—Of history*. Oxford University Press.

Galbraith, J. K. (1990). *A tenured professor*. Houghton Mifflin.

Greenspan, A. (2007). *The age of turbulence: Adventures in a new world*. Penguin.

Isidore, C. (2010, December 20). Stimulus price tag: $2.8 trillion. Retrieved August 12, 2012, from http://money.cnn.com/2010/12/20/news/economy/total_stimulus_cost/index.htm?eref=mrss_igoogle_business

Kaufman, H. (2008, December 6–7). How the credit crisis will change the way America does business. *Wall Street Journal*, A11.

Krugman, P. (2009). *The return of depression economics and the crisis of 2008*. W.W. Norton.

Martin, J. (2001). *Greenspan: The man behind money*. Perseus.

Mayer, M. (1990). *The Greatest-ever bank robbery: The collapse of the savings and loan industry.* Charles Scribner's Sons.

McElvaine, R. S. (1984). *The Great Depression: America, 1929–1941.* Times Books.

McLean, B., & Nocera, J. (2010). *All the devils are here: The hidden history of the financial crisis.* Penguin.

Morgenson, G. (1998, September 24). THE MARKETS; Seeing a fund as too big to fail, New York Fed assists its bailout. *New York Times.* Retrieved August 2, 2012, from http://www.nytimes.com/1998/09/24/business/the-markets-seeing-a-fund-as-too-big-to-fail-new-york-fed-assists-its-bailout.html?scp=1&sq=New%20York%20Fed%20assists%20in%20bailout&st=cse

Parker, T. (Writer) Parker, T. (Director). (2009, March 25). Margaritaville (Season 13 Episode 3). In T. Parker & M. Stone (Executive Producers), *South Park.* Comedy Central.

Posner, R. A. (2009). *A failure of capitalism: The crisis of '08 and the descent into depression.* Harvard University Press.

Santow, L. J. (2009). *Do they walk on water? Federal Reserve Chairmen and the Fed.* Praeger.

Strunk, N., & Case, F. (1988). *Where deregulation went wrong: A look at the causes behind the savings and loan failures in the 1980's.* United States League of Savings Institutions.

Thrush, G. (2017, January 30). Trump vows to dismantle Dodd-Frank "disaster." *New York Times.* Retrieved June 27, 2018, from https://www.nytimes.com/2017/01/30/us/politics/trump-dodd-frank-regulations.html

U.S. Securities and Exchange Commission. (2008, September 19). *SEC halts short selling of financial stocks to protect investors and markets.* SEC.gov. Retrieved August 11, 2012, from https://www.sec.gov/news/press/2008/2008-211.htm

Wolfers, J. (2014, October 29). The Fed has not stopped trying to stimulate the economy. *New York Times.* Retrieved November 14, 2014, from https://www.nytimes.com/2014/10/30/upshot/the-fed-has-not-stopped-trying-to-stimulate-the-economy.html

Zaki, Z., & Gomstyn, A. (2009, November 18). Goldman Sachs apologizes, gives back. *ABC News.* Retrieved August 26, 2010, from http://abcnews.go.com/Business/goldman-sachs-apologizes-back/story?id=9114765

CHAPTER 13

Tired of Sleeping: Trumped Up Trickle Down

The film, *Idiocracy* (Judge), satirically envisions a future that is not brighter, stronger, and better, but one that is the end result of a society on a trajectory of rapid, but unmistakable intellectual and moral decline (Judge 2006). In the film, two individuals were placed in cryostasis, and they awakened 500 years later to a world that was decidedly "stupider." The story works through a series of biting critiques of the political system, the court and prison systems, the police, the military, the medical community, the media, and corporate America in this imagined future. In each case, the depth of human ignorance and ineptitude were laid bare. In this dystopian world, a man named Dwayne Elizondo Mountain Dew Herbert Camacho had been elected President of the United States. President Camacho rose to power because of his celebrity status as a five-time professional wrestling Smackdown champion, and porn superstar. He openly consumed alcohol and swore in public, and he regularly fired his machine gun to get people's attention in the U.S. Congress' House of Representin'. His political speeches were marked by shallow and empty promises, his political appointments were often based on unabashed nepotism and cronyism, and he clearly had no idea how to run a country.

In the first 2016 Presidential debate, Hillary Clinton claimed that Donald Trump's economic proposals were little more than "Trumped up trickle down" (Tankersley, 2016). While this contention was an oversimplification, Secretary Clinton's remarks alerted us to an important point: much of what Donald Trump was proposing was torn from the political

G. D. Klinger et al., *Money Talks*,
https://doi.org/10.1007/978-3-031-00816-0_13

and economic playbook of Ronald Reagan. As we noted earlier, candidates during the Republican primaries were eager to prove that they were more like Reagan than any of the other candidates. Indeed, one of the primary debates actually took place in the Reagan Presidential Library with Ronald Reagan's Air Force One as the backdrop. Marco Rubio wasted no time in invoking the spirit of President Reagan. In introductory remarks, he commented, "I'm honored to be here at the Reagan Library, at a place that honors the legacy of a man who inspired not just my interest in public service, but also our love for country" (Reagan Library Debate, 2015). Not to be outdone, Scott Walker went a step further claiming that he was like Reagan in many important ways: "You see, in my lifetime, the greatest president was a governor from California. Ronald Reagan knew how to go big, and go bold. He understood the essence of moving this country forward, and that's what I did when I took on the status quo in my state, and the Washington-based special interests" (Reagan Library Debate, 2015). John Kasich upped the ante with a personal anecdote: "I think I actually flew on this plane with Ronald Reagan when I was a congressman, and his goals, and mine, really much—are pretty much the same. Lift Americans, unify, give hope, grow America, and restore it to that great, shining city on a hill. Yes, he was a great one, and I learned much from watching him" (Reagan Library Debate, 2015). Walker, Kasich, Rubio, Ted Cruz, and Jeb Bush invoked Reagan's name to support their positions later in the debate, as well. Toward the end of the debate, Rand Paul noted, "I met Ronald Reagan as a teenager, and my family, we're big supporters of him when he ran against Gerald Ford. He was the grassroots, running against the establishment, and I'll never forget that. … I'm a Reagan conservative" (Reagan Library Debate, 2015). Ben Carson reflected, "I was a radical Democrat before I started listening to Ronald Reagan. And he didn't sound like what they said Republicans were" (Reagan Library Debate, 2015). Finally, Chris Christie remarked, "I turned 18 in 1980, and my first vote was for Ronald Reagan. Boy, am I glad I did. And I think the country is, too" (Reagan Library Debate, 2015).

My point here is that while perhaps the Republican primary candidates intentionally invoked the spirit of Reagan given his now mythological status, they were almost forced into a situation where they had to do this given the way the debate was framed. Indeed, holding the debate in the Reagan Presidential Library instead of, for example, one of the Bush Presidential Libraries, created a backdrop that was difficult for the candidates to ignore. And if that was not enough, debate moderator Jake

Tapper led the candidates with questions, especially toward the end of the debate that forced them to address the issue. At one point, Tapper presented the candidates with a question about climate change and asked candidates, "[Reagan's former Secretary of State George] Schultz asks, why not take out an insurance policy and approach climate change the Reagan way?" (Reagan Library Debate, 2015). And near the end of the debate, and before the final commercial break, Tapper foreshadowed the final questions of the debate: "Coming Up, Ronald Reagan is looming large over this debate. So how Reaganesque exactly are these Republicans? We will find out next" (Reagan Library Debate, 2015).

The only issue is, however: none of these candidates measure up to the legacy of Ronald Reagan, least of all Donald Trump, who did not mention Reagan explicitly throughout the entire debate, and I am not alone in that opinion. Mark Weinberg, who served President Reagan in various capacities including Special Assistant, Deputy Press Secretary, and Director of Public Affairs, noted, "In every election since Ronald Reagan's passing, Republican Presidential aspirants pretend to know what he might do, say, or think. Though most of the candidates preparing to gather at the Reagan Presidential Library for their second primary debate had very little, if any, personal contact with Reagan, they invoke his name as if they knew him" (Weinberg, 2015). Significantly, he continued, "[M]ost, if not all, of the Republican candidates have, in many respects, been the anti-Reagan in terms of their conduct on the campaign trail." Specifically, he noted that Reagan never: (1) insulted other Republican candidates, (2) focused on the past, and (3) attacked the press (unless Mrs. Reagan was negatively portrayed) (Weinberg, 2015). On the last point, he observed, "To the contrary, [Reagan] had a very healthy respect for a free press, viewed it as an essential element of a democracy and accepted tough questioning and reporting as coming with the territory" (Weinberg, 2015).

This being said, however, based on what we have learned throughout this book, Ronald Reagan perhaps unwittingly, but unmistakably, set the stage for a Trump presidency. Indeed, as we noted earlier, he similarly set the stage for Jesse "The Body" Ventura becoming Governor of Minnesota, and Arnold Schwarzenegger becoming the Governor of California, among others, and he is the reason why other celebrities like Oprah mused about making a presidential run in 2020, and Kid Rock joked about a run for the U.S. Senate. Although Donald Trump did not explicitly mention Reagan in the primary debate at the Reagan Presidential Library, it is unrelentingly clear that he is attempting to mimic both Reagan's political spirit and Reagan's economic policies in advancing his agenda.

On the first point, one of the main reasons Trump rose to popularity initially was his celebrity status, something that was also true of Reagan, although perhaps to a lesser extent. While Reagan was a radio personality and Hollywood actor earlier in his life, he earned his stripes in politics for many years before making his successful presidential run in 1980. Donald Trump, on the other hand, had no political experience whatsoever proving the point that our move to pure imagology in politics has accelerated in recent years. Instead, Trump is known for his appearances on World Wrestling Entertainment, including WrestleMania XXIII's "Battle of the Billionaires" when he shaves WWE owner's Vince McMahon's head. And Trump Plaza in Atlantic City was the host for WrestleMania IV and V. Indeed, Lavie Margolin (2017) chronicles the parallels between McMahon and Trump's rise to power in his lighthearted and self-published book, *Trumpmania: Vince McMahon, WWE and the making of America's 45th President.* Trump is also well known for his reality television show, *The Apprentice*, where he was fixated on his ratings much in the same way he was for his major political speeches and events as president. In fact, Trump very famously trolled Arnold Schwarzenegger, who was his replacement on *The Apprentice* for ratings that did not measure up to his despite the fact that Trump's ratings on the show were very low, as well. Finally, Trump is also well known for his beleaguered and largely discredited for-profit "Trump University" that was the subject of a lawsuit filed by the New York Attorney General's office for illegal business practices, and two separate class action lawsuits filed in federal court based on the claims that students were regularly defrauded, and that the business used misleading marketing practices, and unethical sales tactics. Trump settled all three lawsuits for $25 million shortly before becoming president. Trump University only operated for five short years, from 2005 until 2010, before closing its doors for good. In the first question of the primary debate at the Reagan Presidential library, Jake Tapper asked Carly Fiorina if she was comfortable with Donald Trump having his finger on the nuclear codes. She replied, "You know, I think Mr. Trump is a wonderful entertainer. He's been terrific at that business" (Reagan Library Debate, 2015). Of course, part of his rise to fame has also been tied to his development of commercial real estate, vacation properties, and casinos, but even that work is linked more to his ego, image, and brand than it is to promoting the public goods.

On the second point, Trump seems to have borrowed three main tropes and topoi from Reagan's political and economic playbook, namely, tax reform premised on trickle-down economics, deregulation, and the demonization of historically disenfranchised individuals and groups. Importantly, the use of the Reagan Presidential Library for the primary debate not only framed the way the debate evolved, but it also framed the role that the GOP candidate for president was expected to fill: to be a "real" Republican, this candidate was supposed to be like, act like, think like, and importantly, talk like Reagan. Trump, it seemed, was up for the challenge, although he never explicitly credited Reagan as a source, or inspiration for his ideas and policies. Ian Bremmer (2018) concluded, "[O]n policy, Trump has governed mostly as a garden-variety conservative Republican. He has rolled back Obama-era regulations, particularly on energy and the environment, signed a tax bill that sharply cut corporate taxes … enforced immigration laws. … [and he] has pushed to increase defense spending" (p. 40). The conservative think tank, the Heritage Foundation has claimed that the Trump Administration has pursued policies that have "hewed remarkably close" to its policy recommendations, enacting two-thirds of its most prominent proposals (Peters, 2018, p. A17). That surpassed even Reagan who, according to Heritage, enacted only 49% of Heritage's policy prescriptions, and who has long been considered the "conservative gold standard" (Peters, 2018, p. A17). Although never explicitly acknowledging Reagan's political and economic tropes, and topoi, it is clear that Trump has borrowed liberally from his rhetorical and policy legacy. Indeed, even his trademark campaign slogan, "Make America Great Again," was nearly the same phrase that Reagan used during his 1980 presidential campaign: "Let's Make America Great Again." Trump told the *Washington Post* in 2017 that he did not realize that Reagan had used the phrase until about a year earlier, and that he had come up with it on his own, but faulted Reagan for not trademarking it (Tumulty, 2017). After he lifted it, unwittingly or not, from Reagan, Trump did precisely that: he trademarked the slogan on July 14, 2015, and filed cease and desist orders against Ted Cruz and Scott Walker when they used the phrase in their campaign speeches (Tumulty, 2017).

Beyond his campaign slogan, Trump borrowed his deregulatory initiatives from Reagan, as well. As we saw earlier, deregulation was one of Reagan's primary policy initiatives. Trump jumped on the deregulation bandwagon early and often. Early in his presidency, on January 30, 2017, Trump signed an executive order aimed toward increased deregulation. At the signing ceremony, Trump boasted, "This will be the largest cut by far in terms of regulations," and that "if there's a new regulation, they have to knock out two. But it goes way beyond that" (Mufson, 2017). He continued, "[W]e'll be reducing [regulations] big league and their damaging effects on our small businesses, our economy, our entrepreneurial spirit. And it's been very badly damaged. So the American Dream is back" (McCaskill & Nussbaum, 2017). A year later, Trump mobilized a suspiciously vague anecdote in his 2018 State of the Union Address to champion the cause of deregulation: "We built the Empire State Building in just 1 year—is it not a disgrace that it can now take 10 years just to get a permit approved for a simple road?" (Trump, 2018).

The "eliminate two regulations for every new one" trope is a commonplace that Trump turns to time and again. At a Republican retreat in February 2018, Trump claimed, "We've eliminated more regulations in our first year than any administration has ever eliminated. And that means four years, eight years, or, in one instance, 16 years" (Qiu, 2018). Besides being hyperbolic, it is telling to note that no U.S. president has ever served for 16 years! Earlier, at the World Economic Forum held in Davos on January 26, 2018, Trump took the hyperbole a step further: "I pledged to eliminate two unnecessary regulations for every one new regulation. We have succeeded beyond our highest expectations. Instead of 2 for 1, we have cut 22 burdensome regulations for every one rule" (Qiu, 2018). While it takes very creative accounting to get to that 22-to-1 ratio, the scope of Trump deregulatory initiatives cannot be underestimated:

> On regulation Mr. Trump has stayed much closer to his campaign rhetoric. Government agencies have all but stopped writing new rules. The clean power plan ... is being unwound. The Federal Communications Commission has voted to repeal net neutrality rules. The administration let Mr. Obama's proposed rule on overtime pay die in court and delayed new regulations governing retirement advice. Numerous smaller rules have been postponed or weakened, too. At minimum, deregulation has made business owners swoon. ("No discredit," 2018, p. 23)

Trump is not only pushing deregulatory efforts upon government agencies but also staffing these agencies with political hacks, government insiders, and administrators who are openly hostile to their agencies' mandate, such as Scott Pruitt former head of the Environmental Protection Agency who resigned under public pressure, Secretary of Energy Rick

Perry, and Secretary of Education Betsy DeVos, to name a few. Within weeks of taking office, President Trump assembled teams to "aggressively scale back government regulations" (Ivory & Faturechi, 2017). Significantly, these teams' work "is being conducted in large part out of public view and often by political appointees with deep industry ties and potential conflicts" (Ivory & Faturechi, 2017). The *New York Times* and *ProPublica* have identified 71 appointees to these teams; 28 of them have potential conflicts (Ivory & Faturechi, 2017). The conflicts reach into the Environmental Protection Agency, Housing and Urban Development, the Energy Department, the Agriculture Department, the Interior Department, the Education Department, the Defense Department, and the Department of Homeland Security. In one representative case, Samantha Dravis, the chair of the E.P.A. deregulation team, "was the top official at the Republican Attorneys General Association. Ms. Dravis was also president of the Rule of Law Defense Fund, which brought together energy companies and Republican attorneys general to file lawsuits against the federal government over Obama-era environmental regulations" (Ivory & Faturechi, 2017). Notably, the Republican Association also received funding from Freedom Partners, an organization backed by the Koch brothers. Unsurprisingly, Ms. Dravis worked for Freedom Partners, as well (Ivory & Faturechi, 2017).

She is not alone. Public Citizen has identified no fewer than 44 administration officials that come from Koch-backed political organizations. U.S. Senator Sheldon Whitehouse identified several other billionaires with blatant conflicts of interest who have lobbied Trump for specific deregulatory relief that enrich them personally, such as Carl Icahn, who bought one of Trump's Atlantic City casinos out of bankruptcy, contributed the maximum he legally could to the Trump campaign, and was temporarily named a "special advisor on regulation" to the president before hastily resigning amid conflict of interest allegations. Then there's coal magnate Bob Murray, who donated \$1.3 million to Trump's inauguration and leading Super Political Action Committee, and submitted a four-page "wish list" of deregulatory and related policies to President Trump that would directly benefit him, his company, and the coal industry generally (Whitehouse, 2018).

Overall, the damage being done in the name of deregulation has gutted, eliminated, or overhauled years' worth of regulatory efforts designed to protect the environment, ensure worker safety, and safeguard consumers. *The Economist* has reported, "The bureaucracy is so understaffed that it is relying on industry hacks to draft policy. They have shaped deregulation and written clauses into the tax bill that pass costs from shareholders to society" ("One year old," 2018, p. 11). Further, "[Trump's] antipathy toward regulation has invigorated animal spirits, but at an unknown cost to the environment and human health" ("One year old," 2018, p. 11). Paul Krugman (2018) contended that Trump's economic deregulation is nothing less than a direct assault on consumers, especially the poor: "Even the administration's de facto financial regulation—its gutting of consumer financial protection—should be seen largely as an attack on the least well off, since poor families and less educated workers are the most likely victims of exploitative bankers" (Krugman, 2018).

Deregulation is not the only front in President Trump's "War on the Poor." His tax relief efforts benefit the wealthy, and corporations, more than they do those who need it the most. On December 22, 2017, President Trump signed the Tax Cuts and Jobs Act. As a result of this Act, the corporate tax rate was decreased from 35% to 21% and is permanent. Individual tax rates were reduced by an average of 3%, but expire at the end of 2025, and envision a net tax increase in 2027. As such, the corporate tax cut really constituted the center of the initiative, both in the short and long term. Further, the nearly uniform average reductions for individuals at all income levels clearly favored the wealthy given the progressive nature of the income tax system. For example, in 2019, an individual in the bottom 10% of income bracket would average a $50 tax cut, while a person in the top 1% gets a $34,000 tax cut. In a revealing public gaffe, House speaker Paul Ryan infamously deleted a tweet telling the story of a woman and her gratitude for her increase in wages: $1.50 a week. He quoted the following along with a link to the full article: "A secretary at a public high school in Lancaster, PA, said she was pleasantly surprised her pay went up $1.50 a week … she said [that] will more than cover her Costco membership for the year" (Tatum, 2018). The annual cost of a basic Costco membership is $60. Overall, according to the Congressional Budget Office, businesses receive an $890 billion benefit or 63%, individuals $441 billion or 31%, and estates $83 billion or 6% (Congressional Budget Office, 2017).

It is important to note that the overall fiscal impact of the plan will be especially pronounced on two fronts: the budget deficit and, ironically, the trade deficit. On the former, the Congressional Budget Office claimed that the Act would add over $2 trillion to the national debt over the next ten years (Congressional Budget Office, 2018, p. 129). The Trump

Administration argues that the tax cuts will spur economic growth, increasing the tax base, and that will more than offset the cost of the tax cuts, a core argument of supply side, or "trickle down" economics.

On the other front, the Tax Bill will also arguably increase the trade deficit. In one economic simulation, the Penn Wharton Budget Model "projects that the tax plan approved by the House on Thursday will increase the trade deficit by about $800 billion over 10 years" (Appelbaum, 2017). Binyamin Appelbaum observed, "[A] larger trade deficit is not a byproduct of the tax plan—it is the heart of the plan" (Appelbaum). Significantly, foreign investors hold about 40% of the federal debt (Appelbaum) and stand to benefit the most from the increase in the trade deficit.

Another important element of this plan is the impact of the corporate tax break. The Trump Administration argues that workers stand to benefit the most from this tax break insofar as the corporations will use these windfalls to increase wages and benefits, another classic justification for trickle-down economics. As part of its public relations push to continue to sell the tax reform package, the White House published a "Fact Sheet" entitled "President Donald J. Trump's Tax Reform is Delivering for All Americans" on March 7, 2018. It begins with a quotation from President Trump, who proclaimed, "At the center of America's resurgence are the massive tax cuts that we just passed before Christmas" ("Fact sheet," 2018). The site then includes a smattering of anecdotal and unrepresentative examples of companies that are passing along some of their tax windfalls to workers in the form of small one-time bonuses (e.g., American Airlines), increased wages (e.g., Walmart), or new jobs (e.g., Charter Communications). One company that did not make the list was Hostess, who generously gave a one-time $750 cash bonus to their employees, $500 toward their 401(k) contributions, and free Hostess treats for a year (Bach, 2018). To sweeten the deal, so to speak, Hostess management is selecting a "product of the week" so all employees will enjoy some variety in their sugarcoated bonuses (Bach, 2018). In his *Confessions*, Jean-Jacques Rousseau (2008) wrote of a "great princess" who, upon learning that the peasants had no bread, famously quipped, "[L]et them eat cake/brioche." In this case, it is quite literal: let them eat Hostess snack cakes! (Fig. 13.1).

Despite the anecdotal evidence, and the public relations pitch, the evidence indicates that the people who benefit the most from these corporate tax cuts are company executives, and shareholders. Stephen Gandel (2018)

Fig. 13.1 President Ronald W. Reagan welcomes Donald J. Trump to the White House. (Maidun Collection/Alamy Stock Photo)

of *Bloomberg* contended, "While more than half of the companies have announced one-time bonuses, and a handful have said they are giving out actual raises, those payouts have generally been small compared with announced buybacks. What's more, most companies, even those that have detailed their plans, look to be saving more than what they plan to spend. … Overall, companies have announced plans for just less than 80 percent of their tax savings." Instead of passing these new windfalls along to workers in the form of additional compensation, or consumers in the form of lower prices, most U.S. corporations are planning to increase their dividends, and stock buybacks, and the group that benefits most from this is the shareholders. While lip service is paid by President Trump and others about the benefits of a boom in stocks for retirement plans, wealthy investors hold the vast majority of stocks. Indeed, Paul Krugman (2017) estimated that, "[T]he richest 10 percent of U.S. residents account for about 80 percent of American owned stocks." Further, Krugman cited Steven M. Rosenthal of the Tax Policy Center who observed, "35 percent of U.S. equities are now owned by foreigners, triple the level during the

Reagan years" (Krugman, 2017). So, it is not just wealthy domestic investors who benefit the most from the Tax Cuts and Jobs Act, but wealthy foreign investors, as well. Stephen Gandel reported, "[A]bout 60 percent of [corporate tax savings] are going to shareholders, compared with 15 percent for employees" (2018). And the Center on Budget and Policy Priority claimed, "Mainstream estimates conclude that more than one-third of the benefit of corporate rate cuts flows to the top 1% of Americans, and 70% flows to the top fifth" (Center on Budget & Policy Priority, 2017).

There is an additional economic effect for those in lower economic brackets, as well. Assuming President Trump's tax reform plan does not create the ballyhooed economic effect of stimulating economic activity and broadening the tax base, as was the case with Reaganomics, somebody has to pay for the projected net loss of $2 trillion in revenue. And that will inevitably come in the form of spending cuts on social programs, and other regressive tax increases, such as sales and use taxes. On this point, the Center on Budget and Policy Priority noted, "Corporate rate cuts could even *hurt* most Americans since they must eventually be paid for with other tax increases or spending cuts" (Center on Budget & Policy Priority, 2017). The Editorial Board of the *New York Times* wrote a succinct and distressing summary of the overall impact of the tax reform initiative: "[T]he Republican tax bill will widen inequality by lavishing breaks on corporations and the wealthy while taking benefits away from the poor and the middle class" (2017).

So, how does one sell a tax reform package that does not directly benefit the overwhelming majority of people of the United States and actually costs them more in the long run? How does one counter widely circulated and well-supported claims that the Act primarily benefits corporations and the wealthy? In President Trump's case, you roll out a simple but powerful rhetorical cocktail. He is no novice on this front; indeed, he has demonstrated knack for selling a shoddy idea and product to an unsuspecting audience, as evidenced by the outcome of the judicial proceedings against Trump University. In this particular instance, President Trump blended together tropes of economic disinterest and false contentions about backlash from the wealthy.

At an event in my home state of Indiana on September 27, 2017, Trump posited, "It's not good for me. Believe me. My plan is for the working people, and my plan is for jobs. I don't benefit" (Murray, 2017). That same day, he tweeted, "This is the right TAX CUT @ the RIGHT TIME. We will ALL succeed & grow together—as one team, one people,

& one American family. #TaxReform" (Trump, 2017a). He mobilized the "team" and "family" metaphors specifically to get as many people as possible to buy into his unadorned bandwagon appeal. At a rally in Missouri on November 29, 2017, in an effort to drum up support for the tax cut bill, President Trump claimed, "Hey, look, I'm president, I don't care anymore. Some of my wealthy friends care. Me, this is a higher calling, do we agree?" (Tankersley, 2017). He repeated the claim that he would not personally benefit from the tax reductions: "This is going to cost me a fortune, believe me" (Berenson, 2017). Further, he contended, without any evidence, "Actually, the rich people actually don't like me, which is sort of interesting, and that's fine" (Tankersley, 2017). Of course, NBC estimated that Trump and his family could save more than $1 billion under the bill the House passed based on his 2005 tax returns (Murray, 2017). We do not know the actual impact based on his current tax situation because he continues to steadfastly refuse to release his tax returns, despite his promise during the campaign to do so, bucking historical convention and basic norms of transparency. On December 22, 2017, the day he signed the Act, President Trump tweeted, "Our big and very popular Tax Cut and Reform Bill has taken on an unexpected new source of 'love'—this is big companies and corporations showering their workers with bonuses. This is a phenomenon that nobody even thought of, and now it is the rage. Merry Christmas!" (Trump, 2017b). The Grinch, as we already know, can be very persuasive; just ask Cindy Loo Who.

President Trump took a rhetorical victory lap in his speech at the Davos Economic Forum in January 2018. Like Reagan, he unabashedly turned to a telling water metaphor to describe the economic impact of his tax reform program:

> What happened is something really special. Once we got it going, it was going, and I wouldn't say a total surprise, but one of the big things that happened and took place is AT&T and some others came out very early and they said they were going to pay thousands and thousands of dollars to people who work for their companies. You have 300,000, 400,000, 500,000 people working for these companies, and all of a sudden it became a big beautiful waterfall where so many companies are doing it. ("Remarks," 2018)

President Trump appropriated the cascading waterfall trope, and earlier the "showering" of corporate love trope in an effort to repackage and resell Reagan's discredited trickle-down economic policies. As we will come to learn, as we have empirically, there is no shower, and no waterfall, and any water of life that does flow from the master class's table is literally just a trickle.

That being said, perhaps the most unsettling of Trump's Reaganesque tropes is the demonization of historically disenfranchised individuals and groups. In his highly regarded book, *Faces of the Enemy*, Sam Keen (1986) noted that nothing mobilizes an ideological agenda more than convincing your audience that they are being confronted by an enemy "other" (p. 29, p. 100). For Reagan, as we previously identified, one of the enemies was so-called welfare mothers who were cheating the system. Trump, on the other hand, has moved well beyond the limited construction of the enemy crafted by Reagan. In Trump's case, the enemies were immigrants, Muslims, and people from developing countries. On this point, *The Economist* reflected, "Donald Trump won the presidency promising to keep out unwanted foreigners and expel those with no legal right to be in the country. Some of his ideas for doing that, such as building a wall on the Mexican border, and barring citizens of some Muslim countries, are unworkable, discriminatory or both" ("Let Salvadorians stay," 2018).

In his presidential announcement speech, on June 16, 2015, Trump infamously attacked Mexico in particular. He complained, "When Mexico sends its people, they're not sending their best. They're not sending you. They're not sending you. They're sending people who have lots of problems, and they're bringing those problems with us. They're bringing drugs. They're bringing crime. They're rapists" (Lee, 2015). The *Washington Post* investigated Trump's incendiary claim equating illegal immigrants to crime, and found, "[N]o solid data support it, and the data that do negate it. Trump can defend it all he wants, but the facts just are not there" (Lee, 2015).

Undeterred, Trump took his thinly veiled racist trope even further, personally attacking a U.S. Citizen and sitting U.S. District Judge, Gonzalo P. Curiel. At a campaign rally in San Diego on May 27, 2016, Trump characterized Judge Curiel, who was presiding over a class action fraud case involving Trump University, as "very hostile," a "hater of Donald Trump" who should be "ashamed of himself" (Editorial Board, 2016). He continued, "I think it's a disgrace what he is doing." Trump unconscionably added that Judge Curiel "happens to be, we believe, Mexican" (Editorial Board, 2016). While Judge Curiel's parents did emigrate from Mexico and later become American citizens, he was born, raised, and educated in my home state of Indiana, attending Indiana University for both college and law school. Not only was the criticism of a sitting federal judge utterly unprecedented for a presidential candidate, but it was also overtly racist. Indeed, even stalwart supporter and Trump apologist Speaker of the House Paul Ryan admitted that Trump's comment demeaning Judge Curiel was a "textbook definition of a racist comment" (Steinhauer et al., 2016).

Trump's targeted, anti-immigrant rhetoric, was a foreshadowing of what was to come. While he continued his attacks on Mexico, he expanded the scope and intensity in his construction of the enemy other. One of the more telling maneuvers was his January 2017 Executive Order that banned foreign nationals from seven predominantly Muslim countries from entering the United States for 90 days, suspended all Syrian refugee travel to the United States indefinitely, and prohibited all other refugees for 120 days. Successfully challenged in several courts, the Trump Administration proffered two new revised versions of the travel ban. The third version, that now included North Koreans and certain government officials from Venezuela, a shrewd political and legal move to make the policy seem less like a "Muslim ban," per se, recently passed Constitutional muster on a narrow 5–4 vote in the U.S. Supreme Court in the divisive case *Trump v. Hawaii*. As we will see in a moment, the timing of this opinion is revealing, with oral arguments on April 25, 2018, and the opinion itself delivered on June 26, 2018.

In the interim, Trump broadened his public demonization of immigrants from other countries. Josh Dawsey (2018) of the *Washington Post* reported that when lawmakers were discussing protections needed for immigrants from "Haiti, El Salvador and African countries" at a recent meeting at the White House, on January 11, 2018, President Trump reportedly fumed, "Why are we having all these people from shithole countries coming here?" Trump then proposed, "[T]he United States should bring in more people from countries such as Norway" (Dawsey, 2018). Trump unapologetically doubled down on racist rhetoric, and it was a harbinger of what was to come.

At one of his trademark rallies in West Virginia on April 12, President Trump was scheduled to give a talk on the merits of his signature tax reform legislation. After declaring the speech "boring," and tossing his prepared text to his audience, Trump vowed to "tell it like it is." He warned, "We cannot let people enter our country—we have no idea who they are, what they do, where they come from. We don't know if they're murderers, if they're killers, if they're MS-13" (Davis, 2018a). He fondly recalled his claim during the campaign when he called immigrants "rapists," and outrageously claimed, without evidence, that while in transit, immigrant women were "raped at levels they have never seen before" (Davis, 2018a). He promised his wildly supportive audience, "This is the kind of stuff and crap that we're allowing into our country and we can't do it."

Shortly thereafter, on May 16, at a roundtable discussion in the White House with state and local leaders about California's immigration policies, and related topics, President Trump equated immigrants to animals: "You wouldn't believe how bad these people are. These aren't people, these are animals, and we're taking them out of the country at a level and at a rate that's never happened before" (Davis, 2018b). It is here that Trump crossed a significant rhetorical boundary. It is one thing to call the enemy other a murderer, rapist, or drug dealer, but to characterize another person as something less than human is a shift that is ripe with chilling implications.

The stage had been set, and in the course of a week, in mid-June, he took his demagoguery to the next level. He started out slow. On June 18, Trump tweeted an intentionally vague warning, "We don't want what is happening in Europe to happen to us!" (Graham, 2018). The next day, on June 19, President Trump tweeted, "Democrats are the problem. They don't care about crime and want illegal immigrants, no matter how bad they may be, to pour into and infest our Country, like MS-13" (Graham, 2018). Referring to immigrants as "animals" who were "infesting" our country, according to David Graham in *The Atlantic*, "drives full-throttle toward the dehumanization of immigrants, setting aside legality in favor of a division between a human us and less-human them. What are infestations? They are takeovers by vermin, rodents, insects. The word is almost used exclusively in this context. What does one do with an infestation? Why, exterminate it, of course" (Graham, 2018). On June 24, President Trump tweeted, "We cannot allow all of these people to invade our country." Now immigrants were not just cast as vermin "infesting" our country, they were simultaneously caricatured as alien invaders. As alien, or even foreign invaders, they cannot and should not be afforded basic human rights. Indeed, Trump continued, "When somebody comes in, we must immediately, with no Judges or Court Cases, bring them back where they came from" (Griffiths, 2018). For the politically astute, it should not go unnoticed that, perhaps with the midterm elections in mind, Trump consciously cast Democrats as defenders of these alleged rapists, murderers, drug dealers, criminals, and animals that were infesting and invading our country, purposefully undermining their political credibility, and placing them at potential risk, as well.

Two days after his dehumanizing "tweetstorm," the Supreme Court handed down the decision in *Trump v Hawaii*, giving the impression that Trump was perhaps implicitly threatening the Court with what we call an "appeal to the gallery" fallacy. The fallacy, derived from a historical legal context wherein the peasants in old courtrooms were confined to the gallery, refers to advocates who believed that they were losing their case on the merits and would then make an outrageous claim to rile up the gallery, creating the fear of a mob uprising if the judge, or jury, decided contrary to the gallery's wishes. At the very least, in short order, Trump placed the issue of immigration front and center as he continued to manipulate the public agenda, and one must presume that even Supreme Court justices, despite their claims to be apolitical, are not immune from the news cycle. Conversely, and perhaps more importantly, the Court's decision, undeniably functions as an exclamation point to Trump's dehumanizing tweetstorm regarding immigrants, and enables him to deploy more of the same in the future.

While Reagan carefully crafted an enemy other during his tenure as president, including, somewhat ironically, the Soviet Union, whom he once dubbed the "Evil Empire," Donald Trump has escalated the rhetorical war on his enemy other, a denigrating, dehumanizing, and demonizing discourse that befits only the worst fascist demagogues, not the leader of a free country whose national poem and motto, *New Colossus*, enshrined on a plaque mounted inside the pedestal under the State of Liberty, proclaims:

> "Give me your tired, your poor,
> Your huddled masses, yearning to breathe free,
> The wretched refuse of your teeming shore.
> Send these, the homeless, tempest-tossed to me,
> I lift my lamp beside the golden door!"

Daniel Kreps (2016) interviewed Mike Judge and Etan Cohen, the director and writer of *Idiocracy* in a June 2016 article for *Rolling Stone*. The prompt for the article was ostensibly the fact that Judge and Cohen "reteamed to pen a series of anti-Donald Trump campaign ads starring the film's wrestler-turned-president, [President Camacho] played by Terry Crews" (Kreps, 2016). Comparing President Trump to President

Camacho, they commented, "The most dangerous contrast to Trump is that Camacho actually realizes he needs advice from other people, and knows that he's not the smartest guy in the room" (Kreps, 2016). Although *Idiocracy* is an incisive satire set 500 years in the future, much of it cuts pretty close to the bone today. Writer Etan Cohen recognized as much in a tweet that garnered a lot of attention: "I never expected #idiocracy to become a documentary so soon" (Kreps, 2016). He continued, "We just thought it would take much, much longer to get to this point. Obviously, when writing the movie, we knew that that was true about TV and pop culture. But it was a crazy joke to think that it could be extrapolated to politics. It seems to be happening really rapidly" (Kreps, 2016).

Given the rapid conflation of reality and fiction, we bear a special responsibility to track, decipher, and engage arguments that move us closer to *Idiocracy*, political and economic arguments that have no discernable warrants, limited and unrepresentative evidence, and disquieting claims. When public arguments regarding immigration, deploying tropes of "invasion" and "infestation" from "shithole" countries, discourse that smacks of the racist fascistic rhetoric Adolph Hitler deployed when he described Jews, Gypsies, and others as vermin, sludge, lice, and parasites, discourse that engendered unfathomable tragic consequences, and discourse that has justified tearing children from their parents while effectively imprisoning both while denying them basic, fundamental, and inalienable human rights, the need for intervention and counter-narratives is more pronounced and urgent. It becomes much easier to slip through biased tax reform packages, and harmful deregulatory agendas, when people are distracted by and mobilized against the "barbarians at the gate," or in this case, the wall, a timeless, but effective rhetorical strategy. The need for greed—cloaked by and perhaps even nurtured by hatred, fear, and exploitation—has thrived during the Trump presidency. And it has significantly contributed to the toxic political and economic miasma that we outlined at the start, a miasma 40 years in the making, and one that invites and portends calamitous consequences. In his message before the start of the World Cup in 2014, Pope Francis humbly reflected, "To win, we must overcome individualism, selfishness, all forms of racism, intolerance and manipulation of people" ("Pope to World Cup," 2014). Like Jimmy Carter's near the start of this story, Pope Francis' words were almost prescient given the unsettling events in the years that would follow.

References

Appelbaum, B. (2017, November 17). Trump's tax cuts are likely to increase the trade deficit. *New York Times.* Retrieved June 29, 2018, from https://www.nytimes.com/2017/11/17/us/politics/tax-cuts-trade-deficit-trump.html

Bach, N. (2018, February 2). Free twinkies for a year? Hostess sweetens worker's tax reform bonus. *Fortune.* Retrieved June 29, 2018, from http://fortune.com/2018/02/02/hostess-tax-reform-bonus-cash-free-twinkies/

Berenson, T. (2017, November 29). President Trump says, wrongly, that he won't benefit from the Republican tax bill. *Time.* Retrieved June 29, 2018, from http://time.com/5041919/donald-trump-tax-reform-bill/

Bremmer, I. (2018, January 22). Tweets aside, Trump has mostly governed like a garden variety Republican. *Time*, 40–41.

Center on Budget and Policy Priorities. (2017, October 11). Corporate tax cuts mainly benefit shareholders and CEOs, not workers. Retrieved June 29, 2018, from https://www.cbpp.org/research/federal-tax/corporate-tax-cuts-mainly-benefit-shareholders-and-ceos-not-workers

Congressional Budget Office. (2017, November 26). *Reconciliation recommendations of the Senate Committee on Finance.* Retrieved June 29, 2018, from https://www.cbo.gov/publication/53348

Congressional Budget Office. (2018, April). *The budget and economic outlook: 2018–2028: Appendix b: The effect of the 2017 tax act on CBO's economic and budget projections.* Retrieved June 29, 2018, from https://www.cbo.gov/sites/default/files/115th-congress-2017-2018/reports/53651-outlook-appendixb.pdf

Davis, J. H. (2018a, April 5). Trump veers from tax script to blast democrats on immigration. *New York Times.* Retrieved July 24, 2018, from https://www.nytimes.com/2018/04/05/us/politics/trump-democrats-immigration-votes.html

Davis, J. H. (2018b, May 16). Trump calls some unauthorized immigrants "animals" in rant. *New York Times.* Retrieved July 24, 2018, from https://www.nytimes.com/2018/05/16/us/politics/trump-undocumented-immigrants-animals.html

Dawsey, J. (2018, January 18). Trump derides protections for immigrants from "shithole" countries. *Washington Post.* Retrieved June 27, 2018, from https://www.washingtonpost.com/politics/trump-attacks-protections-for-immigrants-from-shithole-countries-in-oval-office-meeting/2018/01/11/bfc0725c-f711-11e7-91af-31ac729add94_story.html?utm_term=.f8cf137bd032

Editorial Board. (2016, May 31). Donald Trump and the judge. *New York Times.* Retrieved July 28, 2018, from www.nytimes.com/2016/06/01/opinion/donald-trump-and-the-judge.html

Editorial Board. (2017, December 16). The tax bill that inequality created. *New York Times*. Retrieved July 29, 2018, from https://www.nytimes.com/2017/12/16/opinion/sunday/tax-bill-inequality-created.html

Fact sheet. (2018, March 7). Whitehouse.org. Retrieved July 29, 2018, from https://www.whitehouse.gov/briefings-statements/president-donald-j-trumps-tax-reform-delivering-americans/

Gandel, S. (2018, March 5). Five charts that show how companies are spending their tax savings. *Bloomberg*. Retrieved July 29, 2018, from https://www.bloomberg.com/opinion/articles/2018-03-05/five-charts-that-show-where-those-corporate-tax-savings-are-going

Graham, D. A. (2018, June 19). Trump says democrats want immigrants to "infest" the U.S. *The Atlantic*. Retrieved July 27, 2018, from https://www.theatlantic.com/politics/archive/2018/06/trump-immigrants-infest/563159/

Griffiths, B. D. (2018, June 24). Trump: "We cannot allow all of these people to invade our country." *Politico*. Retrieved July 27, 2018, from https://www.politico.com/story/2018/06/24/trump-invade-country-immigrants-667191

Ivory, D., & Faturechi, R. (2017, July 11). The deep industry ties of Trump's deregulation teams. *New York Times*. Retrieved July 27, 2018, from https://www.nytimes.com/2017/07/11/business/the-deep-industry-ties-of-trumps-deregulation-teams.html

Judge, M. (Director). (2006). *Idiocracy* [Film]. 20th Century Studios.

Keen, S. (1986). *Faces of the enemy: Reflections of the hostile imagination*. Harper Row.

Kreps, D. (2016, June 3). "Idiocracy" team readies anti-Donald Trump campaign ads. Retrieved September 14, 2017, from https://www.rollingstone.com/politics/politics-news/idiocracy-team-ready-anti-donald-trump-campaign-ads-153797/

Krugman, P. (2017, October 26). Trump's $700 billion gift to wealthy foreigners. *New York Times*. Retrieved June 29, 2018, from https://www.nytimes.com/2017/10/26/opinion/trump-taxes-wealthy-foreigners.html

Krugman, P. (2018, April 26). Trump's war on the poor. *New York Times*. Retrieved June 27, 2018, from https://www.nytimes.com/2018/04/26/opinion/trumps-war-poor.html

Lee, M. Y. H. (2015, July 26). Donald Trump's false comments connecting Mexican immigrants and crime. *Washington Post*. Retrieved July 26, 2015, from https://www.washingtonpost.com/news/fact-checker/wp/2015/07/08/donald-trumps-false-comments-connecting-mexican-immigrants-and-crime/

Let Salvadoreans stay. (2018). *The Economist*. Retrieved June 27, 2018, from www-economist-com.eu1.proxy.openathens.net/leaders/2018/01/11/let-the-salvadoreans-stay

Margolin, L. (2017). *Trumpmania: Vince McMahon, WWE and the making of America's 45th President. Lavie Margolin.*
McCaskill, N. D., & Nussbaum, M. (2017, January 30). Trump signs executive order requiring that for every one new regulation, two must be revoked. *Politico.* Retrieved July 24, 2018, from https://www.politico.com/story/2017/01/trump-signs-executive-order-requiring-that-for-every-one-new-regulation-two-must-be-revoked-234365
Mufson, S. (2017, January 30). Trump wants to scrap two regulations for each new one adopted. *Washington Post.* Retrieved July 24, 2018, from https://www.washingtonpost.com/news/energy-environment/wp/2017/01/30/trump-wants-to-cut-two-regulations-on-businesses-for-every-new-one-imposed/?utm_term=.9343adf162e8
Murray, M. (2017, November 16). Trump and his family could save more than $1 billion under house tax bill. *NBC News.* Retrieved June 29, 2018, from https://www.nbcnews.com/politics/first-read/trump-his-family-could-save-more-1-billion-under-house-n821491
No discredit where none is due. (2018, January 13–19). *The Economist*, 23.
One year old. (2018, January 13–19). *The Economist*, 11.
Peters, J. W. (2018, January 23). Think tank says Trump has hewed to its ideas. *New York Times*, A17.
Pope to World Cup: Overcome racism, greed in sport. (2014, June 12). *USA Today.* Retrieved July 24, 2018, from https://www.usatoday.com/story/sports/soccer/2014/06/12/pope-to-world-cup-overcome-racism-greed-in-sport/10361029/
Qiu, L. (2018, February 23). Trump says "No president has ever cut so many regulations." Not quite. *New York Times.* Retrieved June 27, 2018, from https://www.nytimes.com/2018/02/23/us/politics/trump-says-no-president-has-ever-cut-so-many-regulations-not-quite.html
Reagan Library Debate. (2015, September 16). Retrieved July 24, 2018, from https://cnnpressroom.blogs.cnn.com/2015/09/16/cnn-reagan-library-debate-later-debate-full-transcript/
Remarks and a question-and-answer session at the World Economic Forum in Davos, Switzerland. (2018, January 26). *The American Presidency Project.* Retrieved July 24, 2018, from https://www.presidency.ucsb.edu/documents/remarks-and-question-and-answer-session-the-world-economic-forum-davos-switzerland
Rousseau, J. (2008). *Confessions.* Oxford University Press. (Original work published 1790).
Steinhauer, J., Martin, J., & Herszenhorn, D. M. (2016, June 17). Paul Ryan calls Trump's attack on judge "racist," but still backs him. *New York Times.* Retrieved June 28, 2018, from https://www.nytimes.com/2016/06/08/us/politics/paul-ryan-donald-trump-gonzalo-curiel.html

Tankersley, J. (2016, September 26). Clinton coins phrase "Trump-ed up trickle down." *Washington Post*. Retrieved July 24, 2018, from https://www.washingtonpost.com/politics/2016/live-updates/general-election/real-time-fact-checking-and-analysis-of-the-first-presidential-debate/clinton-coins-phrase-trump-ed-up-trickle-down/

Tankersley, J. (2017, November 29). A "main street" tax speech becomes a Trump riff on the rich. *New York Times*. Retrieved June 29, 2018, from https://www.nytimes.com/2017/11/29/us/politics/a-main-street-tax-speech-becomes-a-trump-riff-on-the-rich.html

Tatum, S. (2018, February 5). Paul Ryan deletes tweet about tax cuts after twitter backlash. Retrieved July 3, 2018, from https://edition.cnn.com/2018/02/03/politics/paul-ryan-tweet-tax-cut-backlash/index.html

Trump, D. [@realDonaldTrump]. (2017a, September 27). *This is the right TAX CUT @ the RIGHT TIME. We will ALL succeed & grow together—as one team* [Tweet]. Twitter. Retrieved July 3, 2018, from https://twitter.com/realdonaldtrump/status/913187235452690432?lang=en

Trump, D. J. [@realDonaldTrump]. (2017b, December 22). *Our big and very popular Tax Cut and Reform Bill has taken on an unexpected new source of 'love'* [Tweet]. Twitter. Retrieved July 3, 2018, from https://twitter.com/realdonaldtrump/status/944187730564714497?lang=en

Trump, D. J. (2018, January 31). State of the Union 2018: Read the full transcript." CNN.com. Retrieved July 3, 2018, from https://www.cnn.com/2018/01/30/politics/2018-state-of-the-union-transcript/index.html

Tumulty, K. (2017, January 18). How Donald Trump came up with "Make America Great Again." *Washington Post*. Retrieved July 24, 2018, from https://www.washingtonpost.com/politics/how-donald-trump-came-up-with-make-america-great-again/2017/01/17/fb6acf5e-dbf7-11e6-ad42-f3375f271c9c_story.html

Weinberg, M. (2015, September 16). The GOP field doesn't understand Ronald Reagan. I know – I worked for him. *Politico*. Retrieved August 24, 2016, from https://www.politico.com/magazine/story/2015/09/gop-debate-reagan-213148/

Whitehouse, S. (2018, February 21). Sen. Whitehouse: Trump is in the back pocket of billionaires. Retrieved March 7, 2018, from https://www.cnn.com/2018/02/21/opinions/trump-billionaire-influence-opinion-whitehouse/index.html

CHAPTER 14

Epilogue: We Can't Make It Here—Moving Beyond the Free Market

The stories we read and the songs that we sing are windows into the culture in which we find them. They reveal values and ethical tensions that shape the way that we see ourselves, and live our lives. Throughout this book, I have interwoven stories from popular culture that frame flashpoints at important junctures in American economic and political history. Although each of these purposefully chosen cultural references supports particular points developed in each of the chapters of this book, for me, the most compelling and relevant narrative themes for the argument that I am making here flowed from the pen of Theodor Geisel, better known as Dr. Seuss.

One of the more powerful stories from Dr. Seuss (1971) that has shaped the way I view the exploitative nature of the free market from a very young age was *The Lorax*. Released in 1971, when I was 5 years old, it was one of the first books that I remember reading as a child. This simple tale, much more than just a children's book, lays bare the inherent tensions between an unregulated free market, and a deeper environmental consciousness. In this much-loved book, Dr. Seuss tells the story of the Once-ler, a character motivated by greed, selfishness, and a complete disregard for the consequences of his actions. The Once-ler clear-cut the Truffula trees in order to make "Thneeds that everyone, EVERYONE, *EVERYONE* needs," or so he believed (1971, p. 49). Of course, people did not really need Thneeds; they were luxury items that presumably

G. D. Klinger et al., *Money Talks*,
https://doi.org/10.1007/978-3-031-00816-0_14

generated enormous profit for the Once-ler. The Lorax, who spoke for the trees, accused the Once-ler of being "crazy with greed," and observed, "no one on earth … would buy that fool Thneed!" (p. 24). They were products that did not seem to generate any inherent social worth, and came at tremendous environmental costs. The costs did not stop with the clear-cutting of the Truffula trees, regrettable in its own right, the production processes created poisonous byproducts, what Dr. Seuss called "Smogulous Smoke," "Gluppity Glup," and "Schloppity-Schlopp," and displaced species such as the Brown Bar-ba-loots, the Swomee-Swans, and the Humming-Fish from their natural habitats. The Once-ler did not stop until the last Truffula tree had been chopped with a final "sickening smack," the mammals, birds, and fish had all left, and there was nothing left to exploit. The Once-ler then closed his Thneed factory, and his employees moved on to next place to repeat the cycle, leaving a trail of toxicity and destruction in their wake. Although he felt a tinge of sadness at the time, the Once-ler justified his actions based on the belief that "business is business! And business must grow regardless of crummies in tummies, you know" (p. 37). Consequently, he "biggered" his factory, "biggered" his roads, "biggered" his wagon, and "biggered" his loads. And, of course, he "biggered" his money that, he believed, is something that "everyone needs" (p. 39).

The story ends on a hopeful but vague note when the well-intentioned young boy in the book wondered what he could do to reverse the damage that had been done. The now retired and reclusive Once-ler, displaying a long overdue sense of guilt and regret, introduced his young interlocutor to a small pile of rocks left behind by the Lorax engraved with a single word: *"Unless."*

One of the more difficult things for social critics is to turn their attention to affirmative paths forward. Many critics feel that the criticism itself has served an important social function, but readers, not to mention editors, often demand more. In the final chapter to his highly regarded book, *Technopoly*, Neil Postman (1993) reached the same crossroads. He mused:

> Anyone who practices the art of cultural criticism must endure being asked, What is the solution to the problems you describe? Critics almost never appreciate this question, since, in most cases, they are entirely satisfied with themselves for having posed the problems, and, in any event, are rarely skilled in formulating practical suggestions about anything. (p. 181)

In the epilogue to this book, I cautiously turn my attention to the same dynamic, and try to answer the charge issued by Dr. Seuss (1971) at this end of *The Lorax*. Importantly, I have chosen to do so by dropping academic apparatuses, policy prescriptions from experts, and other evidence from the public sphere. Instead, I turn to the resources of common sense, and an innate moral sensibility unencumbered by the traditional need to support my observations with the research and arguments of others. In short, what follows are open ideas about how we can change our way of thinking about the role of economics in our everyday lives as we chart our way forward.

Unless we collectively renounce the principles of greed, self-interest, profiteering, and deregulation, *unless* we collectively put policies in place that permanently check the excesses of the free market, and ensure a more just and equitable distribution of wealth, we are doomed to repeat the disastrous and unsustainable boom-bust cycle of market capitalism. As consolidation and monopolistic practices continue to grow, I worry that the boom-bust cycle will be even more pronounced in the years to come making the Great Recession of 2008 seem like a minor economic downturn.

Specifically, I offer the following 12 prescriptions for further reflection:

1. We must disabuse ourselves of the myth of the "free market."
2. We must stop the demonization of regulation.
3. We must check back reliance on government-directed entitlement programs.
4. We must support legislation that ensures that every person willing and able to work earns a living wage.
5. We must enhance and enforce existing legislation that prevents monopolies, and the construction of business entities that are "too big to fail."
6. We must re-examine the role of the Federal Reserve Bank in the economy, and our society.
7. We must temper the permeation of gambling in all aspects of our lives.
8. We must teach our children to play games and engage in activities that encourage cooperation, collaboration, and synergy rather than those that engender division, domination, and exploitation.

9. We must recover the positive messages embedded within religion while rejecting the deleterious consequences of institutional misinterpretations and misapplications of these messages.
10. We must stop the demonization of others, and reject the rhetoric of division, and the politics and economics of war.
11. We must change the standards of success in society away from individual material accomplishment toward collective well-being.
12. We must give feminine values a chance to move us in a different direction insofar as masculine principles have taken us to a point where our very existence is at risk.

I will leave the specifics of how we incorporate these ideas into our everyday lives to policy analysts, and enlightened legislators. For me, the process begins by a single change of mind, a change of heart, and a change of perspective. The need for this change is urgent because the miasma that I allude to throughout this book is becoming more pronounced, and our very existence is now at risk. Our current path is simply unsustainable, and substantially more must be done to move us in a different direction.

In 2011, my nephew was diagnosed with childhood leukemia. He was 5 years old at the time, the same age I was when I first read *The Lorax.* I watched with dismay as this strong and courageous young man went through the debilitating process of chemotherapy to fight the cancer. He emerged from his long and painful series of treatments free from the clutches of this affliction, ringing a bell as a symbol of his complete remission before being discharged from Riley Children's Hospital in Indianapolis. The celebration and relief was short lived, however, when we learned that the leukemia had returned. This led to another round of treatments, even more potent and aggressive than before, involving both radiation and an extremely painful umbilical cord transplant that actually changed his blood type. Happily, he emerged from this second round of treatments in complete remission, this time for good. He did not know it at the time, but this brave young man taught me an invaluable life lesson: when confronted by a powerful disease, an appropriate and vigorous treatment regimen can help to cure the disease, but only through strength in the midst of adversity, and perseverance in the face of what may initially appear to be a hopeless situation.

On one of the visits to see my nephew in the hospital, I found a book by Dr. Seuss (2011) that I had not seen before laying on a table in his room called *The Bippolo Seed and Other Lost Stories.* Although drawn from stories that were previously published elsewhere in more obscure outlets, the book itself was published in 2011, the year my nephew was first admitted to the hospital. While he lay recovering, I flipped through the pages of this book, and was immediately drawn to the primary "lost story" in this book. Like *The Lorax*, *The Bippolo Seed* tells a cautionary tale of the consequences of a community infected with greed. I scribbled down a few lines and feel that they are perhaps the best way to conclude my narrative here.

The Bippolo Seed featured a conversation between a duck named McKluck and a scheming cat. The duck found a rare seed of a Bippolo Tree that could grant wishes. Originally, the duck was interested in growing enough food for a week, but the cat encouraged the duck to think beyond those immediate needs. Instead of simply obtaining enough food for a week, McKluck, now seduced by greed, wished for even more:

> 'I wish,' yelled the duck, and he started to scream, 'For eight thousand buckets of purple ice cream! A trunk full of toothpaste! A big kitchen sink! And lots of brass keyholes! And gallons of ink! I wish for two boatloads of Baked Boston Beans! And, also nine carloads of sewing machines!' Then his mouth started steaming, his tongue got so hot, [b]ut the more that he wished, the more greedy he got. 'I wish,' shrieked the duck, 'for a million silk towels! And three million cages for very big owls! And forty-five thousand, two hundred and two hamburger buns! And a bottle of glue! And four million satin lined red rubber boots! And five million banjos! And six million flutes! Oranges! Apples! And all kinds of fruits! And nine million Hopalong Cassidy suits!'. (Dr. Seuss, p. 5)

The cat, in short, prodded McKluck to be motivated by greed rather than immediate need. To this end, the cat slyly suggested:

> 'When you grow all that food in your Bippolo Tree, you can go into business ... in business with me! We'll *sell* all that food. You'll be rich!' laughed the kitty, 'why you'll be the richest young duck in the city!' 'Hmm ...,' said the duck, and he wrinkled his brow. 'I never thought much about money till now. But, golly, you're right. With some money, gee whiz, [w]hy I'd be the happiest duck that there is!' (3)

Distracted by grandiose dreams of getting rich quick, and "dizzy and crazy with greed," McKluck lost the seed, and ended up with nothing (6). The moral to this story, of course, is that greed and a love of money do not guarantee happiness. While ostensibly a children's tale, the lessons apply quite aptly to the rise of greed, self-interest, and a disregard for consequences in our lives. The path to true happiness follows a different course, one that deploys love, altruism, and a care for others as our moral compasses as we chart our way forward through the difficult challenges that continue to confront our world.

References

Dr. Seuss. (1971). *The Lorax.* Random House.
Dr. Seuss. (2011). *The Bippolo Seed and other lost stories.* Random House Books for Young Readers.
Postman, N. (1993). *Technopoly: The surrender of culture to technology.* Vintage.

Index[1]

[1] Note: Page numbers followed by 'n' refer to notes.

G. D. Klinger et al., *Money Talks*,
https://doi.org/10.1007/978-3-031-00816-0

E